READING
THE BIBLE
BOOK BY
BOOK

RICHARD H. HIERS

READING THE BIBLE BOOK BY BOOK

An Introductory Study Guide to the Books of the Bible with Apocrypha

FORTRESS PRESS
PHILADELPHIA

COPYRIGHT © 1988 BY FORTRESS PRESS

Library of Congress Cataloging-in-Publication Data

Hiers, Richard H.
Reading the Bible book by book.

Includes index.
1. Bible—Introductions.   I. Title.
BS475.2.H54   1988   220.6'1   87–45893
ISBN 0–8006–2074–7

Printed in the United States of America   1-2074
95   94   93   92   91   3   4   5   6   7   8   9   10

to
Delton L. Scudder

CONTENTS

PREFACE

And he rose and went. And behold, an Ethiopian, a eunuch, a minister of Candace the queen of the Ethiopians, in charge of all her treasure, had come to Jerusalem to worship and was returning; seated in his chariot, he was reading the prophet Isaiah. And the Spirit said to Philip, "Go up and join this chariot." So Philip ran to him, and heard him reading Isaiah the prophet, and asked, "Do you understand what you are reading?" And he said, "How can I, unless some one guides me?" And he invited Philip to come up and sit with him. (Acts 8:27–31)

As has been noticed since early times, the Scriptures are difficult to understand without guidance from others. The title of this volume is intended to suggest that readers may find my book helpful as an introduction to any or all of the biblical writings, taken separately or in any sequence that may be desired. The short, introductory treatments of each of the biblical books are written as independent essays; readers will not need to have plowed through preceding sections in order to grasp what is being said in any one of the essays. On the other hand, those who wish a broad overview of biblical history, literature, and religion may find it worthwhile to read through this book as a whole either before or after more focused study of particular biblical books or passages. Special features of the book and some suggestions as to study strategies are indicated below (Introduction, pp. 1–5).

The present volume is a sequel to an earlier introduction, *Reader's Guide to the Bible* (Nashville: Abingdon Press, 1978). The principal merit of the earlier book may have been that it told less than the reader wished to know. It was meant as a bare outline of main points in connection with each biblical book. Here, however, meanings and themes are described much more fully, numerous important and often dramatic scenes are highlighted, and more attention is given to comparing intrabiblical perspectives on various religious beliefs, concerns, and practices.

I am indebted to innumerable former teachers, fellow students, colleagues, and friends who have shared their perceptions with me in both formal and informal settings during some thirty years of study and teaching in the biblical field. I am also grateful to many whose work I know mainly or only through their publications. And we all may thank those scholars and other persons of generations before us who have understood and given guidance, going back even to the days of the biblical writers, if not quite, perhaps, to the time of Adam and Eve!

Here I want to thank the many persons who have encouraged my efforts in connection with this work, especially John M. Bullard, Corbin S. Carnell, Austin B. Creel, Joseph F. Douthitt, Pierce S. Ellis, Jane Gale Hiers, Lucy Hiers, John A. Hollar, Joy and B. Davie Napier, Minor F. Watts, and Jim and Louise Williams. My preeminent colleague Theodor H. Gaster has contributed many insights from his rich store of learning. Michael Eldridge, another special colleague, has diligently worked through several sections of the present manuscript, and provided numerous helpful comments. I thank all for their support and assistance; but none is to blame for any possible (or impossible) shortcomings that may remain.

RICHARD H. HIERS

University of Florida
July 15, 1987

ABBREVIATIONS

Abbreviations

Old Testament Apocrypha

New Testament

TABLE OF DATES

3000 B.C.	End of Stone Age; beginning of Bronze Age; Canaanites settled in the "land of Canaan"
2700–2200	Age of the pyramids in Egypt
2500–1500	Mohenjo-daro (Indus Valley) civilization in India
1800	Code of Hammurabi established in Babylonia
1800–1500	Stonehenge monuments erected in Britain
1800–1400	Period of the patriarchs: Abraham, Isaac, Jacob, Joseph
1500	Invasion of India by Aryans
1500–1230	Israelites in Egypt
1375–1358	Reign of Ikhnaton, Pharaoh of Egypt; prevalence of sun worship
1290–1223	Reign of Ramses II, Pharaoh of Egypt; extensive building program
1230	Exodus from Egypt by Israelites across the Red Sea
1230–1200	Israel in the wilderness: law received by Moses
1200	Settlement/conquest of Canaan by Israelites; occupation of coastal plain of Canaan by Philistines
1200–1000	Period of the judges; Philistines gain ground
1100	End of Bronze Age; beginning of Iron Age in Egypt and Mesopotamia
1000	Reign of Saul, king of Israel; defeat of Israelites by Philistines
995–965	Reign of David over both Judah and Israel; beginning of United Kingdom; subdues Philistines
965–926	Reign of Solomon over Judah and Israel; builds Temple; alienates Israelites

926	Secession of Northern Kingdom (Israel); end of United Kingdom
926–722	Period of the divided kingdom: Israel and Judah now separate nations
853	Formation of alliance against Assyria by Judah, Israel, and Syria
750	Founding of Rome
740	Appearance of earliest classical prophets: Hosea, Amos, Isaiah
738	Tribute paid to Assyrians by Israel
734	Siege of Jerusalem by Syria and Israel
722	Defeat and annexation of Israel (Northern Kingdom) by Assyria; end of Northern Kingdom
701	Siege of Jerusalem by Assyrians
700	Scythian rule established in Russia
622	Deuteronomic reform under King Josiah
612	Fall of Nineveh (capital of Assyria) to Babylonians
609	Josiah killed in battle by Egyptians
600	Birth of Zarathustra (Zoroaster)
598	First deportation of people from Jerusalem to Babylon
586	Conquest of Jerusalem by Babylon; end of Southern Kingdom; destruction of the temple; beginning of the exile
560	Birth of Buddha
550	Birth of Confucius
550–540	Period of the prophecies of "Second Isaiah"
540	Defeat of Babylonians by Persians
538	Decree of Cyrus; end of exile
515	Temple rebuilt by authority of Zerubbabel and Joshua the high priest
470	Birth of Socrates
444	Jerusalem's walls rebuilt by authority of Nehemiah
427	Birth of Plato
400	The law promulgated by Ezra
384	Birth of Aristotle
331	Defeat of Persians by Alexander the Great
326	Invasion of India by Greeks
300–198	Jewish people under Egyptian (Ptolemaic) rule
221–207	Great Wall of China built
198–168	Jewish people under Syrian (Seleucid) rule

168–64	Maccabean period: Jewish independence regained
64	Palestine annexed by Romans
55	Invasion of Britain by Julius Caesar
27 B.C.–A.D. 14	Reign of Augustus, first Roman emperor
6 B.C.	Birth of Jesus
A.D. 64	Christians persecuted in Rome by authority of Nero
66–70	Jewish war for liberation from Rome
70	Jerusalem captured, temple destroyed by Romans
79	Eruption of Mount Vesuvius, which buries Pompeii
96	Christians in Asia Minor persecuted by Romans
100	Native cultures well established in Central and South America

INTRODUCTION

This short, introductory volume is intended to provide those who may be reading any or all of the books of the Bible, including the Old Testament Apocrypha, for the first time or so, with some sense of their historical contexts, their major literary forms, and their authors' or editors' principal concerns. No particular religious tradition or denominational background is presupposed, and none is especially recommended here. As a convenience, however, the symbols B.C. and A.D. will be used rather than B.C.E. (Before the Common Era) and C.E. (Common Era).

It is expected that the reader will wish to give her or his attention primarily to the biblical text itself. The chapters of this book, therefore, are quite limited in length and indicate only the basic features of each biblical book. Significant biblical passages that illustrate various points are frequently cited, usually in parentheses, but in most instances these are only some of the relevant texts. The reader is often referred to similar or contrasting statements or ideas found in other biblical writings, usually by means of the abbreviation *cf.* ("compare"). Since many readers will not be studying the entire Bible, each chapter of the present volume is meant to be understandable by itself, so some matters are repeated from time to time.

A few words are in order as to the organization and contents of the present volume. The table of contents (p. vii) sets out the general framework. Next follows a list of the books of the Bible with their abbreviations in the order in which they are treated here, showing page numbers where each book is introduced. Readers may wish to attach a tab to the first page of this list for easy reference, since the order in which the books of the Bible appear varies considerably from

one version of the Bible to another. The situation is further complicated by the fact that Jewish or Hebrew Bibles include neither the Old
Testament Apocrypha nor the New Testament, while Christian Bibles
all include the New Testament but differ as to which, if any, of the
apocryphal writings are to be regarded as Scripture. A table of dates
immediately precedes this introduction. Since most of the biblical
writings refer to or were written in the context of particular events,
readers will find it helpful to refer to this table from time to time.

Part 1 begins with an overview of the Old Testament, followed by
units introducing each of the OT books, which are considered in the
conventional order found in Protestant Bibles from the King James
Version (KJV) to the Revised Standard Version (RSV) and the New
English Bible (NEB).

After a brief introduction, Part 2 introduces the OT Apocrypha,
which includes the deutero-canonical writings, as they are characterized in Roman Catholic tradition. Until the sixteenth century, the
apocryphal writings were included within the OT section of all Christian Bibles. Even modern versions differ as to their placement: the
NEB locates the Apocrypha between the OT and the NT, while the
New Oxford Annotated Bible (NOAB) sets the Apocrypha apart—
with a new system of paginations and separate maps—following the
NT. Since the apocryphal writings by and large were composed and
reflect historical developments between the time the latest OT books
were written and the beginning of the NT period, we have followed
the example of the NEB, and most earlier Protestant Bibles, in placing
our treatment of the Apocrypha between those on the Old and the New
Testament sections. Moreover, we have construed the Apocrypha in
the broad sense, so as to include not only the deutero-canonical
writings, that is, the apocryphal books that Catholicism regards as
fully canonical or scriptural, but also 1 and 2 Esdras and the Prayer of
Manasseh, which Catholicism views as not fully canonical; 3 Maccabees and Psalm 151, which are contained in Eastern Orthodox Bibles;
and even 4 Maccabees, to which the Greek Orthodox church accords a
secondary status.

Part 3 introduces the NT and the various books it comprises. These
were all relatively early Christian writings, but not necessarily the
earliest: for example, some non-canonical (non-scriptural) writings
such as *1 Clement* and the *Epistle of Barnabas* may have been composed before 1 and 2 Timothy and 2 Peter. We have therefore used the
alternative rubric, "canonical early Christian writings."

Part 4 provides three background essays: the first on major events and periods in biblical history; the second on some of the principal literary and editorial features of biblical writing; and the third on central themes in biblical religion and faith. The book concludes with a topical index. Boldface citations there refer to pages where technical terms that may be unfamiliar to many readers are defined or explained. Such definitions are generally included in parentheses on the pages cited.

I here offer a few suggestions as to study strategies. Whether the reader is beginning serious or adult-level Bible study for the first time, or has already been engaged in such study for a while, there is no substitute for careful reading of biblical text. My treatment of a given book may aid, but ought not replace such reading. The following procedure is recommended for people who wish to study a particular book. If you are interested in Job, for example, begin by reading my introductory chapter on Job, noting the main sections, themes, and so forth, to look for. Then turn to the Book of Job itself, visualize the scenes, empathize with the various characters presented, note any questions prompted by the reading, and ponder from time to time what main point or points the writer was trying to get across to the original readers. It may be helpful then to reread my introductory treatment of Job to see if it addresses or clarifies any problems or questions that came to mind while reading the biblical text.

The three background essays in Part 4, while not mandatory, may help readers see the biblical books in broader contexts. Since, to a great extent, biblical faith came to expression in connection with events—past, present, and anticipated—the first essay, which traces the basic features of the historical context, is especially important. Most of the biblical writings are parts or examples of broader categories of biblical literature. The second essay indicates some of these connections, along with other literary considerations. The third essay indicates the religious context in which the perspectives of many of the biblical writings may be seen, sometimes in near or complete unanimity, sometimes representing contrasting beliefs and affirmations.

There are several ways to use these essays. Since they all refer to a wide range of events, writings, and beliefs, they may be more helpful after the reader has worked carefully through several of the books of the Bible with their introductions. On the other hand, reading these essays before undertaking more detailed study of particular books could provide a useful overview. Or they can be read and reviewed from time to time during the course of one's study of the Bible.

Should the reader come across unfamiliar terms, he or she may wish to consult the topical index, looking particularly for boldface citations to definitions or explanations given elsewhere in the book. The glossary function of the boldface citations in the topical index should serve to provide much of the information that otherwise might have been footnoted. Also, modern annotated study editions of the Bible often provide helpful, detailed notes. Citations to secondary literature are also kept to a minimum here. The fact that hundreds of scholarly books and articles on biblical books, passages, and topics are published each year makes it impractical to include such citations in this relatively brief introductory volume.

Those who wish to examine the biblical text and related issues more thoroughly will find many helpful multivolume commentaries, such as the Anchor Bible, the Interpreter's Bible, the Proclamation Commentary series, and various single-volume introductions to the Old and New Testaments, as well as more specialized treatments of biblical history, literature, religion, and theology. The *Interpreter's Dictionary of the Bible* (ed. George A. Buttrick and Keith R. Crim, 5 vols. [Nashville: Abingdon Press, 1976]) and the new *Harper's Bible Dictionary* (ed. Paul J. Achtemeier [New York: Harper & Row, 1985]) provide short, instructive topical essays and notes. The latter is probably the best popular reference work to which the general reader can turn for more information.

As study Bibles, the *New Oxford Annotated Bible with the Apocrypha* (NOAB), the Revised Standard Version (Oxford, 1977), and the *Oxford Study Edition of the New English Bible with the Apocrypha* (Oxford, 1976) provide generally reliable translations, supplementary essays, annotations, maps, and introductory paragraphs. Be forewarned, however, that the NOAB's notes and comments sometimes present a simplistic and traditionalist Christian viewpoint which may offend non-Christians and tend to blur or bypass important problems in interpretation. The Revised Standard Version (RSV) gives a more literal and precise translation, and preserves some flavor both of the old King James Version (of 1611; KJV) and certain Hebrew expressions. The New English Bible (NEB), on the other hand, often renders the meaning of some passages more imaginatively and clearly than the RSV, but occasionally presents questionable conjectures in the form of translations. The notes provided in the Oxford Study edition of the NEB often give less information than those given in the Oxford Annotated edition of the RSV. Quotations here are from the RSV, unless otherwise noted, even where the language of the RSV fails to be inclusive as to gender. The forthcoming edition of the RSV is expected to remedy that defect.

I have attended especially to the basic beliefs and concerns indicated in each of the biblical writings, but have intentionally avoided attempting to intimate what meanings the texts should have for modern readers. The present significance of biblical texts may be very important. My view, however, is that each reader's own understanding—and faith-understanding—will be better served by beginning with the effort to grasp what meanings the biblical speakers, writers, and editors may have found and expressed in and for their times. In this way, the book may serve indirectly to suggest the continuing and contemporary relevance of many biblical texts, for those who appreciate the intentions and meanings of the biblical writers in their own time will be better able to recognize how those intentions and meanings may relate to matters of faith and life today. But it is essential to be and remain open to the biblical text and the biblical authors' intentions. Lack of interest in or respect for what the biblical authors intended can all too easily result in substituting the modern reader's notions and prejudices for the biblical authors' beliefs and concerns. The present book will be useful, I hope, to persons studying either independently or in church seminars or college classes.

THE OLD TESTAMENT,
OR HEBREW SCRIPTURES

AN OVERVIEW

The term Old Testament was coined by Christians to distinguish the Scriptures Christianity had inherited from and shared with Judaism from those written by and for the emerging Christian communities in the first and second centuries A.D. To the present time, many Jews prefer to use expressions like the Hebrew Scriptures or, simply, the Bible, since what Christians call the New Testament is not part of Jewish Scripture or canon of sacred writings. According to ancient tradition, leading Jewish rabbis who met in Jamnia ca. A.D. 90 determined which of the many writings that had been considered inspired or authoritative at one time or another in Jewish circles should be included in or excluded from the Jewish canon. Those writings which were included at Jamnia constitute the present Jewish Scriptures. In the sixteenth century A.D., Martin Luther decided that the Christian OT should be limited to the writings accepted by the Jamnia rabbis.

Jewish tradition divided its sacred writings into three categories: the Law, the Prophets, and the Writings (or Holy Writings). The Law included the first five books, Genesis through Deuteronomy, which in traditionalist Judaism (and traditionalist Christianity) came to be called the five books of Moses and among scholars are known as the Pentateuch ("five books"). In Judaism these writings are also known as the Torah ("law") and are regarded as the basis for Jewish life. The Talmud ("teaching") and later rabbinical commentaries concentrate on interpreting the meaning of the Torah for Jews who wish it to guide their lives. The Prophets included the historical books, Joshua, Judges, 1 and 2 Kings, and 1 and 2 Samuel, as well as the lengthy books of Isaiah, Jeremiah, and Ezekiel, and the shorter writings contained in the Book of the Twelve, that is, Hosea through Malachi.

The Writings comprised all other books, such as Psalms, Proverbs, Ruth, Job, and Esther.

The Bibles of first- and second-century Christianity included the Greek Septuagint (often designated LXX) and some other Greek versions. These Scriptures included several writings omitted by the Jamnia rabbis. There was as yet no generally accepted collection of writings known as the New Testament. One of the early so-called Christian fathers, Marcion, may have made the first collection of Christian Scriptures, ca. A.D. 140. Marcion observed that the world as he knew it was marked by misery, violence, death, and decay, and doubted that the God who had made it could be good. He also noted that according to Jewish and Christian Scriptures, which were not yet known as the OT, Yahweh delighted in bloody sacrifices. He concluded that the God of these Scriptures was a malevolent deity, quite different from the One whom Christianity had come to worship. Marcion proposed to dispense with both Jewish Scriptures and the God known through them. The rest of Christianity decided not to go along with Marcion, branded him a heretic, and affirmed that the God known in the Bible was the God of Christianity and that what later came to be known as the OT was to be part of the Christian Bible.

Exactly which books or writings constituted the OT was a matter of some disagreement among later Christians. The Septuagint included a number of writings that for one reason or another—including the fact that, at the time, they were not known to exist in Hebrew or Aramaic —the rabbis at Jamnia excluded from their canon. These writings, now referred to as the Apocrypha, included such important works as Ecclesiasticus, the Wisdom of Solomon, Tobit, and Judith, and they continued to be regarded as Scripture by nearly all Christians until the time of the Protestant Reformation, when they were relegated to the apocryphal category by Protestants. Most of the writings of the Apocrypha remain in Catholic and Eastern Orthodox Bibles to the present time. At least some of another group of OT writings also, for a while, served as Scripture for many early Christians—those writings now designated the Pseudepigrapha. Jude (an NT book), for instance, quotes one of these writings, *1 Enoch*, as Scripture. *Second Enoch, 2 Baruch*, the *Book of Jubilees,* and the *Testament of the Twelve Patriarchs* are other particularly important pseudepigraphic writings. Several of the writings in the Pseudepigrapha include Christian commentary, and some of them may have been written by Christians. (See the introduction to Part 2 concerning editions of OT Pseudepigrapha.) The writings sometimes characterized as the OT Apocrypha are treated in Part 2 of this study guide. It is not thereby implied that they have any less historical or religious value than those we now turn to, which all Jewish and Christian communities consider to be Scripture.

The first half of the OT consists mainly of stories and historical reports arranged roughly in chronological order, beginning with the creation and the appearance of the first life forms, humanity among them, and following the course of events in the life of the Hebrew, Israelite, Judahite, and Jewish people down to approximately 400 B.C., the era of Nehemiah and Ezra. Here we have what probably were three separate collections of stories and historical tradition:

1. The Tetrateuch ("four books," Genesis through Numbers), which were put in their present form by Priestly editors (commonly designated P or R^P; ca. 400 B.C.)

2. The Deuteronomic history book (comprising Deuteronomy, Joshua, Judges, 1 and 2 Samuel, and 1 and 2 Kings), assembled and edited by a writer or writers influenced by the Deuteronomic reform who lived toward the end of the exile (commonly designated the Deuteronomic theologian or the Deuteronomic historian, DH; ca. 550 B.C.)

3. The unit (consisting of 1 and 2 Chronicles, Ezra, and Nehemiah), assembled and edited by an unknown writer (commonly designated the Chronicler, who sometimes is thought to have been Ezra; ca. 350 B.C.). This third unit provides a brief summary (and revision) of history from the earliest times through the period of the exile, and adds new accounts of the return of the exiles and the reconstitution of Jerusalem and the temple through the time of Nehemiah and Ezra.

The second half of the OT includes a variety of writings, some —such as Amos and Hosea—dating from as early as the eighth century B.C. The most notable groups include the Book of Psalms, the wisdom writings (Proverbs, Ecclesiastes, and Job), the three longer prophets (Isaiah, Jeremiah, and Ezekiel), and finally, the prophets of the Book of the Twelve (Hosea through Malachi). In addition we find Esther, which follows Nehemiah, perhaps because both purport to have been written in the Persian period; the Song of Solomon, which follows Ecclesiastes and like it was thought from early times to have been written by Solomon; Lamentations, which follows Jeremiah both because it was once commonly believed that Jeremiah had written it and because it describes the course of events in Jerusalem after the beginning of the exile; and Daniel, which probably dates from the second century B.C. but purports to have been written in the time of the Babylonians and thus appropriately follows Jeremiah and Ezekiel. Though not part of the Book of the Twelve, Daniel is similar in content to some of the more apocalyptic prophets contained therein, and so is plausibly placed next to it. Had the Book of the Twelve not already been closed, or completed, before Daniel was written, Daniel might have been included in it. All of the present OT writings are placed in settings which suggest they were composed by ca. 400 B.C. Later Judaism evidently considered sacred only those writings that were written by that time. Most of the apocryphal and pseudepigraphic writings similarly are ascribed to relatively ancient authors or seers.

Studying the Bible would be simpler if the traditions about a given period all dated from that period. Such, however, is not the case. Thus the first story we find in the Bible, the first creation narrative (P), probably was not written down until ca. 400 B.C., whereas the second creation account (J) may have been written as early as 950 B.C. The point to bear in mind is that a given tradition should be seen not only as a recollection of what took place at the time the events supposedly happened but also—often primarily—as a source of insight into the religious and cultural beliefs and concerns of those who set the tradition down. Thus, though the P story may tell us very little about how the world came into being many millennia ago, it provides a great deal of information about the beliefs and concerns of Jewish leadership in Jerusalem ca. 400 B.C. From this perspective, all biblical traditions are of historical and religious value—even if they tell us more about the times in which they were written than about the times or events they describe. Therefore, even 1 and 2 Chronicles are important sources, at least for Jewish beliefs and practices ca. 350 B.C.

Frequently, of course, the records are contemporary with, or at least close in time to, the events described: the court history in 2 Samuel 11—20 and 1 Kings 1—2; much of the tradition in prophets such as Amos, Hosea, Isaiah, Jeremiah, Nahum, and Obadiah; and the memoirs of Nehemiah, for example. Nevertheless, students will find it helpful to keep track not only of the main outline of historical periods and events but also of the approximate dates (as they can best be determined) and perspectives of the biblical sources or writers to whom we are indebted for this great wealth of tradition.

To assist readers in finding their way through the long and complex periods in which the OT events occurred and were remembered, a table of dates has been provided (see pp. xv–xvii above) and a summary of major events and periods in biblical history has been included in Part 4 (see pp. 207–13 below). Readers are urged to consult these resources frequently, particularly since much of the OT faith developed in the context of events: those remembered from the past, those experienced in the present, and those anticipated for the future.

THE OLD TESTAMENT

GENESIS

Genesis 1—11 forms the prologue and setting for all that follows in the Bible. Here we see the story of early humanity before the days of the first fathers and mothers of Israel. The two creation stories which it contains complement each other. In the first story, 1:1—2:4a (P), the transcendent God calls creation into existence by his word, summoning the waters and the earth to bring forth all other kinds of living creatures, and last of all makes "man"—male and female—in his own image. Afterward, God affirms that everything he has made is very good, and he rests on the seventh (sabbath) day. In the second, but more ancient creation story, 2:4b–25 (J), Yahweh-God forms "man" (*adam*) from the dust of the ground (*adamah*) and puts him in the Garden of Eden to tend it. Yahweh-God then forms the beasts and birds from the ground—in the same way he made man—with the purpose of giving man a companion and helper (2:18–24). Man names the beasts and the birds, but they do not fill the empty place in his life. Therefore Yahweh-God makes woman (*ishshah*) from the rib of the man (*ish*). "This at last" was the companion the man was looking for. The Hebrew word for man, *ha adam* (translatable also as "earth creature"),* becomes in English the proper name Adam. The narrator explains the affinity between later men and women: originally they were "one flesh." Explanations like this of existing phenomena on the basis of what happened to people in primordial times are

---

*See Phyllis Trible, *God and the Rhetoric of Sexuality* (Philadelphia: Fortress Press, 1978), 72–105. Trible suggests that in the J narrative *ha adam* does not become male until woman is made from its ribs.

referred to as etiological explanations or stories. Many such stories or comments appear in Genesis.

In Genesis 3 (J continued), the woman, persuaded by the serpent, and then the man, who needs no further persuasion, break the one commandment given them, by eating the forbidden fruit, that of the "tree of knowing good and evil." Immediately they experience their nakedness, and they try to hide from Yahweh-God when they hear him walking in the garden "in the cool of the day." The man blames the woman (and Yahweh, who gave her to him), and the woman blames the serpent. (The serpent is not identified with Satan either here or anywhere else in the OT; the serpent is merely the most subtle of all the wild creatures Yahweh has made. [Gen. 3:1; cf. Wisd. of Sol. 2:24].) All three are subjected to various penalties. The man and the woman are expelled from the garden, but Yahweh-God provides them with warm clothes. Now they are mortal, for their way to the tree of life, of which they have not yet eaten, is barred (3:22–24). But the human experiment is not put to an end. Now the man and the woman come together and have offspring (4:1–2).

In Genesis 4 (J), Cain is jealous because Yahweh has favored Abel's offering but has rejected his own. He tries to overrule Yahweh's choice and make himself number one by killing his brother, thereby committing the first fratricide. Yahweh banishes Cain from his homeland but tries to protect him from vengeance at the hands of Abel's kinsmen by somehow marking him. Cain's descendant Lamech, who in J tradition appears to be the father of Noah, likewise kills a man (another homicide) and then brags about it to his wives. The P tradition introduces Seth, a more auspicious forebear of Lamech and thus of Noah and later mankind, in 4:25—5:27. The P tradition generally has a more optimistic view of human nature and destiny than the J material. In Genesis 6—9 (where J and P are intertwined) Yahweh-God finds the human imagination "only evil continually" (J) and decides to destroy all flesh, but Noah (a righteous man, according to P) is spared, along with his family and an ark full of two (P) or seven (J) pairs of each kind of animal, bird, and "everything that creeps on the ground." Some of those additional pairs are required in the J narrative because in that version Noah sacrifices one or more of all the clean (ritually suitable) animals and birds immediately after leaving the ark (Gen. 8:20). The additional pairs enable all species of life to survive, so that they may be fruitful and multiply upon the earth, and so that Yahweh may make his covenant with them as well as with Noah and his descendants (Gen. 8:15–19; 9:8–16).

In the last of these stories from Genesis 1—11—the episode of the Tower of Babel (J)—Yahweh confuses and scatters mankind, which, heedless of Yahweh, has tried to secure a great name and destiny for itself by building a city and a tower "with its top in the heavens" (11:4).

The J stories present a discernible theology of history: humanity violates the conditions of life before Yahweh, experiences disruption of community and alienation or distancing from Yahweh, yet is permitted to continue to exist, though under increasingly circum-scribed conditions. Once living in peace and harmony with each other and with Yahweh in the garden, humans are now divided, "scattered abroad," unable to understand one another's language. It is in this setting that Abram (later called Abraham) appears. He is born, mar-ries, and goes with his family from Chaldea to Canaan in the closing verses of chap. 11. By structuring the traditions in this way, the narra-tor implies that Abraham is somehow to be understood as Yahweh's answer to the fractured and alienated condition of humanity. This interpretation is made more explicit in the first few verses of chap. 12. Before turning to these verses, some further attention is due to Genesis 1—11.

Minor details suggest that the stories in Genesis 1—11 once circu-lated separately. Wives of Cain and Seth, and would-be avengers of Abel, appear from nowhere. Noah is said to be the "first tiller of the soil" (9:20), but Adam and Cain both tilled it before him. Humankind is twice separated by languages and locations (chaps. 10, 11). Lam-ech's sons are described as the fathers of all nomads, musicians, and metalworkers (4:19–22), but as the story is told, they would all have perished in the flood. Neither the first collector and arranger of the J stories nor R^P, who later edited Genesis, seems to have been bothered by these apparent inconsistencies. Their concern, evidently, was not so much with literal history as to preserve these old traditions and, through them, to understand and explain the meaning of the human situation in their own times. To the extent that these traditions were regarded as ancient, they were taken to be authoritative and not to be discarded—even though they might fail to present a completely coher-ent narrative.

The mythical fragment about the sons of God (who resemble the lustier type of Greek deities) and the daughters of men (6:1–4) is only partly "broken," or assimilated to the more developed biblical faith. The new race of demigods resulting from the infusion of immortality into humankind might have lived forever were it not for the limit of

120 years—a limit exceeded by only a few subsequent biblical figures. Presumably the Nephilim (who were, apparently, these mixed divine-human progeny under a different name) would have perished in the great flood, which follows immediately, but they appear later on (e.g., in Num. 13:33). Etiological interests recur frequently in Genesis 1—11, typically in the form of answers to implicit questions about why things are as they are: Why do men and women desire to be "one flesh"? Why do snakes have no legs? Why do women have pain in childbearing? Why must men toil for their bread? Why must all men and women die? Why are the nations divided?

Genesis 1—11 records these ancient, and also some not so ancient, stories about the origins and early days, years and millennia of humankind—and of other life forms or creatures as well. These chapters form the prelude to the biblical traditions that follow. Beginning in Genesis 12, attention shifts to the story of Israel, starting with its forebears: the fathers and mothers of that special people who, through them, and through Yahweh's blessings and for his own purposes, are called into being.

In Gen. 12:1–3, Yahweh calls Abram (later renamed Abraham) to leave his hometown in Haran and go to the land of Canaan, and promises to make him a great nation and to make his name great (cf. 11:4). Yahweh promises that Abram will be a blessing to, or the envy of, other nations. Yahweh also blesses Sarai (later called Sarah), Abram's wife, and promises—notwithstanding her advanced age— not only that she will bear a son but also that she will become the mother of kings and nations and that Yahweh will establish his covenant with her son Isaac (Gen. 17:15–21). The remainder of the biblical story—both in Genesis and in the Bible as a whole—records the partial fulfillment of these commands and promises. Abraham is the central figure in chaps. 12—26. Isaac appears mainly to connect Abraham with Jacob, whose dealings with Esau and Laban are described in chaps. 27—35. There are few independent traditions about Isaac, and he appears mainly as a passive and shadowy figure. Sarah, Rebekah, and Rachel, on the other hand, emerge as definite and significant persons in the course of events. The account of God's covenant of circumcision with Abraham (Gen. 17:1–4) probably comes from P, which characteristically is interested in ritual or "priestly" matters. Most of the remaining Genesis traditions come from J, but some E material appears, often blended with J as JE. Chapters 20 and 22 appear to derive mainly from E. Both P and E traditions in Genesis generally use the divine name Elohim, translated as "God." In Genesis, the J tradition is distinguishable by its use of the divine name Yahweh, translated as "the LORD." It is sometimes said that J tradition is earlier than E material, and that the two collections of tradition are to be dated ca. 950 and 850 B.C. respectively. The more significant point is that J represents Southern or Judahite tradition, while E consists of Northern or Israelite materials. The symbols J and E, like P, are used sometimes to designate the collectors and editors of these respective materials, and sometimes to refer to the biblical texts attributed to these collectors and editors.

Abraham and Jacob are remembered for their faithfulness and obedience to God but also for their mistrust and (esp. in the case of Jacob) deceit. These modes of response almost alternate in the Abraham stories. Abraham goes, as Yahweh commands (12:4), but fearing for his life, lets Pharaoh take Sarai as wife (12:10–20). Later, after separating from Lot, Abraham is promised all the land he sees, along with innumerable descendants. He goes and builds an altar to Yahweh (13:8–18) but then doubts that Yahweh-God will give him the promised offspring (15:2–3) and so has a child by another woman (16:1–4). On the positive side, again, Abraham agrees to be circumcised (chap. 17), and Yahweh promises that, notwithstanding her advanced age, Sarah will bear him a son (18:10–15). (Though Sarah laughs at the idea, Abraham apparently preserves a straight face.) Yahweh honors Abraham by consulting him about the fate of Sodom, and Abraham, to his credit, goes so far as to remind Yahweh to "do right" and not destroy the righteous with the wicked (chap. 18). But then, again fearing for his life, Abraham gives Sarah over, this time only briefly, to the Philistine king Abimelech (chap. 20). Isaac at last is born (chap. 21), and in due course Abraham meets the supreme test of faith by making ready to sacrifice this special and only son through whom alone, it seems, the promise of Gen. 12:2a can be fulfilled.

Time passes, and Isaac grows up. Abraham grows old. He sends his servant to find a wife for Isaac from among his kinsmen. The servant travels to Nahor, near Haran. There he prays for guidance and comes upon Rebekah, Abraham's grandniece and Laban's sister (24:1–15). The narrator emphasizes that the decision to marry Isaac is up to Rebekah (24:5, 8, 58). They marry and have twins, Jacob and Esau. The boys grow up, and Jacob becomes the central narrative figure. Jacob coolly extorts Esau's birthright (25:29–34), deceives his blind, old, dying father, Isaac, in order to swindle Esau out of his blessing, and then prudently goes to visit Uncle Laban in Haran to escape Esau's revenge (chap. 27). There Jacob falls in love at first sight with his cousin Rachel while also noticing the size of her father's herds—a sure sign of his wealth (29:9–11). Laban, the Aramean, who also has an eye for acquirable wealth (24:29–31), tricks Jacob into marrying another daughter first, and thus into fourteen years of indentured service (29:15–30). Years go by. Jacob has nine sons and a daughter and gains title to most of Laban's movable property (with God's help, of course). He correctly senses that Laban's sons are displeased and that the time has come to leave. One day while Laban is away, Jacob steals off with everything he claims (chaps. 30—31). Laban's posse overtakes Jacob, but warned by God in a dream (31:22, E) and unwilling to bring harm to his own daughters and grandchildren, Laban in exasperation calls on God to keep an eye on Jacob, in the words of the Mizpah benediction (31:49–50). Jacob returns to Canaan, anxiously sending large bribes ahead to placate Esau (32:1–21). An ancient myth (largely unassimilated) about a night demon tells of Jacob's wrestling at Peniel (face [or presence] of an *el* [or god]) with a man or god who must flee before daybreak. This being blesses Jacob and renames him Israel (32:22–32, JE). Here, as elsewhere in Genesis, etiological interests are apparent. In P, Jacob is renamed Israel under less primitive circumstances, near Bethel (35:9–15).

The story of Shechem's rape of Jacob's daughter Dinah, his subsequent love for her, and her brothers' vicious revenge is told in chap. 34. Jacob objects to his sons' conduct on prudential, not moral, grounds (34:30). A separate story is set out in chap. 38, that of Judah, who has married a Canaanite woman, and his daughter-in-law Tamar, who cleverly compels him to observe the traditional requirement of levirate marriage after her husband dies and his other sons fail to do their duty. (See also Deut. 25:5–10; Ruth.) Here the obligation of the brother-in-law (*levir,* in Latin) is assumed by the widow's father-in-law.

The saga of Joseph and his brothers in Genesis 37, 39—50 is one of the early masterpieces of world literature. J and E traditions are carefully blended. (In J, which is the Southern or Judahite source, Judah protects Joseph, who is sold to Ishmaelites; in E, it is Reuben who pleads for Joseph, who is sold to Midianites. Here, as elsewhere in the E tradition, God typically communicates with people through the medium of dreams.) In the story, Jacob's doting affection for Joseph (one of the two sons of his beloved Rachel), which he expresses by dressing him up like little Lord Fauntleroy (37:3–4), together with Joseph's tactless recitation of his seemingly pretentious dreams, prompts his brothers to try to get rid of him. Joseph survives, is taken to Egypt, recognized there for his ability to interpret dreams, and made czar of agriculture. Worldwide famine brings all the earth, including his brothers (who are not bright enough to think of the idea themselves, Gen. 42:1–2), to Egypt to buy grain. This gives Joseph opportunity to get back at them—and curiously, to add to the misery of his father, to whom he has neglected to send word that he has been alive and well in Egypt all these years (chaps. 42—44). Theologically, Joseph's achievements there represent God's providential care for Israel and all the families of the earth (41:57; 45:5–7; 50:20) and thus an early, partial fulfillment of the promise in J traditions that the descendants of Abraham, Isaac, and Jacob would be a blessing (Gen. 12:2–3; 26:4; 28:14). Historically, the Joseph story serves to bring Jacob and his family from Canaan into Egypt, where the story of Israel begins in the Book of Exodus.

EXODUS

Two important eras and two decisive events are remembered in Exodus: the eras of Israel in Egypt and of Israel in the wilderness; the events of God's delivering Israel out of Egypt and of his giving Israel the law. The traditions, including some quite early ones, are preserved by J, E, and P. E introduces the divine name Yahweh ("the LORD") in 3:13–15. J used this name from the start (Gen. 2:4b); in P it is first revealed in Exod. 6:2–3. Previously both E and P have used the name Elohim (originally a plural form meaning "gods," but in biblical times a proper name for God).

At the end of Genesis, Jacob (or Israel) and his family are sojourners (resident aliens) in Egypt. According to Exodus 1, the people of Israel multiply greatly and, under a new Pharaoh (possibly Ramses II, ca. 1290–1223 B.C.) who fears their growing numbers, are made slaves. Now they groan in bondage, crying to God for help (2:23) —though later, in the wilderness, their recollection of life in Egypt will be much more positive (Exod. 14:10–12; 16). Moses, who has married Zipporah, the daughter of a Midianite priest (named Jethro in E, Reuel in J), is called by God to lead the Israelites out of Egypt. Moses is reluctant to accept this assignment, but Yahweh answers all his objections and appoints Moses' brother Aaron to assist him (3:11—4:17). An early and largely unassimilated myth tells of Moses' vicarious circumcision along the way whereby Zipporah shrewdly thwarts Yahweh's arbitrary attempt to kill him (4:24–25, J—the remains of another story about a night demon; cf. Gen. 32: 24–32).

Moses and Aaron proceed to perform wonders and evoke plagues to impress Pharaoh with God's power. (In J, Moses speaks and God sends the plagues; in E, Moses raises his hand or rod; and in P, Aaron wields the rod. The P tradition views Aaron as the father of all later priests and tends to emphasize his importance.) Pharaoh, however, is unimpressed until God sends the "destroyer," killing the firstborn of the Egyptians but "passing over" the houses of Israel (12:21–24, J). (The P account is concerned with how the Passover ceremony is to be observed in later generations, 12:1–20, 40–51.) All now looks hopeful for the Israelites. But then Yahweh hardens Pharaoh's heart, the better to "get glory" over him (14:4), and Pharaoh sends a great army after the terrified Israelites. Nevertheless, Yahweh rescues them by the Sea of Reeds (Red Sea). One version visualizes a "wall of water" on either side of the escaping Israelites that engulfs the pursuing Egyptians. The early song attributed to the prophetess Miriam (15:20–21) pictures the action somewhat differently. Whatever the case, the exodus ("way out," "departure" in Greek) is commemorated in many later writings as a major milestone, indeed, as the event in which God called Israel into existence as a people (e.g., Deut. 5:6; Hos. 11:1; Isa. 43:15–17; 51:10). Thus it can be said that the history of Israel as a people, if not yet a nation, begins with the exodus from Egypt.

The wilderness epoch is marked by complaining (chap. 16) and apostasy (chap. 32) on the part of the Israelites. Leviticus, Numbers, and Deuteronomy also describe Israel in the wilderness and the laws God gives to Moses there for Israel. The Covenant Code, delivered orally to Moses on the mountain (Mount Sinai in J), is reported in chaps. 20—23 (E). This first codification of Israelite law may date from as early as ca. 1100 B.C. In the memory and faith of Israel, it was not just any god but the God who brought them out of Egypt who gave this law (20:2).The first two of the Ten Commandments or Decalogue require exclusive fidelity to this God; the last eight serve to promote and preserve the well-being of the community. The Third Commandment (20:7) probably warns against committing perjury (cf. Jer. 5:2). The Fourth Commandment proclaims the Sabbath as a day of rest not only for Israelite families but also for their servants and cattle, and for sojourners. The Fifth and Tenth Commandments refer to inner attitudes. Numerous other commandments follow in chaps. 21—23; these too require faithfulness to God and proper observance of sacrifices and festivals, but primarily they require the maintenance of right relationships within the community. Thus one can speak of the vertical and horizontal dimensions of Israelite law: what is owed to God, and what is owed to neighbor. The community laws specify what is to be done if wrongdoing occurs; for example, injuries to animals or to slaves or to other persons must be remedied by due restitution. Criminal and civil laws are not differentiated. The "law of retaliation" applies only when a pregnant woman is injured by brawling males (Exod. 21:22–25). Slaves, widows, orphans, sojourners, the poor, and both domestic and wild animals are to be protected and provided for (see, e.g., 21:20, 26–27; 22:21–27; 23:4–5, 9–12). All these commandments, not just the Ten, are remembered as the words and laws of Yahweh. (In traditional Judaism, the total number of commandments in the several books of the law is said to be either 613 or 623.) After receiving these commandments, as the story is told, Moses records them and reads this "book of the covenant" to the Israelites. They pledge their obedience, and he consecrates them with the "blood of the covenant" (24:3–8).

Chapters 25—31 and 35—40 (P) mainly contain laws and descriptions of the design of the tabernacle and its furnishings, the duties and prerogatives of Aaron and his sons (the only persons who may be priests, according to P), and procedures for the ordination of priests. Chapters 32—34 consist principally of J and E traditions, including the famous episode of the golden calf (chap. 32). Here Moses barely dissuades Yahweh from destroying Israel (32:7–14), and Aaron, rather lamely, "explains" the presence of the calf: "I threw [the gold] into the fire, and there came out this calf" (32:24). Yahweh speaks with Moses "face to face" (33:11), or as another tradition has it, Moses sees Yahweh's back but not his face (33:20–23). In chap. 34, Moses (again, as the story is told) goes up Mount Sinai to receive another and somewhat different set of commandments, sometimes called the ritual Decalogue (34:11–28, J). It is possible that chap. 34 gives another ancient version of the tradition of making covenant which is found in chaps. 19—24 (E).

LEVITICUS

The title of this biblical book is misleading: Levites are mentioned only in 25:32–33. The book primarily contains laws concerning priests, sacrifices, festivals, and ritual purity. Biblical tradition to ca. 450 B.C. does not distinguish between priests and Levites: in these early traditions, if a man is a priest, he must be a Levite, that is, from the tribe of Levi. The distinction first appears in the P tradition, ca.

400 B.C. Leviticus includes two major literary components: the Holiness Code (H) in chaps. 17 through 26, and P laws (part of the Priestly Code, or PC) in the other chapters. All purportedly were spoken by Yahweh to Moses in the wilderness (1:1). Like most of Exodus, Numbers, and Deuteronomy, Leviticus is set in the wilderness period (ca. 1230–1200 B.C.). By the time the Pentateuch was put in its final literary form (ca. 400 B.C.), Jews generally believed that all legal traditions, including those that modern scholars date well after the time of Moses, were revealed to Moses and transmitted by him to Israel during the wilderness years.

H, the third codification of Israelite-Judahite law, may have been composed by rural priests or Levites ca. 650 B.C.—about the same time that J and E, the Southern and Northern narrative traditions respectively, were being combined to form JE. The Northern kingdom, Israel, was then defunct, and the Southern kingdom, Judah, had fallen heir to Northern traditions that it preserved by weaving them together with its own. (The first codification was the Covenant Code; the second was the Deuteronomic Code, D.) The laws in H stress Yahweh's holiness and the requirement that Israel be holy (*qadosh*), that is, separate or different from the ways of other nations (18:3; 19:2; 20:23–26). Commonly the laws in H are sanctioned by the refrain "I am Yahweh your God." They pertain to sexual practices, priestly purification, sacrifices, and festivals, but also to love of neighbors (19:18) and strangers (19:34) and to justice, including obligations to the poor and to sojourners (19:33–34; 23:22; 24:22). The lex talionis or law of retaliation (24:19–20; cf. Exod. 21:22–25) applies only to disfigurement (mayhem in modern American statutes), but an implicit principle of limited retribution or compensation also appears in several other laws (e.g., 24:17–18, 21). In chap. 25, the land is to keep Sabbath: whatever grows by itself the seventh year is to provide food for citizens, slaves, sojourners, domestic animals, and wildlife (25:2–7; cf. Exod. 23:10–11). The jubilee law requires the return of unredeemed rural property to original owners and the freeing of indentured servants in the fiftieth year. Leviticus 25:10a is the text inscribed on the Liberty Bell. The underlying rationale for the land ethic of Leviticus 25 is that ultimately the land belongs to Yahweh, not the people: "The land is mine; for you are strangers and sojourners with me" (25:23). Chapter 26 consists of admonitions about the life-and-death importance of keeping the commandments, ordinances, and statutes set out in H.

In Leviticus, as in Exodus and Numbers, we see large segments of the fourth and most extensive collection or codification of law, sometimes designated the Priestly Code, or PC. The PC describes mainly burnt, cereal, peace, sin, guilt, thank, and wave offerings —several of which are not mentioned in the earlier codes. The PC, like P tradition generally, differentiates between priests and Levites, relegating the latter to the role of assistants to the former. Several laws focus on what Aaron and his sons (the priests—now distinguished from Levites) are to do with the blood, fat, kidneys, livers, entrails, etc., of the sacrificial animals. Choicer portions belong to the priests as their due (7:28–36). Clean and unclean animals are to be differentiated (chap.11). Priests and others are to attend to human diseases and discharges with various therapeutic procedures and offerings (chaps. 13—15). Procedures for the Day of Atonement (Yom Kippur) are described in chap. 16: various animals are to be sacrificed at the tabernacle or tent of meeting (which functions in P and PC as an early prototype of the temple at Jerusalem), and a goat is to be sent to Azazel, a wilderness spirit of some sort, to make atonement (thus the later expression "scapegoat"). No one may eat the blood of either domestic or wild animals, "for the life of every creature is its blood" (17:10–14). Because life comes from God, it must be returned to him, by pouring the blood out on the ground. (According to P, early humanity and all other creatures originally were vegetarian; see Gen. 1:29–30. After the flood, in P tradition, humans might eat flesh but not "with its life, that is, its blood," Gen. 9:4. According to Acts 15:20, 29, early Christians were to abstain likewise.)

NUMBERS

Israel is still in the wilderness, between Egypt and the promised land. Several narrative sections, mainly J and E, are included in chaps. 11—14, 16, 20—25, and 32. The greater part of the book continues the P laws (Priestly Code or PC), which appear at length from Exodus 25 through Leviticus and Numbers. PC was the fourth major collection or codification of law, set down ca. 400 B.C., probably by priests who presided over the offering of sacrifices at the temple in Jerusalem. These laws are typically presented as instructions spoken by God to Moses, supplementing those initially given on Mount Sinai. The entire Tetrateuch or first four books (Genesis, Exodus, Leviticus, and Numbers) was probably edited by R^P, the Priestly redactor or editor, ca. 400 B.C.

This book's title derives from P's characteristic interest in the numbers, names, and locations of the Israelite tribes, their leaders, and their families. The P laws relate mainly to sacrificial offerings and ritual purity. P distinguishes priests (Aaron and his sons) from Levites. The latter were to attend to the tabernacle and its furnishings and merely assist the priests (1:47–53; 3:5–37; 18:2–7). The distinction between priests and Levites does not appear in writings dated before ca. 450 B.C. P narratives refer frequently to the tabernacle or tent of meeting (which is rarely mentioned, if at all, in the earlier J, E, or DH traditions). This was visualized as a portable prototype of the Jerusalem temple, which, when the P authors were writing, had been the only proper place of worship for over two hundred years. P seems to have assumed that Judah and the Jewish people had always been obliged to worship in just one place: first the tabernacle, and then, when it was built, the temple.

Primary responsibilities and perquisites are reserved for priests (e.g., chaps. 4, 18). Special P laws in Numbers also include the cereal offering of jealousy, a kind of trial by ordeal for a wife whose husband suspects her of infidelity (chap. 5); the law of the Nazirite, a temporary ascetic withdrawal for either men or women (chap. 6); Passover, which must be kept also by sojourners (chap. 9); laws of inheritance, including provisions for daughters if there were no sons (chap. 27; cf. Job 42:15, which says that Job provided for both his sons and his daughters); keeping vows or making contracts—women's subject to fathers' or husbands' approval (chap. 30); and establishing cities of refuge, and other cities for Levites (chap. 35; cf. Deut. 18:1–8; 19:1–10). P narratives include accounts of the stoning of a violator of the Sabbath (15:32–36), and the fate of Korah and other misguided Levites who dared pretend to priestly status (chap. 16). The famous Aaronic benediction is in 6:24–26.

J and E narratives report Israel's repeated complaining about life in the wilderness and their hankering for the good old days in Egypt. Fed up with all the complaining, Moses on one occasion proposes to disown Israel (chap. 11); another time Yahweh determines to disinherit them, and Moses only just barely persuades him to relent (chap. 14). Miriam and Aaron protest Moses' marriage to a black (Cushite) woman, and envy his unique status as prophet and leader. In punishment, Miriam is turned snow white with leprosy until Aaron petitions Moses and prays to God for forgiveness (chap. 12). Israelite scouts report that Canaan is fruitful, but filled with big, strong inhabitants (chaps. 13—14). Only Caleb and Joshua are confident that they can occupy it. Again (chap. 20, E and P) the people of Israel pine for the comforts of Egypt. Following Yahweh's instructions, Moses strikes a rock that brings forth water (20:2–11, 13; cf. Exod. 17:1–7)—an act of faithlessness, according to later tradition, which thus explains why Moses was not allowed to enter the promised land. (Num. 20:12; Deut. 32:48–52)

Chapters 22—24 (J and E) picture Balak's persistent efforts to induce the (non-Israelite) prophet Balaam to curse Israel. Balak is king of the land of Moab, which the Israelites are passing on their way to Canaan. Their presence makes him nervous, so he sends for Balaam, a professional execrator. As the story is told—possibly combining two different versions—it is unclear whether God wishes Balaam to go or not. According to Num. 22:20, God tells Balaam to go ahead. Yet two verses later, God is angry because Balaam has gone, and Yahweh's angel blocks the path. Balaam's ass, seeing the angel, refuses to proceed. Balaam, who does not see the angel, beats the ass, whereupon she reproaches Balaam for so treating her. Balaam shows no surprise at hearing her speak, and concedes that she is in the right, especially after the angel becomes visible to him, too, and points out that she has saved his life. Balaam proceeds to the capital of Moab, but insists that he can only speak what Yahweh commands. To Balak's utter exasperation, Balaam repeatedly pronounces blessings on Israel rather than curses, even adding one final, gratuitous blessing after Balak has dismissed him (24:10–19). The episode's point comes in the comforting assurance that there is no enchantment or divination against Israel (23:23). Strangely, P tradition later condemns Balaam (31:8, 16), possibly confusing Balaam, son of Beor, with the story of Israel's apostasy at Baal-Peor (25:1–5).

The Book of Numbers concludes the collection of traditions about early times which was edited in priestly circles, ca. 400 B.C. What follows is an earlier collection of traditions, commonly designated the Deuteronomic history book, which begins with the Book of Deuteronomy.

DEUTERONOMY

The title means "second law." Chapters 5 and 12—26, together designated the Deuteronomic Code (D), constitute the second major codification of Israelite law, the first being the Covenant Code (Exodus 20—23). Much of chaps. 12—19 was evidently added well after the codification of the laws in the rest of the book. The original codification, which incorporated most of the Covenant Code, may have been made as early as the period of the judges. Most of the book purports to have been spoken by Moses to Israel in the wilderness.

Chapters 1—4 are an introduction by the Deuteronomic editor (also known as the Deuteronomic theologian or Deuteronomic historian, or simply, DH) both to the book of Deuteronomy and to the entire Deuteronomic history book, which, omitting Ruth, extends through 2 Kings. Some modern scholars posit two different Deuteronomic editors, one ca. 600 B.C., the other ca. 550 B.C. For simplicity, we refer only to one such editor, theologian, or historian, designated here as DH, who wrote ca. 550 B.C. DH drew on earlier Southern or Judahite traditions (J, down to ca. 950 B.C., A, thereafter) and Northern or Israelite accounts (E, down to perhaps ca. 850 B.C., B thereafter) and some other sources, and arranged them in their present order, commenting occasionally, particularly in Deuteronomy, Judges, and 1 and 2 Kings. DH was looking back into history, trying to make sense of what had occurred. Drawing on the prophets, who had explained the meaning of events in their own times in accordance with Yahweh's righteousness, DH retrospectively viewed the frequent disasters that had come upon Israel and Judah as Yahweh's punishments for their forsaking him and the requirements of the Covenant. Writing in the middle of the sixth century B.C., DH apparently regarded the Deuteronomic requirement that Israel worship only in one place (implicitly, Jerusalem) as a key criterion in appraising the kings of Israel and Judah. DH was probably unaware that this requirement (along with a series of laws making various accommodations to it) was added to the text of Deuteronomy less than a century earlier. In these first chapters, Moses reviews previous events in the wilderness (where the Israelites are still wandering), emphasizing the need to keep Yahweh's ordinances and statutes, including the Ten Commandments (4:13–14), which are repeated in chap. 5. According to this editor, the Covenant was made at Mount Horeb, not Mount Sinai (5:2; 29:1). Perhaps these are different names for the same mountain.

Chapters 6—11 include a series of sermons calling for fidelity to Yahweh and his "commandments, statutes, and ordinances." Some material may derive from an ancient ceremony of covenant renewal (see Deuteronomy 27; Josh. 8:30–35; 24:1–28), practiced perhaps as early as the time of the judges (ca. 1200–1000 B.C.). The great commandment to love God is included in 6:4–5. These sermons insist that Yahweh is bringing Israel into the land of Canaan for his own purposes, particularly, his love for them, not because of their importance or merit (7:6–9; 9:4–8). They warn that once Israel is in the land, the people shall surely perish if they neglect the Commandments and worship other gods. Cultic credos recalling the people's history (6:20–23; 26:5–9) may have been recited at the ancient ceremony of covenant renewal. These sermons—which may either go back to the time of the old ceremony or come largely from the pen of DH— express the understanding that Yahweh gave the law to the people of Israel for their own good because of his love for them: the law serves beneficially to structure the community; moreover, by keeping the law, Israel can avoid incurring Yahweh's wrath. In addition, Yahweh loves the sojourner; therefore the Israelites should do likewise (10:18– 19; cf. Lev. 19:33).

Chapters 5 and 12—26 recapitulate the Covenant Code, but with many additions. The added laws pertain both to sacrifices and festivals, but also to justice and compassion within the community. A number of new laws give expression particularly to Yahweh's compassion for people and also animals.

The principal innovation is the idea that when the Israelites enter the promised land, they are to destroy all the shrines where the indigenous peoples serve their gods, and thereafter worship at only one place, implicitly, Jerusalem (12:2–14). Jerusalem is not named, probably because the authors of this new requirement were aware that the Israelites did not even occupy that city until the time of David (2 Sam. 5:6–9), and that the temple was not built there until the reign of Solomon (1 Kings 6). According to earlier legal and historical traditions, the Israelites had been free to worship at many places, and had done so without qualms (e.g., Judg. 17:7–13; 1 Sam. 2:12–17; 9:12–13; 14:33–35). The new law requiring centralized worship evidently was introduced prior to or in connection with the Deuteronomic reform carried out under King Josiah of Judah, ca. 622 B.C. (see 2 Kings 22:1—23:25).

Now that worship is permitted only in Jerusalem, a number of adjustments are required. In view of the fact that many live far from Jerusalem, provision is made for local slaughter of animals for food (12:15–16, 20–22). The major festivals, however, are to be observed in Jerusalem by all males every year (16:5–17; cf. Tob. 1:6). Tithes of crops that prove too bulky to be carried to Jerusalem may be sold and the proceeds used to buy food to "eat before Yahweh" there (14:22–27). The closing of the local shrines meant that the Levites who have been priests there are out of work. Provisions are made to meet their needs: they may sell their patrimony and move to Jerusalem, where they are supposed to have the same duties and rights as the

Levites who are priests there (18:6–8); those who remain in their towns or local rural areas, now having no livelihood, are to be provided for along with widows, the fatherless, and sojourners (12:18– 19; 14:27–29). Secular judges are to be appointed to replace the local Levites, who, as priests, formerly were available to settle claims (16:18–20; cf. 17:8–13); and secular cities of refuge are to be set aside to replace the cultic shrines which previously served as sanctuaries for persons who committed manslaughter (19:1–10). The requirement that Yahweh be worshiped only at the one place is intended to counter the Judahites' continuing tendency to worship deities other than Yahweh at these local shrines.

The *herem*, meaning the sacred destruction or slaughter of the indigenous peoples of Canaan, also is stipulated in order to prevent apostasy that might result from contact with them. The *herem* is a recurrent theme in Deuteronomy and the Deuteronomic history book. To what extent it accurately represents ancient Israelite practice is uncertain. Judges 1:27–35 and some other texts suggest that it was not carried out systematically. Certain related neighboring peoples were to be tolerated, but excluded from the Israelite community (23:3–8).

Other laws provide protection for the poor (15:7–11), laborers (22:8; 24:14–15), slaves and escaped slaves (15:12–18; 23:15–16), newly married males (24:5), day laborers (24:14–15), debtors (24: 10–13), sojourners, orphans and widows (24:19–22), and offenders (25:3). These laws, some of which derive from Exodus 20—23, emphasize Yahweh's compassion or love for his people. Some are also concerned with conservation and respect for animal life (20:19; 22:1–4, 6–7; 25:4).

Chapter 27 ordains a ceremony in which Israel gathers at Shechem to ratify the covenant, invoking curses on those who violate the laws (cf. 11:26–29). Chapters 28—30 (probably composed by DH) reiterate the life-and-death importance of faithfulness to Yahweh and his commandments (e.g., 30:15–20; see also 32:45–47).

Chapters 32 and 33 include, respectively, a psalm attributed to Moses, and Moses' blessing of the tribes of Israel (cf. Jacob's blessing of the tribes, Genesis 49). In 32:48–52, Yahweh tells Moses that he will see the promised land, but not go there. Chapters 31 and 34 (J and E) report Moses' appointment of Joshua to be his successor and Moses' death at the age of one hundred and twenty (cf. Gen. 6:3).

Deuteronomy concludes the Pentateuch, the five books of the Law or Torah, popularly ascribed to Moses. Several hundred verses of these books are attributed to Moses in the text, for example, his two psalms or songs (Exod. 15:1–18; Deut. 31:30—32:43) and numerous speeches to Israel and conversations with Yahweh and others. But nothing in these texts suggests that Moses was thought to have authored any of the first five books as such. Deuteronomy is also the first part of the Deuteronomic history book, which also includes Joshua, Judges, 1 and 2 Samuel, and 1 and 2 Kings. The Book of Joshua continues the narrative from Deuteronomy 34, which is set in the closing years or months of the wilderness era.

JOSHUA

The book has two main sections. In the first section (chaps. 1—12) Joshua brings the Israelites out of the wilderness and into the promised land, which, with Yahweh's help, they conquer. In the second (chaps. 13—21) the land is apportioned among the various Israelite tribes. Principal sources include J (the Southern or Judahite tradition set down perhaps ca. 950 B.C.) and E (the Northern or Israelite tradition possibly recorded ca. 850 B.C.). Here the Deuteronomic editor (DH) continues his retrospective account of Israel's history that began with the Book of Deuteronomy. Writing ca. 550 B.C., DH contributes several interpretive and summary passages.

DH conveys the impression that Israel completely overran the land, killing off all the indigenous peoples. Theologically, DH characterizes these events as the fulfillment of all the promises to the fathers: Yahweh thus gave the people this land as their possession or inheritance, and gave them rest (1:13–15; 11:23; 21:43–45). Several passages, however, indicate that the conquest was less than complete (e.g., 11:22; 13:2–7, 13; 15:63; 16:10). Modern historians dispute whether Israel's occupation of the land was primarily through conquest or by more peaceful settlement of largely unoccupied areas. The reported tribal allotments are probably somewhat idealized; very likely, the several tribes managed to settle where they could, with periods of conflict as well as times of peaceful relations with their neighbors (thus, e.g., 17:11–18; 19:47; Judges 1).

Various DH passages emphasize the *herem*, which required the killing of indigenous peoples, presumably lest any survivors tempt the Israelites to worship their gods (10:28–40). Nevertheless, in later years, Israelites, Judahites, and Jews evidently would be tempted again and again to worship other gods: we find such practices condemned (and sometimes ridiculed) from Hosea and Isaiah, through the times of Ezekiel and Second Isaiah, on down to relatively late writings such as the Wisdom of Solomon, the Letter of Jeremiah, and Bel and the Dragon. Various passages probably attributable to DH affirm that if Israel would keep the laws of "this book" (probably referring to Deuteronomy), they would prosper (1:7-8); but if they served the gods of foreign peoples or intermarried with foreigners, they would "perish quickly from off the good land" (23:1-16).

Early traditions (mainly J and E) recall a number of memorable scenes: the harlot Rahab's clever protection of the Israelite spies at Jericho—hiding them on the roof, then letting them down by a rope from her window in the city wall, and finally marking her window by a scarlet cord (chap. 2); Israel's crossing the Jordan river on dry ground while the ark—symbolizing the power and presence of Yahweh—causes its waters to stop, piling up in a heap (chaps. 3—4); and the dramatic capture of Jericho, as its walls fell flat (though without harming Rahab or her household) after the trumpets blew and the people shouted (chap. 6). (Archeological evidence suggests that Jericho was last destroyed long before the time of Joshua, so some interpreters propose that the story originally had to do with another city conquered by Israel.) The story of the capture of Ai by ambush and the slaughter of all its inhabitants—all while Joshua holds out his javelin—is told in chap. 8. Joshua then builds an altar at Shechem, and holds a ceremony of covenant ratification there, featuring the reading of "the book of the Law" (8:30-35). The Gibeonites (Hivites), a nearby tribe, wishing to be spared the notorious *herem*, send a peace delegation who, equipped with moldy bread and worn-out clothes, pretend to have come from a far country (chap. 9), and thereby beguile the Israelites into making a covenant to let them live. The five Amorite kings who attacked Gibeon for making peace with Israel are then defeated by Yahweh and Israel on the day the sun and moon stood still (10:1-15). Joshua's headquarters for a time was at Shiloh (18:1-10), but Shechem was the main place for tribal meetings to renew the covenant (chap. 24). Here we find another cultic credo whereby the people of Israel were to recite the historic deeds of Yahweh on behalf of his people (24:2-13). An oath of fidelity to Yahweh and his law is also part of this ceremony (24: 14-27, E).

JUDGES

The Israelites are now in Canaan, having conquered or settled the land. But the Canaanites and other peoples have "persisted in dwelling" there, and, together with several neighboring nations, cause Israel much grief. Israel's political structure—such as it was—in this era (ca. 1200–1000 B.C.) was that of a federation of tribes loosely united, but occasionally divided against one another. The main institutional expression of their unity was the periodic ceremony of covenant renewal usually held at Shechem, which is evidenced in Deuteronomy 11 and 27, and Joshua 8 and 24, though not mentioned in the Book of Judges. An editor, possibly DH, comments thematically in the concluding chapters of this book, "In those days there was no king in Israel; every man did what was right in his own eyes" (21:25). From this perspective we may infer that the politics of "rugged" or autonomous individualism failed to cope with the serious problems which were gradually overwhelming the nation. What Israel needed, it seemed, was a strong central government, namely, a king. The editor/commentator clearly recognized that the Israelite federation was unable to ·cope either with external enemies or with internal dissensions.

As to external enemies, at first Israel manages to hold its own. Under the leadership of Deborah, a prophetess and judge (4:4–5), certain Israelite tribes get together and defeat a coalition of Canaanite kings. This is when the heroine Jael dramatically kills the Canaanite general Sisera while he sleeps (4:21) or drinks out of a "lordly bowl" and so is unable to see the blow coming (5:25–27). The Song of Deborah, one of the earliest fragments of Biblical tradition, records that some Israelite tribes failed to come when they were called (5:13–18), clearly a bad sign for the future of the federation. Through a surprise attack featuring some startling special effects in the middle of the night, Gideon, leading troops from the tribes of Manasseh, Naphtali, and Asher, is able to prevail over Midianite invaders (chaps. 6—7), but he refuses to be made king on the grounds that only Yahweh should have that honor (8:22–23). Jephthah and the Gileadites (here represented as one of the tribes of Israel) manage to subdue the Ammonites, though Jephthah's tragic vow costs the life of his daughter, his only child (chap. 11). The Israelite tribe of Ephraim, though summoned to help, fails to come (12:2). The Philistines, however, soon prove too much for Israel. The stories of the exploits of Samson, the physically powerful but mentally and morally negligible hero, serve as a distraction to their original listeners and readers; but they do not alter the fact that the Philistines have become rulers over Israel (15:11) and will remain so for a time.

The federation is also unable to deal with problems of internal disorder. The Ephraimites, aspiring to the grandeur of being number-one tribe in Israel (cf. Gen. 48:8–20), and perhaps desiring a share in the spoils of battle, berate Gideon for not calling them to help fight the Midianites. His diplomatic answer averts conflict (8:1–3), but when the Ephraimites repeat their performance with Jephthah, who has just defeated the Ammonites, bloody civil war breaks out in Israel, even while the Philistine menace grows on the horizon (12:1–6). In the particularly gruesome series of stories which conclude the book (chaps. 17—21), the tribe of Benjamin is nearly destroyed in a fratricidal frenzy by the rest of Israel. It is rescued from extinction only by the Israelites' last-minute anguish at the idea that a tribe should be lacking in Israel (21:3), and by their proceeding to massacre another Israelite tribe (Jabesh-gilead) and forcibly abduct young women from an old Israelite town (Shiloh) in order to obtain wives for the surviving Benjaminite males (chap. 21). Clearly the storyteller meant to justify the establishment of the monarchy in Israel as a way out of the moral and political chaos characteristic of the time of the judges.

The Deuteronomic historian (DH) structures the period in terms of a cyclical theology of history, as set forth at 2:11–23: Israel commits apostasy by worshiping other gods; Yahweh punishes Israel through plundering or domination by enemy nations; the Israelites cry or groan under oppression; Yahweh has pity on them and delivers them through a judge who, either single-handedly or as leader of one or more tribes, overcomes the enemy of the moment, and then rules for a time "judging" all Israel. The judge dies, Israel again commits apostasy, and the cycle repeats itself, again and again. In this framework DH presents such diverse figures as Ehud, Shamgar, Deborah, Gideon, Tola, Jair, and Samson. (Some of these may have been local or tribal leaders at one time or another, but it is unlikely that any of them actually judged or ruled over all Israel.) For a while, Gideon's son, Abimelech, sets himself up as king over part of Israel, rules by brutal violence, and then perishes, unlamented by all, when an unnamed woman drops a millstone on his head (chap. 9). Otherwise, the tribes are held together, at best, by their common interests, tradition, and devotion to Yahweh.

RUTH

This short story, set in the chaotic and slaughterous "days when the judges ruled," is all the more remarkable in that its gentle heroine is not an Israelite, but a Moabite. Moreover, she turns out to be King David's great-grandmother.

The author's references to Israelite custom in "former times" (4:7) might suggest that he or she was writing relatively late in the history of Judah. The present story presupposes David's rise to fame (4:17–22), and interpreters who view it as a polemic against the kind of ethnocentrism, if not xenophobia, represented in Ezra and Nehemiah, date it in postexilic times. Probably the law (or practice) of levirate marriage has evolved since its earlier formulation in Deut. 25:5–10. But the same considerations could suggest that at least the core of the story may be relatively ancient. No eyebrows are raised when Judah marries a Canaanite woman, or when Moses marries a Midianite (Genesis 38; Exodus 2, 18; but see Numbers 12 and Judg. 14:1–3). The story of Ruth may antedate the rise of the kind of intense ethnocentrism found in postexilic times. Conceivably, the law of levirate marriage set out in Deut. 25:5–6 was meant to *limit* the obligation to the brother(s) of the deceased, as against the kind of custom represented in Genesis 38 and Ruth, where the obligation extends to a widow's father-in-law or any (nearest) kinsman. In any case, it is not possible to date the story of Ruth with certainty.

The practice of levirate marriage is presupposed. (*Levir* is a Latin term for brother-in-law.) According to Deut. 25:5–6, if a married man dies without a son, his brother is obliged to marry the widow, and their first son is to bear the dead brother's name. It was probably understood that the child of such a union would inherit from his father. From the story of Judah and Tamar (Genesis 38), we learn that the obligation might devolve on a second brother-in-law or even the father-in-law. At the time of the story of Ruth, we see that the obligation (or privilege) extends to the nearest male kinsman.

In the story of Ruth, a man from Judah, his wife Naomi, and two sons sojourn in Moab, where the man dies, as do the sons, after marrying young Moabite women. Naomi's daughters-in-law, Orpah and Ruth, both propose to go with Naomi, who now plans to return to Judah. She urges them to remain with their parents in Moab, since she has no husband, and tells them they ought not wait to remarry until any sons she might yet have could grow up. Nevertheless, in her famous statement of steadfast devotion, "Entreat me not to leave you . . ." (1:16–17), Ruth insists on abiding with Naomi. Together they return to Judah. There Ruth gleans, as she is entitled to do under the law (Deut. 24:19–22), in the fields of Boaz, an older man who takes kindly to her. Evidently Ruth does not yet know that Boaz is a kinsman of her deceased husband (2:19–20).

Winter is coming, and Naomi advises Ruth how to let Boaz know that she would like him to become her husband (3:1–4). Ruth approaches Boaz at night on the threshing floor, and he is delighted by her proposal (3:6–11); but there is a complication, namely, a still nearer kinsman who, in effect, holds the first option. The next morning, Boaz goes with this kinsman to the city gate and gathers a quorum or minyan of ten elders, who form a kind of court of record. Hinting that no sensible man would want to marry Ruth, "that Moabite woman," and thus be obliged to provide an inheritance for her offspring, Boaz elicits the kinsman's refusal. The kinsman now takes off his own sandal—an interesting vestige, perhaps, of the harsher requirement set out in Deut. 25:8–10. Now Boaz can exercise the "right of redemption" himself.

Ruth and Boaz receive a special blessing from the elders and all those at the gate (4:11–12) and are married. Their son is to be the grandfather of the great King David. This circumstance and the favorable representation of Ruth here contrast notably with the negative view toward Moabites expressed in Deut. 23:3–4 and toward marriage with foreigners generally in several other biblical writings (e.g., Ezra 9—10; Neh. 13:23–31; Add. to Esther 14:15). That David later leaves his parents for safekeeping as guests of the king of Moab may confirm his Moabite lineage (1 Sam. 22:3–4).

1 SAMUEL

Eli and Samuel are introduced both as priests who preside over the "yearly sacrifice" at Shiloh, and as judges (5:18; 7:15). Samuel is also described as a prophet (3:20) or seer (9:19). The book depicts an era in which Israel is at war against the Philistines. Desperately, the Israelites bring their secret weapon, the ark (representing Yahweh's presence and power), out against their enemy—who has been oppressing them since the days of the judges—but to no avail. The Philistines defeat Israel, and capture Shiloh and even the ark (chap. 4). Old Eli falls dead, and his daughter-in-law, dying in childbirth, hopelessly names the new baby Ichabod ("Gone is the glory," 4:21–22). Following these events are tales about the Philistine god Dagon's obeisance to the ark and the Philistines' returning it to the Israelites (chaps. 5—6). These probably were told with the idea of providing consolation to latter-day Israelites by showing that Yahweh was still powerful, even though Israel had been ignominiously defeated. Although Israel experiences some relief in Samuel's time (chap. 7), the Philistines continue to rule the land (13:19–22). Samuel's sons, like Eli's, are corrupt, so in order to provide needed leadership for the nation, Samuel anoints Saul and later David as kings. Duplicate and sometimes triplicate versions of several episodes are reported, deriving from J, E, and other sources or commentators. Though they are part of the Deuteronomic history book, 1 and 2 Samuel contain little obvious commentary by DH.

Northern tradition (E) views the people's desire for a king as rejection of Yahweh. According to this tradition, Samuel opposes the idea of kingship and yields only reluctantly (8:1–9; 10:17–24), warning as to what it will be like to have a king (8:10–18), thereby reflecting both Israel's commitment to the theocratic ideal (cf. Judg. 8:23) and also, probably, its unhappy experience under Solomon's tyrannical rule (see 1 Kings 5:13–14; 12:3–4). In Judahite tradition (J), however, Samuel anoints Saul without hesitation, as Yahweh commands, after Saul comes to him looking for his father's lost asses (chap. 9). Judah's experience of kingship under David and Solomon was more positive when J was writing, ca. 950 B.C.

Saul's career begins ca. 1000 B.C. after the manner of the judges, with his bold rescue of Jabesh-gilead from the Ammonites (chap. 11). Under Saul, Israel gains initial successes against the Philistines, which are all the more remarkable considering the extent of Philistine power and control at the time (13:19–23). Saul nevertheless fails to satisfy Samuel (13:8–15; chap. 15), who denounces him and anoints David to be king in his place. It is a long time, however, before David actually becomes king.

Notwithstanding Samuel's opposition, Saul manages to free part of Israel from Philistine domination. David, a Judahite, appears as one of Saul's warriors. One version of David's rise to prominence is the perhaps legendary story of his victory over the Philistine giant, Goliath (chap. 17; but see 2 Sam. 21:19, where someone else is credited with having killed Goliath). In time, Saul becomes jealous of David's popularity (18:7–8) and suspects, perhaps correctly, that David hopes to supplant him as king. David learns of Saul's resolve to kill him, and escapes with the assistance of his wife, Michal, Saul's daughter (chap. 19). Seeking refuge in Gath, a Philistine city, David is recognized as the famous champion Philistine-slayer. To escape retribution, he pretends to be crazy. (In the ancient Near East, madmen were thought to be touched by divine power, and were treated with caution.) Achish, king of Gath, exclaims that he already has enough madmen in his entourage (21:10–15), so David is allowed to move on. David then gathers a band of debtors and malcontents, the beginning of his own standing army (22:1–3). Saul now obsessively tracks David through the wilderness, while the Philistine storm clouds gather against Israel.

Chapter 25 indicates David's modus operandi at this time. He sends ten of his band to ask the wealthy Nabal for a "donation" on the basis that they have "protected," that is, not yet stolen, his sheep or attacked his shepherds. After Nabal indignantly (and imprudently) declines to be shaken down, and sends David's men away empty-handed, his intelligent (and beautiful) wife Abigail quickly makes amends. When he learns what has happened, Nabal dies of what once was called apoplexy. David then takes Abigail as one of his wives. Soon David becomes a vassal or mercenary of the Philistine king Achish and spends his time raiding non-Israelite villages, all the while telling Achish that he has been plundering Judahites and related peoples. Samuel is now dead, so unlike Saul (chap. 15), David is not obliged to destroy the spoils, as required by the *herem* doctrine; instead he uses them to maintain his army and give presents "to his friends, the elders of Judah" (chap. 27; 30:26–31), who later show their appreciation by making him king. David kills the men and women of the villages he has raided, not because of the *herem*, but to prevent their telling on him to Achish (27:8–12). Dead men and women tell no tales.

The Philistines are now ready to fight Saul and the army of Israel, and Achish is ready to have David join them in the campaign. Some of the Philistine lords question David's loyalty, however, so he and his men are sent back, just in time as it turns out, to retrieve their wives, children, and possessions which have been carried off by some Amalekites (chaps. 29—30). While David is thus honorably occupied, the Philistines crushingly defeat Israel on Mount Gilboa. Saul and most of his sons perish, but their bodies are respectfully buried by the grateful men of Jabesh-gilead. Once again, there is no king in Israel.

2 SAMUEL

This might well be entitled the Book of David. It reports David's rise to power following Saul's death, his great achievements, as well as his great offenses against his subjects and against Yahweh, and subsequently, the various catastrophes which are interpreted as Yahweh's judgments against him. David's story begins in 1 Samuel and ends in 1 Kings 2. Second Samuel is part of the Deuteronomic history, which starts with the Book of Deuteronomy and (excepting Ruth) extends through 2 Kings. The main source in 2 Samuel is J, though there is also some E. The court history (chaps. 11—20; 2 Kings 1—2) may be an earlier piece preserved by J, or perhaps composed by J himself.

It is no simple matter for David, a Judahite, to become king of Israel. Though he is quickly made king of Judah, he becomes king over Israel only after several complications are resolved (chaps. 2—5). His reign over both kingdoms ca. 990–965 B.C. marks the beginning of the united monarchy. But it is a precarious unity. During David's reign, the North (Israel) makes two serious efforts at secession (chaps. 15—18; 20). As a Judahite, David needs to convince the Israelites that he is a legitimate successor to Saul. His famous lament over Saul and Jonathan (chap. 1) may have been published with this purpose in mind. His message to the men of Jabesh-gilead (2:5–7), one of the Israelite tribes (Judg. 21:8), clearly invites them to regard him as their king. War games in which twelve men from each side kill each other with swords (chap. 2) degenerate into war between Israel and Judah (chap. 3), no doubt to the great amusement of the Philistines. Saul's general and cousin, Abner, disgruntled because Ishbosh, Saul's oldest surviving son and Israel's nominal king, has reproached him for going to bed with Saul's concubine, proposes to bring Israel over to David's side. Significantly, David stipulates that first Michal, Saul's daughter (for whom David otherwise has shown little regard), must be restored as his wife (3:13). Evidently David wishes to be in a position to gain Israel's loyalty by qualifying as Saul's son-in-law, and thus as a member of the royal family of Israel. Abner delivers Michal to David, persuades the elders of Israel to accept David as their king, and promises to gather all Israel to David to make a covenant with him as such. But then David's commander, Joab, prompted by jealousy and desire for revenge, murders Abner, thereby creating a major public relations problem. David orders public mourning, composes a lament, and makes it clear to the Israelites that he is innocent of Abner's death (3:31–39)—but without lifting a finger to punish Joab, whose services he still needs. Next, two assassins, sensing David's ambition and hoping that he will reward them, bring him the head of Ishbosheth. David has them publicly executed and Ishbosheth's head buried with honors. Persuaded at last, Israel makes him their king, too (5:1–5).

David and his men take Jerusalem from the Jebusites, making it the capital of the now united kingdom. In short order he proceeds to defeat or otherwise come to terms with the Philistines and most of the other erstwhile enemy nations—a remarkable accomplishment considering the Philistines' initial, virtually complete supremacy. The prophet Nathan, according to a relatively late source, declares that David's house and kingdom will "be made sure for ever" (chap. 7). Seemingly to secure this end, David hands Saul's two remaining sons and five grandsons over to the Gibeonites for execution on the pretext that they have an old grievance to settle against Saul (21:1–14; cf. 9:1). Shimei, a kinsman of Saul's, accuses David of murdering Saul's family and reigning in its place (16:5–8). David does spare Mephibosheth, Jonathan's lame son, but keeps him under house arrest (chap. 9).

Second Samuel 11—20 and 2 Kings 1—2 constitute the great literary, historical, and theological masterpiece of the period. The writer of this court history may well have been a contemporary of David's and Solomon's, and some scholars suggest that he was none other than J, who collected and edited Southern tradition ca. 950 B.C.

The writer describes the course of events with exceptional economy of words: "It happened, late one afternoon." David commits adultery with Bathsheba. On learning that she is pregnant, he tries to cover his tracks by sending for Uriah, her husband, so that the latter will go home and "father" the child. But, in striking contrast to David, Uriah is too devoted to his comrades in the field to indulge in such pleasures. So David cynically sends him back with a message instructing Joab to arrange to have Uriah killed in battle. Afterward, David takes Bathsheba as another of his wives. The prophet Nathan then tells David the parable of the little ewe lamb, thereby catching the conscience of the king and causing him to pronounce judgment upon himself. Nathan declares that the sword shall not depart from David's house (chap. 12), and the ensuing events recapitulate David's offenses.

In what follows, we see not only a series of events which implicitly represent Yahweh's judgment against David in the form of evil arising against him out of his own house (12:11); we also see David's sons struggling for power. In theory, the oldest son succeeds the king once he dies. But David, though increasingly decrepit, is in no hurry to die. His oldest son, Amnon, rapes David's daughter, Tamar. Two full years later—and thus with premeditation or "in cold blood"— Absalom, the next oldest son, has Amnon murdered. After further maneuvering (15:1–9), Absalom declares himself king, precipitating renewed war between Israel and Judah. Joab, going against David's order to spare Absalom, has him killed. For a while Israel and Judah again are ruled by David (chap. 19). But the kingdom again comes apart as the Israelites once more secede, this time under the leadership of Sheba, a man of Saul's tribe (chap. 20). The stories in 1 Kings 1—2 will complete the pattern of evil arising against David out of his own household. Adonijah, now David's oldest surviving son, expects to be king soon, since the old man is about to die. But Solomon's mother and the prophet Nathan conspire to bring about a palace revolution that leapfrogs Solomon onto the throne. Solomon then conducts a bloody purge of possible rivals and dissenters, including his own brother Adonijah.

Chapters 21—24 assemble miscellaneous leftover traditions about David: stories about Philistine giants (including Goliath, here reportedly killed by a certain Elhanan), a psalm virtually identical to Psalm 18 (22:2–51); another psalm purporting to be the last words of David (23:1–7); a catalogue of David's mighty men; and the story of his numbering Israel and Judah, inspired by God (cf. 1 Chron. 21:1, which credits Satan with the inspiration), but nevertheless sinful, and therefore punished by plague (chap. 24).

1 KINGS

The period covered here extends from the last days of David (ca. 956 B.C.) through the reign of Ahab (ca. 875–850 B.C.) and includes the era of Solomon, the breakup of the united kingdom, and reports of intermittent warfare among Israel, Judah, and Syria. Early prophets figure prominently, anointing, advising, and condemning kings, according to the word of Yahweh. First Kings is part of the Deuteronomic history book (edited by DH) that begins with Deuteronomy and ends with 2 Kings. Sources include Southern or Judahite (J and A) and Northern or Israelite (E and B) traditions, among others. DH's commentary on the kings and their faithfulness (or lack thereof) to Yahweh appears fairly regularly in summary formulas (15:9–15, 33–34; 22:41–46).

As the book opens King David is now quite old and somewhat senile, but has not appointed a successor. His oldest surviving son, Adonijah, assuming that his father will soon be dead, celebrates in anticipation of his own installation as king (1:5–10). David has never been able to cope with Adonijah (1:5–6) or any of his other sons (2 Samuel 13—19). For reasons of his own, Nathan conspires with Bathsheba to beguile the befuddled David into thinking that he has promised that Solomon, a much younger son, will become king (1:11–27). The ruse succeeds, Solomon is quickly enthroned, and David soon dies. Solomon promptly conducts a political purge, sending his henchman Beniah to kill possible rivals and dissenters, including his brother Adonijah and old Joab (even as he clings to the altar, a supposed sanctuary), on various feeble pretexts (chap. 2).

Solomon is remembered for his wisdom, a trait illustrated by his resolution of the competing claims of the two harlots for the one living infant (chap. 3). He is credited with authorship of many wisdom writings, including much of Proverbs, Wisdom of Solomon, and, by implication, Ecclesiastes. He is also famous for the luxury and extravagance of his court (chaps. 4; 10), and as the builder of the temple and several (rather larger) royal palaces (chaps. 5—7). A euphoric commentator epitomizes the era: the people "were as many as the sand by the sea; they ate and drank and were happy" (4:20).

But as the story unfolds, Solomon provokes increasing resentment on the part of the Israelites for the heavy yoke of forced labor he imposes upon them (12:4). DH notes another negative trait, Solomon's unprecedented apostasy, but generously suggests that Solomon's foreign wives were to blame for turning his heart to other gods, and that this happened only in his old age (11:4–8). Nevertheless, DH blames Solomon for the ultimate breakup of the kingdom, interpreting it as Yahweh's judgment against Solomon's apostasy (11:9–11).

Solomon's son and successor, Rehoboam, enjoys playing the role of Oriental potentate even more than his father did. Refusing to heed the Israelites' plea for relief from the harsh treatment they suffered under Solomon, Rehoboam arrogantly tells them that now it will be much worse for them. As a result, "Israel departed to their tents," leaving Rehoboam, and his successors, to rule only over Judah (chap. 12). Thus Israel and Judah, united most of the time under David and his son Solomon, break apart ca. 926 B.C. Never again did a descendant of David rule over Israel.

Jeroboam, anointed by the prophet Ahijah (11:29–39) is made king of Israel. Southern tradition regards him, indeed along with all Israelite kings, unfavorably. DH accuses all northern kings of apostasy: necessarily, none of them worshipped at the Jerusalem temple as required by Deuteronomy 12. DH, writing ca. 550 B.C., assumes that this requirement—then probably less than a hundred years old—was part of the original Mosaic law. Much of the time, during the period of the divided kingdoms that follows, Judah and Israel are at war with one another (14:30). Judah suffers particularly, at first (see Isa. 8:17).

In 922 B.C., the Egyptians raid Judah (14:25–26) and also, perhaps, Israel.

The very idea of kingship is always portrayed as suspect in early Israelite tradition (see, e.g., Judg. 8:22–23; 1 Sam. 8:4–18). None of the Northern kings enjoyed the sense of divine authorization experienced or claimed by the house of David in the South (see 2 Sam. 7:11–17). In the North, kings and their entire families often are assassinated by would-be successors. One such pretender, Baasha, kills off Jeroboam's family and makes himself king, in accordance with the word of Yahweh (15:27–30). The prophet Jehu then denounces Baasha, who dies after a reign of two years. His son Elah and all his male kinsmen are then killed off by Zimri, another pretender, who lasts just seven days (chap. 16). After more civil war, Omri becomes king of Israel—an important one, according to extrabiblical sources. It is he who establishes Samaria as the capital of Israel. Afterwards, the Northern kingdom is frequently referred to as Samaria, as well as Ephraim, and, of course, Israel.

The prophet Elijah is introduced in chap. 17. His special status is shown in a story that tells how ravens bring him food while he is in hiding. His miraculous powers are indicated by his multiplying the contents of a widow's jar of meal and cruse of oil. He also brings her son back to life through prayer and a kind of CPR (17:20–22; cf. 2 Kings 4:32–35).

Omri's son Ahab and his Phoenician wife Jezebel then rule Israel. On Elijah's orders, King Ahab gathers all Israel and four hundred and fifty prophets of Baal to take part in a contest at Mount Carmel (chap. 18). Baal's prophets call on him to light their sacrificial fire, but there is no answer. Call louder, Elijah mockingly urges them. Perhaps Baal is musing, or visiting the outhouse, or asleep. They call louder, and lacerate themselves. Still no answer. Then Elijah calls on Yahweh, whose sacrifice is immediately consumed by fire from heaven. Elijah orders the prophets of Baal killed, and then the rains come, ending the three-year drought Elijah previously called for in order to show that Yahweh, not Baal, sends the rain (chaps. 17—18; in Canaanite religion, Baal was the god of rain, fertility, and life). Jezebel does not share Ahab's Israelitish scruples as to rights of subjects who do not care to comply with royal desires. When Naboth declines to sell his ancestral vineyard, which Ahab covets, she has him framed and summarily executed and "gives" the vineyard to Ahab. Thereupon Elijah pronounces Yahweh's word against them both (21:17–24).

Syria, the small kingdom just north of Israel, at one time is allied with Israel against Judah; at another, with Judah against Israel (16:16–20). On one occasion, after all of three years without war (22:1), Israel plans to seize some territory back from Syria. Ahab calls on Jehoshaphat, king of Judah, who is at this point allied with him as a vassal or junior partner, to join in the campaign against Syria. Unimpressed by the four hundred yes-men prophets in the court of Ahab, Jehoshaphat asks if there is not yet another prophet of Yahweh of whom they may inquire. The prophet Micaiah (the last syllable of whose name, like Elijah's, signifies that he is an adherent of Yahweh) is consulted. Having been warned by one of Ahab's officials not to rock the boat, Micaiah sardonically tells Ahab, "Go up and triumph." But Ahab knows that Micaiah never prophesies good about him, and charges him to tell the truth. Micaiah then declares that Ahab will die in battle. Ahab thinks it is a big joke (22:18), goes to war, is wounded, and dies.

2 KINGS

Second Kings continues the history of Israel and Judah and concludes the Deuteronomic history book. As in 1 Kings, Israelite kings uniformly are condemned for apostasy, while Judahite kings (who at least occasionally worship in Jerusalem) generally receive qualified praise (e.g., 15:1–5; 16:17–20). Major events occur during these years, ca. 850–586 B.C. In 853, at the battle of Qarqar, the three small kingdoms of Syria, Israel, and Judah temporarily succeed in blocking Assyrian expansion into their territory. But the Assyrians reappear over a century later, in 738, and this time Israel must pay tribute to purchase a few more years of independence. Hoping to compel Judah to join them against the advancing Assyrians, Syria and Israel together besiege Jerusalem, ca. 734 (see Isaiah 7—8). But Ahaz, king of Judah, turns to Assyria for help, even paying a large bribe; and Assyria obligingly attacks and overruns much of Syria and Israel (15:29; 16:1–9). In 722 B.C., Assyria moves decisively against Israel, now bringing that kingdom to an end. Never again is there a kingdom of Israel. As Amos has anticipated, it has "fallen, no more to rise" (Amos 5:2). DH interprets this final disaster as Yahweh's judgment for Israel's chronic apostasy (17:7–23). Now only the Southern kingdom of Judah is left.

Judah preserves at least nominal independence for nearly another 140 years. In 701 B.C., Sennacherib's Assyrian army surrounds, but does not enter Jerusalem (see 2 Kings 18:13—19:37; Isa. 36:1—

37:38). King Hezekiah ruled Judah during much of the troubled period, beginning, perhaps, as early as 728 B.C. (18:1, 9–10) until ca. 687 B.C. DH credits him with having been uniquely faithful to Yahweh, who in turn caused him to prosper (18:3–6; cf. 23:25); but Isaiah reproaches Hezekiah, perhaps for having imprudently shown all the royal treasures to a visiting delegation from Babylon (20:12–19). Hezekiah was succeeded by his son, Manasseh, famous chiefly for his apostasy, idolatry, and syncretism (combining the worship of Yahweh with worship of other gods), and for slaughtering innocent people in Jerusalem (21:2–16). Shortly after the long reign of Manasseh—the worst Southern king ever, according to DH (21:1–16)—Josiah is enthroned in Judah. He is the best king in DH's "book" (22:2; 23:25). He restores the temple (ca. 622 B.C.), removing foreign and idolatrous cults in compliance with the newly rediscovered "book of the law," probably Deuteronomy, which now contains the requirement of worship in only the one place (see Deuteronomy 12—19; 2 Kings 22—23). (According to the "pious fraud" theory, the ink was barely dry on the new chapters in Deuteronomy when the book was "found." It may well be, however, that the centralized worship requirement and attendant adjustments in law and cultus were added as part of a reform movement that developed earlier, perhaps during the years of the apostate Manasseh.)

In the late seventh century B.C., Babylon emerges as the great empire in the Near East. In 598, its emperor, Nebuchadnezzar, carries off Jerusalem's treasures, leading families, craftsmen, and King Jehoiachin (24:10–16). Then in 587, Zedekiah rebels against the Babylonians, who, after a terrible year-long siege, destroy Jerusalem, including the temple, and take most of the remaining citizenry to Babylon (cf. Psalm 137). This marks the end of the kingdom of Judah and the beginning of the exile. Never again did a descendant of David sit on the throne of Judah. Nor was there ever again a kingdom of Judah—though in the second and first centuries B.C., there would emerge a Jewish kingdom of sorts that endured some hundred years.

Sources include Northern (B) stories about miraculous deeds by Elijah and Elisha, and considerable Southern (A) material. As in 1 Kings, references are made to no longer extant chronicles of the kings of Israel and Judah. (These are not the same as the books of 1 and 2 Chronicles that are found in the OT.) Two sections duplicate, largely verbatim, portions of Isaiah and Jeremiah: 2 Kings 18:13—20:19 (cf. Isa. 36:1—39:8); and 2 Kings 24:18—25:21 (cf. Jer. 52:1–27).

Second Kings begins with a series of tales about Elijah and his younger associate and successor Elisha. Elijah calls down fire on three platoons of Israelite soldiers who had been sent by King Ahaziah, evidently to arrest him (chap. 1). Accompanied by a group of fifty prophets ("the sons of the prophets") Elijah and Elisha approach the Jordan River. Elijah parts the water with his mantle, and the two prophets cross over. Elijah is then taken up into heaven by a whirlwind, accompanied by a chariot and horses of fire. (The images of entering heaven by crossing the Jordan or by means of a heavenly chariot in Southern spirituals may derive partly from this scene, and partly from Israel's crossing the Jordan on its way to "the Promised Land" [Joshua 3]). Elsewhere, too, Elijah is associated with fire (1 Kings 18). Later traditions look for Elijah, prophet of repentance par excellence, to return to earth before the time of judgment (Mal. 4:5–6; Ecclus. 48:1–11; Matt. 17:10–12). Elisha now proceeds to use his "double share" of Elijah's spirit to perform a series of wonders. He takes Elijah's mantle and parts the Jordan; purifies the water at Jericho with salt; calls two bears out of the woods to attack some small boys who have insulted him by calling him "baldy" (chap. 2); prophesies the defeat of Moab by Israel, Judah, and Edom (chap. 3); multiplies the contents of a widow's jar of oil so she can pay her debts; cures a wealthy Shunammite woman's infertility and restores her son to life; renders edible a pot of poisoned pottage; feeds a hundred men with twenty loaves of bread and some ears of grain (chap. 4); cures the Syrian Naaman's leprosy, but inflicts his servant Gehazi with it for taking graft (chap. 5); retrieves a lost axe head by making it float to the surface of the Jordan River; uses ESP to eavesdrop on the words of the Syrian king; blinds the army of pursuing Syrians, and then orders the king of Israel to give the Syrian army a great feast, after which the Syrians peaceably return home (chap. 6); foretells relief from a great famine (chap. 7); instructs the Shunammite woman on how to survive a seven-year famine; and predicts Hazael's murderous overthrow of the Syrian king Ben-hadad (chap. 8).

As in 1 Kings, the chronology of 2 Kings is complicated by the system of relative dating (e.g., 8:16, 25), and the fact that many kings have similar or identical names. Israel and Judah each have kings named Jehoram, Ahaziah, and Jehoash—not to be confused with Israel's king Jehoahaz; and Judah later has a king named Ahaz, not to be confused with Israel's king Ahab or the kings Ahaziah. Two different kings named Jeroboam rule over Israel. Israel's king Pekahiah is followed by Pekah, while Judah's Jehoiakim is followed by Jehoiachin. The prophet Jehu is to be distinguished from the king by that name. To make matters worse, some kings have more than one name: the kings Jehoram are also known as Joram, and the kings Jehoash as Joash, while Jehoiachin is also known as Jeconiah (1 Chron. 3:16; Esther 2:6) and simply Coniah (Jer. 22:24, 28). Readers are advised to have on hand one of the standard lists of the kings of Israel and Judah (see, e.g., NOAB, pp. 1548–49). Occasionally reports conflict, for instance, as to the year Ahab's son Jehoram began to reign over Israel (1:17; cf. 3:1).

Alliances continue to shift uncertainly, as Syria, Israel, and Judah combine with or against one another and other nations, notably, Edom, Moab, Assyria, and Egypt. Between 926 and 722 B.C., Israel has nineteen kings from nine different dynasties or families, which are commonly overthrown by revolution or assassination. In Judah, on the other hand, the only break in the line of nineteen Davidic kings, beginning with Rehoboam, from 926 to 586 B.C., is Athaliah, the first and only queen in either Israel or Judah (9:29; 11:1–16).

Prophets continue to anoint, advise, and condemn the kings. Jehu's rebellion is instigated by Elisha (chap. 9), and his slaughter of the house of Ahab is said to have Yahweh's prior approval (10:30), though Hosea later declares otherwise (Hos. 1:4–5). Most of the classical prophets appear during the later years of Israel and Judah, the period set out in 2 Kings; they are Amos, Hosea, Isaiah, Micah, Jeremiah, and Ezekiel.

Writing several decades into the exile, perhaps ca. 550 B.C., DH, the historian/theologian/editor of the Deuteronomic history book, tries to make sense of the grand, tragic, and chaotic events and times dating back to the days when Moses and Israel were in the wilderness. This much is clear: Yahweh had made good his promise to bring Israel into the land of Canaan and give it to them as an inheritance and a possession. Had Israel (and Judah) remained faithful to Yahweh and his covenant, they would have continued to enjoy his favor there. But Israel and Judah had worshiped other gods and otherwise failed to obey Yahweh's ordinances, commands, and statutes. Consequently they experienced divine judgment in the form of disaster and defeat at the hands of their enemies. Thus not only the Northern Kingdom (2 Kings 17:7–18), but also the Southern (2 Kings 17:19–20; 24:1–4), perished because their people and leaders had broken covenant with Yahweh. DH concludes his work with the pathetic note that the exiled King Jehoiachin is allowed to live out his life as an honored prisoner of the Babylonians (25:27–30). Yet DH achieved his goal. The kings and their kingdoms were gone—possibly forever—but Yahweh is

still God. All that happened made sense within the framework of the
theology of history presented by DH to his fellow exiles.

1 CHRONICLES

The final editor of 1 and 2 Chronicles, Ezra, and Nehemiah is
usually referred to as the Chronicler. Some interpreters suggest that
Ezra, remembered as "the scribe," might have been the Chronicler.
Whoever brought them together, these four books constitute the third
of the three edited segments of biblical historical tradition that constitute the first half of the OT. Certain evidences, including the distinction between priests and Levites (e.g., 9:10–16) and reference to
Persian coins (1 Chron. 29:7), suggest that Chronicles was written no
earlier than 400 B.C. The present 1 and 2 Chronicles originally formed
a single book. First Chronicles 1—9 provide a genealogical recapitu-
lation of world and Israelite history from Adam to the time of David.
Curiously, the Babylonian exile (ca. 586–539 B.C.) is reported at 9:1,
and vv. 2–34 seem to describe the population of Jerusalem after the
exile. But then the scene shifts to the time of Saul (ca. 1000 B.C.).
Chapter 10 reports Saul's death, and chaps. 11—29 concentrate on
David's reign. Like the priestly authors and editors of much of
Genesis through Leviticus, the Chronicler was interested in genealogies, including those of early humanity, but particularly the sons of
Abraham and Israel. Relatively few women are named; for example,
there is no mention of Eve, Sarah, Rebekah, Leah, Rachel, or Ruth.
Little is said as to what anyone did (apart from having sons) until the
time of David.

Religious functionaries (priests, the sons of Aaron, and Levites,
the sons of Levi) are accorded special prominence (see chaps. 6; 9;
23—26). Levites are particularly important as assistants to priests in
the tabernacle (which, as in P tradition, appears as a portable prototype of the Jerusalem temple), with gatekeepers and musicians also
filling important roles. In all probability these distinctions did not exist
in the time of David and Solomon, but did figure prominently in
temple rituals at the time the Chronicler wrote (ca. 350 B.C.).

Earlier biblical materials are used when suitable to the Chronicler's
purposes. Traditions that might cast doubt on David's virtue are
omitted, such as his working as a mercenary for the Philistines (1
Samuel 27; 29—30), his dancing naked before the ark (2 Sam. 6:12–
22), the Bathsheba-Uriah episodes and David's subsequent condemnation by Nathan (2 Samuel 11—20), and his arranging for the demise

of Saul's family (2 Sam. 21:1–6; cf. 1 Chron. 10:6). There is no mention of warfare between Judah and Israel (cf. 2 Samuel 2—3); instead, even before Saul's death, various Israelite groups seek David as their leader and afterwards unanimously make him their king (chaps. 11—12). David all but builds the temple: he receives the plans from God, works out the details, assembles building materials and workmen, as well as priests and Levites to staff it, and he prays for Solomon to have wisdom to see it to completion (chaps. 22; 28—29).

Satan appears in the Bible for the first time at 21:1. He, rather than Yahweh (cf. 2 Sam. 24:1) incites David to take a census. The Chronicler's theological commentary on history somewhat resembles that of DH, in that Israel and Judah experience catastrophe at the hand of God because of their unfaithfulness (e.g., 5:25–26; 9:1). Like the wisdom writers, however, the Chronicler also suggests that individuals are brought to account for their misdeeds (e.g., 10:13–14). Chronicles may contain accurate information about priestly and Levitical families in the postexilic period. But much seems to derive from pious imagination; for example, the reports that Zeruiah was David's sister (2:16), that Joab was the first man into Jerusalem (11:6), that Reuben lost his birthright because he had committed incest (5:1), that Elhanan killed not Goliath, but his brother (20:5; cf. 2 Sam. 21:19), that over three hundred thousand troops from all twelve tribes of Israel came in full battle dress to make David king (chap. 12), and that David commanded over a million Israelite soldiers and nearly half a million from Judah (21:5).

Solomon, the Chronicler assures us, was chosen by David, God, and the people of Israel (23:1; 29:1, 22); and all the mighty men and all the other sons of David pledged him their allegiance. No mention is made of either the palace revolution that put Solomon on the throne or his purge of dissenters and possible rivals (including Joab and Solomon's own brother Adonijah, 1 Kings 1—2). The idealized view of history presented by the Chronicler has led some interpreters to suggest that he may have meant to picture here a future messianic era, modeled on the golden age of David's kingship.

2 CHRONICLES

The retelling of history begun in 1 Chronicles continues here, down to the time of the exile (ca. 586 B.C.). The book's last verses anticipate the first few of Ezra, which carries the account into the postexilic period. The Chronicler again repeats much of earlier biblical writings (here, 1 and 2 Kings), omitting and supplementing in accordance with his concerns. The Chronicler emphasizes the importance and virtues of Levites (e.g., 20:14–19; 23:4–7; 29:34; 34:12–13). Again, temple worship is the central interest, with special roles assigned to priests and Levites, respectively. (These functionaries are not differentiated in 1 and 2 Kings, or in any other sources written before ca. 450 B.C. It is likely that 2 Chronicles was written ca. 350 B.C., along with 1 Chronicles, as a single book.)

Julius Wellhausen's comment that one might as well try to hear the grass growing as hope to learn anything about history from Chronicles may have been overly severe, though undoubtedly we do have here a revisionist history written from a particular religious and political perspective. In any event, we may learn a great deal from Chronicles about the interests of an important segment of Judaism in the fourth century B.C.

The first nine chapters portray Solomon as an ideal king, who is remembered especially for his construction and dedication of the original temple. Nothing is said about his apostasy, which in 1 Kings 11 is said to be the reason for the breakup of the kingdom of Israel-Judah shortly after his death. Generally the Chronicler holds the view that Judah (the Southern Kingdom) is the true "Israel," and has little to say, and less that is favorable, about the Northern Kingdom. Most of the Southern kings are said to have been good, but attention is directed mainly to religious leaders. Military and political events are less significant than faithful worship of Yahweh expressed through offering sacrifices and other temple rituals, which are carried out under the auspices of the priests and various orders of Levites. When the Chronicler wrote, the Jewish people were no longer an independent nation, but only a province of the Persian, or possibly a later foreign empire, and thus were bound together primarily by religious and cultural ties.

Kings Hezekiah and Josiah are remembered chiefly for keeping the Passover in Jerusalem (chaps. 30, 35). Catastrophes befalling certain kings are explained as God's judgment for sins that go unrecorded in earlier tradition, such as Jehoram's wretched end (chap. 21), Uzziah's leprosy (26:16–20), and Josiah's untimely death at the hands of Pharaoh Neco (35:20–24). On the other hand, Manasseh, the worst king of all according to 2 Kings 21, nevertheless repents, the Chronicler tells us (33:12–17), evidently to account for the extraordinary length of his reign (ca. 687–642 B.C.). These features of Chronicles may have been prompted by familiarity with the emerging orthodox wisdom theology (represented in Proverbs), according to which the righteous are rewarded with long life, while the wicked soon suffer or perish. Several times, however, 2 Chronicles holds out the hope that God will forgive those who repent and pray to him.

Second Chronicles concludes the Bible in modern Hebrew editions, where it is classified with the Holy Writings. Unlike 2 Kings which leaves off in the time of the exile, 2 Chronicles reports the Persian monarch Cyrus's edict of liberation, which, as in Ezra, includes the promise that he will undertake to build a new temple in Jerusalem (36:22–23).

EZRA

The author—probably the Chronicler, who may have been Ezra himself—continues his story from 2 Chronicles, starting with Cyrus's proclamation ending the exile (ca. 538 B.C.), through the rebuilding of the temple (ca. 515 B.C.), and down to the time of Ezra the priest and scribe. It is possible that Ezra was appointed governor of Jerusalem and its environs, which then constituted a Persian province; at any rate, as the story is told, King Artaxerxes has authorized him to teach the returned exiles the laws of God and of Persia, and see that these laws are enforced (7:25–26). It is not clear whether the author was thinking of Artaxerxes I (ca. 465–425 B.C.) or Artaxerxes II (ca. 400–350 B.C.). Most interpreters place Ezra in the latter period. One section is written in the first person, as if indeed by Ezra himself (7:27—9:15).

The writer is mainly interested in the second temple, its reconstruction, furnishings, and staff: all central features of Jewish life in his time (ca. 350 B.C.). As in Chronicles, the people usually are referred to as Israelites (e.g., 2:2; 6:16), though the term Jews also appears here for the first time in the OT (e.g., 4:23; 5:1; 6:7–8). Since Israel and Judah no longer exist as nations, the people's identity now is experienced primarily in terms of their common religion and culture. Thus the temple and ritual observances are of basic importance in Ezra. The author states that the Persian kings Cyrus and Darius not only commanded that the temple be rebuilt, but even proposed to pay all the costs (6:1–12). Even the king of Assyria helps (6:22). Later, the Persian king Artaxerxes sends Ezra to Jerusalem laden with gifts of silver and gold, and with permission to take whatever more he can find "in the whole province of Babylonia" for sacrificial offerings and anything else needed for the temple (chap. 7). Such concern and generous support for the temple on the part of foreign rulers is not recorded anywhere other than in 2 Chron. 36:22–23.

Also in chap. 7, Ezra is associated with the law, particularly with laws relating to temple sacrifices and ritual propriety. Ezra is also represented as the great teacher of Jewish law in Nehemiah 8.

As in Chronicles, the writer likes to count and name "the heads of the fathers' houses" (chaps. 2, 8). Here, too, priests are distinguished from Levites (e.g., 6:16, 18). Priests, Levites, and related temple functionaries are accorded special privileges (7:24). The attention given to Levites has suggested to some interpreters that the author himself may have been a member of that order.

Like Nehemiah before him, Ezra is appalled to find that fellow Jews, especially priests and Levites, have married foreign women, thereby contaminating the "holy race" (9:2) and "holy place" (9:8). He "rends" (tears) his clothes and pulls out his own hair, prays to God (chap. 9), and undertakes to propitiate God by requiring the culprits to make confession, sacrifice rams as guilt offerings, and separate from these foreign women (chap. 10). The book concludes with a list of Levites who, to the author's apparent satisfaction, put away these wives along with their children (10:44).

NEHEMIAH

This book concludes the Chronicler's narration, which began in 1 Chronicles. As in 1 and 2 Chronicles, Ezra, and Numbers, considerable attention is given to the names and numbers of families, particularly Levites and related temple personnel (chaps. 10—12). Nehemiah 7:6–63 duplicates nearly verbatim Ezra 2:1–70. Most other material seems to come from what may have been Nehemiah's memoirs or diary.

Nehemiah, a cupbearer to the Persian king Artaxerxes, hears that things are not well in Jerusalem, even though it has been nearly a hundred years since the end of the exile. He asks God for help and Artaxerxes for permission to go there and take charge of rebuilding the city. Arriving in Jerusalem, he tours it inconspicuously, observes its ruined condition, decides what needs to be done, assembles the local Jews and their leaders, and calls on them to get to work (chap. 2). Under his direction, the city gates are repaired, and in only fifty-two days, the walls are restored—to the dismay of the troika of jealous neighboring provincial officials, "Sanballat the Horonite, Tobiah the servant, and Geshem the Arab." Informed of their plotting, Nehemiah had posted guards and even armed those who worked on the walls (4:6–23). Learning that some Jewish nobles have been exacting interest and foreclosing against fellow Jews, Nehemiah gathers them together, and tells them in no uncertain terms to stop charging interest and to return the properties they have taken. For the record, he notes in his diary that—unlike former governors of Judah—he has refrained from collecting the customary perquisites of office, both because he feared God, and because such servitude would have been a burden on the Jewish people there (chap. 5). His enemies continue to plot against him, and now hire various prophets to try to scare him into hiding in the temple. Scornfully Nehemiah refuses to panic: "Should such a man as I flee?" (6:10–14).

Later, Nehemiah returns to Jerusalem, evidently for a second term as governor. With characteristic vigor he corrects various other abuses, including the sale of fish and produce on the Sabbath, threatening to "lay hands on" any future violators (13:1–22). Finally, discovering that certain Jews have married women of Ashdod, Ammon, and Moab, he "cursed them and beat some of them and pulled out their hair," making them forswear such marriages in the future (13:25). Nehemiah comes across as a forcible and fearless leader, a man of direct and decisive personal action, who was not ashamed to pray to God or ask him to remember him for his good deeds.

Nehemiah probably lived in the time of Artaxerxes I. The restoration of the Jerusalem wall—a major event in postexilic Judaism—is dated ca. 444 B.C. Ezra suddenly appears in chaps. 8—9 as if he were one of Nehemiah's contemporaries, but Ezra's promulgation of the law (perhaps the Pentateuch) by the Water Gate (chap. 8) more likely is to be dated in the time of Artaxerxes II, ca. 400–350 B.C. This scene suggests the central importance of law (Torah) in Judaism of the fourth century B.C. We may see here the beginning of the midrash tradition: paraphrasing translations and interpretations of the law for the edification of the general populace (8:7). The scene is reminiscent of the ancient Israelite ceremonies of covenant renewal, when the law was read and affirmed by those present (Deuteronomy 27; Josh. 8:30–35; 24:1–28).

Together, the books of Ezra and Nehemiah are the last of the historical writings in the OT canon. In Christian Bibles, the writings from Genesis through Nehemiah report events in more or less chronological order. The books from Esther to Malachi are arranged more according to categories of literature than historical sequence, such as wisdom, "Solomonic" writings, psalms, longer prophets, and shorter prophets.

ESTHER

Esther, along with Ruth, Judith, and Susanna, are memorialized in separate books bearing their names. Esther appropriately follows Ezra and Nehemiah, which also are set in the time of the Persian monarch Ahasuerus, or Artaxerxes I or II, and thus sometime between ca. 465 and 350 B.C. The story is more plausibly read as imaginative literature, however, than as objective history. As told, however, it may reflect Jewish experience or fears of persecution in later times. Apart from a quite indirect allusion to God's providence (4:14), the secular tone of the book is remarkable: no one prays; there is no mention of God, the law, the temple, or even the Sabbath; no one keeps kosher; and no eyebrows are raised over Esther's marriage to a Gentile (cf. Additions to Esther). Religious interest is limited to the festival of Purim (9:26–32), which is "explained" in connection with unintelligible references to casting "Pur" (3:7; 9:24). The point of the festival, like that of the book, is clear, however: it is to celebrate the defeat of would-be persecutors of the Jews, epitomized in the despicable Haman.

The story contains several notable, even melodramatic scenes: Queen Vashti's refusal to display her beauty for the entertainment of guests at the king's seven-day banquet, and the consequent consternation in the royal court at the prospect of a women's revolution throughout the empire (1:10–18); Ahasuerus's Miss Universe Pageant, won, of course, by Esther, who is made queen (or number-one harem girl) in place of the now demoted Vashti (2:1–17); Esther's cousin, and guardian, Mordecai's resolute unwillingness to bow before Haman, and that self-important worthy's exasperation at such effrontery (3:2; 5:9, 13); and Esther's brave appearance before the king, who—to her enormous relief—*does* extend his golden scepter, thereby sparing her life, and even offers her half his kingdom (4:10—5:3). In the central, climactic sequence, the king's insomnia prompts him to have "the book of memorable deeds" read; he decides to honor Mordecai (6:1–3), just in time to assign this task to Haman who has arrived bright and early hoping to arrange for Mordecai's execution; Haman, who pretentiously imagines that he, himself, is the one the king means to honor, sketches out a full, public, royal parade featuring himself. But then he learns that he must heap these honors, omitting no detail, on none other than Mordecai, his enemy! The most melodramatic moment in the book, if not the Bible, is Esther's denunciation of Haman, and the king's unfortunate misconstruction of that wretched man's posture as he falls upon her couch to plead for mercy (7:6–8).

In the story, Haman, offended by Mordecai's refusal to bow and scrape before him (3:2–5), persuades King Ahasuerus to "destroy, slay, and annihilate" all Jews. Through Esther's courageous intervention, the king changes his mind, and has Haman hanged on the same gallows he had prepared for Mordecai. Because under Persian law the king's decree, once given, cannot be revoked, he can only grant Esther and Mordecai authority to send word throughout the empire that the Jews are to defend themselves by killing all who may attack them (8:8–14). Construing the edict a bit broadly, Jews then preemptively massacre "those who hated them": eight hundred in Susa, and seventy-five thousand in the provinces, along with Haman's ten sons (9:6–16). A certain morbid redundancy may be noted in the two reports of the hanging of Haman's sons (9:13–14, 25) after they have already been killed (9:6–10, 12).

The story ends with Esther installed in Haman's house and Mordecai wearing the king's signet and royal garb (8:1–2, 15), elevated to the post of second-in-command over all the empire, and eulogized in terms reminiscent of statements reserved in Kings and Chronicles for the kings of Israel and Judah (10:2–3). Probably the story was meant not only to entertain with its humor and melodrama, and to explain the origins of the festival of Purim (which is not grounded in the law or Torah), but also to encourage readers facing persecution in the author's time and perhaps in later times with the hope that they, too, might triumph over their enemies.

JOB

In broad terms, Job represents the wisdom genre of literature. Several segments are indistinguishable in form and substance from material found in Proverbs and Sirach. Yet, as we shall see, there are important differences. The Book of Job could also be classed with the more philosophical biblical writings, especially Ecclesiastes and 2 Esdras, which likewise raise—sometimes rather bluntly—basic questions as to the meaning (or meaninglessness) of life.

Interpreters disagree as to when the book was written, which parts may have been added later, and even its main purpose. Surprisingly, Job is not a Jew but a citizen of Uz (perhaps in Edom); yet he worships Yahweh and leads a life of exemplary righteousness (1:1–5, 8, 22; 2:10; 29:11–17; 31:1–40). The book begins with a prose prologue (chaps. 1—2) and ends with a prose epilogue (42:7–17), both of choice literary and dramatic quality. The chapters between are mainly poetic in form, and include three cycles of discourses in which Job complains and is reproached, in turn, by each of his three friends (chaps. 3—27); a somewhat extraneous psalm in praise of wisdom (chap. 28); Job's concluding summation in his own defense (chaps. 29—31); Elihu's remarks (32:6—37:24); God's two answers "out of the whirlwind" (38:1—40:2; 40:6—41:34); and Job's two replies (40:3–5; 42:1–6).

Textual problems are suspected in the third cycle, in which lines typical of his friends are attributed to Job (24:18–25; 27:7–23; perhaps 26:5–14). The wisdom poem (chap. 28) adds a flavor of orthodoxy to the book, affirming, as do many passages in Proverbs, that the fear of the Lord is (the beginning of) wisdom. Elihu's commentary probably was inserted by a later interpreter to show what the latter considered Job's real fault (surely he must have had one!): his pride (33:17; 37:24). The second of Yahweh's answers, which portrays Behemoth and Leviathan—the latter as a prototype of a medieval or Chinese dragon—probably is a later addition intended to illustrate the limits of human knowledge and power. The prologue and epilogue may have constituted an earlier story that was then expanded by the three cycles of speeches and Yahweh's reply. In the prologue, Job is remarkable for his patience (1:20–22; 2:10); but he is not so characterized in the poetic section (e.g., 21:4). Yet both the prose and poetic sections refer to Job's children (1:13–19; 8:4), his vanishing kinfolk and close friends (19:13–19; 42:11), and both contain masterful touches of irony.

The book is concerned with the problem of evil or theodicy (God's righteousness). Job is uniquely righteous and prospers (1:1–3), as indeed he should, according to orthodox wisdom theology (e.g., Prov. 14:11). He is described as the richest man in all the east. But he then experiences one catastrophe after another: his herds are stolen, his servants are massacred by marauders, his children all die in a windstorm, and he himself is covered with loathsome sores (chaps. 1—2). Such is his misery that his wife advises him to get it all over with: "Curse God and die" (2:9). Job does not curse God, but he does curse the day he was born (chap. 3); he desires to die (6:8–9) and objects that the wicked flourish and the poor perish while God takes no notice (21:7–33; 24:1–12). In particular, Job maintains that he is innocent and that God is punishing him unjustly (10:2–7; 23:10–12). Repeatedly—in language borrowed from the courtroom—Job protests that God is not giving him a fair trial (9:14–19; 23:2–7; 31:35).

Job's "comforters" are adherents of orthodox wisdom theology, according to which God rewards the righteous with long, happy, and prosperous lives, but cuts off the wicked in the midst of their sinning (e.g., 4:7–9). On these premises, they conclude that since Job suffers, he must have sinned. They question whether any man can really be righteous before God (4:17; 25:4–6); assert that Job's children perished because they sinned (8:4); advise him to seek God, that is, to repent (8:5–7; 22:21–30); tell Job that he deserves worse punishment than he has so far received (11:1–6) and that by complaining he is sinning even more (15:2–6); and charge him with numerous fictitious iniquities (22:4–11). Job is not deceived by these "miserable comforters" (16:2). He perceives that they blame the victim because they themselves fear calamity (6:21) and wish to "magnify themselves" against him (19:5). He sardonically denounces their pretensions to absolute wisdom: Too bad, he says to them, that when you die, "wisdom will perish with you" (12:2).

In his answers to Job, Yahweh reviews the wonders of creation, implying that human beings cannot know the ways of God, a point reiterated by Elihu: "Behold, God is great, and we know him not" (36:26). Yahweh's speeches "out of the whirlwind" declare that he has created the world for purposes that go beyond human desires for knowledge and fulfillment (chaps. 38—39; 40:15—41:34). For example, Yahweh has given the wild ass the steppe and saltland for his dwelling place (39:5–8), the eagle the rocky crag (39:27–30), and the mountains for all wild beasts to play upon (40:20). Job acknowledges that Yahweh's ways transcend his understanding, now that he "sees" God. Since no theophany (appearance of God) is reported, "see" may mean that Job understands and accepts Yahweh's transcendence. To the "friends" who have insisted that God has been punishing Job for his sins, Yahweh says, "You have not spoken of me what is right, as my servant Job has" (42:7). Yahweh restores Job's fortunes (exactly doubling the number of animals he had before, 42:10); only then do his relatives and erstwhile friends (who disappeared entirely during the time of Job's poverty and affliction, 19:13–19) turn up to feast (at Job's expense), show him sympathy (which he no longer needs), and bring him gifts (now that he is doubly rich)—again the ironic touches. Job then has another seven sons and three daughters (presumably the ideal numbers of each), and afterward lives 140 more years (notwithstanding the limit of 120 years prescribed in Gen. 6:3). Was all this told with a straight face, or did the author perhaps mean to parody the orthodox wisdom theology—which Job attacks directly in his speeches?

In the epilogue, Yahweh says that Job has spoken rightly about him, but that his comforters have spoken falsely. The comforters had claimed that God always rewards the righteous and punishes the wicked, and that Job was wrong to complain about the way God was treating him. Yet when Job acknowledges that God's ways are unsearchable, his fortunes are restored, as if the orthodox wisdom theology is somehow true after all! Perhaps the author meant that a person is rewarded for faith in God, but that such faith paradoxically includes recognizing that in this life the righteous may have to endure inexplicable catastrophes and tragedies.

Possibly the author meant Job to represent the Jewish people, who collectively experienced suffering beyond what they believed was deserved during several centuries following the exile (cf. Isa. 40:2, where the prophet tells the exiles that they have already received double for their iniquities). Some interpreters see in Job's affirmation "I know that my redeemer lives" (19:25–27) the hope for vindication after death, if not resurrection. (The prospect of resurrection is rarely indicated in the OT: it is hinted at, perhaps, in Ezek. 37:1–14 and Isa. 25:8; but explicitly anticipated only in Dan. 12:2).

As the story is told, it is Satan who first challenges the orthodox wisdom theology: "Does Job fear God for nought?" he asks (1:9). Satan argues that God makes it worth Job's while to be righteous, implying that such righteousness is tainted by self-interest. (Satan, incidentally, is not yet a cosmic principality or even a minor evil being, but only a zealous prosecuting attorney in Yahweh's court. He appears only two other times in the OT: 1 Chron. 21:1; Zech. 3:1–2. There is no mention of "the devil" in the OT; cf. Wisd. of Sol. 2:24.) It is not Satan, however, but Yahweh who initiates the testing of Job by directing Satan's attention to him (1:8). Satan proceeds to wager that once he brings calamity upon Job, Job will turn from Yahweh, and Yahweh accepts the wager. But even then, Satan acts only with Yahweh's permission (1:12; 2:6). Job does not turn from God, but rightly complains that God is not treating him fairly. Thus, whatever else the author may have intended, the story of Job affirms that, appearances notwithstanding, God ultimately is in control of human destiny, and may be trusted even by those who experience devastation.

PSALMS

Psalms generally are prayers or songs written in poetic form, which were either recited by individuals or sung as hymns on various ceremonial occasions. Many are found outside the Book of Psalms, such as the Songs of Moses (Exod. 15:1–18), Miriam (15:21), Deborah (Judges 5), and Judith (Jth. 16:2–17); prayers, such as those found in Jer. 12:1–13, Jon. 2:2–9, and Luke 1:46–55; and whole books, such as Lamentations and Obadiah.

The Book of Psalms presents the biblical faith in microcosm: creation (Pss. 104; 148), history (Pss. 105; 106), the law (Ps. 119), the word of Yahweh (81:8–16), and wisdom (Pss. 1; 37). In and above all, God is besought and praised. The Book of Psalms constitutes one tenth of the OT's pages. As now arranged, its psalms are grouped into five "books," each ending with a distinctive formula of blessing (after Pss. 41; 72; 89; 106). Psalm 150 is the finale to the book as a whole (but see Ps. 151 in the Apocrypha). Numerous psalms traditionally are attributed to David, but many to others, such as Asaph, the sons of Korah, and even Moses and Solomon. Many have no ascription. A later editor would supply what he or she thought appropriate settings for several of the psalms assigned to David (e.g., Pss. 3; 18; 56; 59). Instructions at the beginning frequently appear, advising "the choirmaster" as to hymn tunes (e.g., Pss. 8; 12; 45; 80) or instrumental accompaniment (e.g., Pss. 4; 5; 54). For these and other notations, see the RSV; they are omitted in the NEB. The present Book of Psalms probably was the hymnal and prayerbook of the postexilic (or second) temple. The term *selah* often appears, indicating places where the choir, instrumentalists, or readers should pause a moment before going on. Liturgical directions sometimes are indicated (e.g., 118:2–4; 129:1–2). It is not likely that copies of the psalms were available to the entire congregation. Often the congregation was to repeat a particular response: in· Psalm 136, the repeated response is written out in full. (See also the three repeated refrains in the psalms found in the Prayer of Azariah and the Song of the Three Young Men.) Some psalms borrow from others (e.g., Ps. 53 duplicates Ps. 14, and Ps. 108 evidently is based on Pss. 57:7–11 and 60:5–12). Occasionally the editor who numbered the psalms arbitrarily divided single hymns or poems in two (e.g., Pss. 9—10; 42—43).

Form critics have identified certain types of psalms, particularly *enthronement, royal, lament,* and *thanksgiving.* The first type celebrates God's enthronement in the heavens and his sovereignty over creation and all nations (e.g., Pss. 46; 93; 97). Some of these may derive from an ancient ceremony in which Yahweh was symbolically reenthroned each year. Royal psalms apparently were sung at the coronation of the kings of Judah (Pss. 2; 21; 72; 110). Lament psalms are the most common, the greater number in the form of prayers for help by individuals in distress. Typically these call on God, ask his protection from and vengeance upon personal enemies, pray for deliverance from death (Sheol, or "the pit"), invoke God's steadfast love, and affirm that he will indeed help or has already done so, and that the petitioner will pay his vows, offer sacrifice, or praise God in the assembly (e.g., Pss. 13; 35; 54; 56; 71). Some are less concerned with personal enemies than with forgiveness of sins (e.g., Pss. 38; 51), God's help in maintaining a righteous life (Pss. 119; 141), and anxiety in the face of sickness or the brevity of life (Pss. 39; 88). Like Job, some psalms charge God with neglecting to do justice and call on him to arise and make things right (Pss. 10; 58). Communal laments concern the sufferings of Israel (or Judah, or the Jewish people) as a whole, and often ask God to crush the nation's enemies (Pss. 60; 80; 83). Some evidently refer to the exile experience (e.g., Pss. 74; 79; 137; see also the Book of Lamentations).

Psalms of thanksgiving or praise, both individual and communal, also are numerous. Usually these offer thanks to God for deliverance from enemies or Sheol, for forgiveness, or for victory against national enemies (e.g., Pss. 9; 18; 98; 116). Some of the hymns praise God for his greatness as manifested in creation (Pss. 95; 104; 147; 148), for his mighty deeds in history (Pss. 66; 105), or for both (Ps. 136). Like the Yahweh speeches in Job, the creation psalms affirm that Yahweh's concerns extend beyond human needs and desires: he causes "the grass to grow for cattle" (104:14); "rocks are a refuge for badgers" (104:18); young lions seek their food from God (104:21); he gives food to the beasts (generally) and young ravens (147:9); the sea teems with innumerable "living things both great and small," and Yahweh made Leviathan, the great sea creature, "to sport in it" (104:25–26).

Many psalms, however, do not fit into these categories. Some are of mixed character, that is, both lament and thanksgiving (Pss. 40; 89; 139), royal and lament (61), or thanksgiving and enthronement (103). Moreover, various other types can be identified: wisdom (Pss. 1; 37; 49; 112), moral admonition and exhortation (Pss. 15; 32; 52; 62; 81; 128), and encouragement or hope (Pss. 91; 100; 121; 125). Psalm 23 voices confidence in God's continuing providential care. Several eulogize Zion, Jerusalem, or the temple, the national and religious capital (Pss. 48; 84; 87; 122; 132). Zion, the mountain in Jerusalem on which the temple was built, sometimes stands for the temple, sometimes for the whole city of Jerusalem. Some of these psalms may have been sung by people coming to Zion to offer sacrifices or participate in the three main ceremonies that, under seventh-century Deuteronomic law, were to be observed there (see Deuteronomy 12; 16). In Psalm 82, God addresses the unrighteous gods (probably those of other nations) in the heavenly council. Another unusual psalm advises a king's new bride as to her prospective role (45:10–17).

Like the prophets, the psalmists place differing values on sacrificial worship and hold divergent views as to the relation between Israel and other nations. Portions of several psalms oppose or transcend sacrificial offerings (40:6; 50:9–15, 23; 51:16–17; 69:30–31; 141:2), while other passages commend sacrifices (20:3; 50:8; 51:19; 66:13–15). Psalms 68; 72; and 149 hope for Israel's triumph over foreign nations, while others call upon all nations, and even all creation, to praise the Lord (Pss. 67; 87, NEB; 117; 148; 150).

PROVERBS

Proverbs is the principal example of wisdom literature in the OT. Wisdom writers' reflections generally are presented in poetic form, in which each statement typically is followed by a repetition of the underlying idea, but in different terms or imagery. Frequently the wisdom writers use aphorisms or short, often pungent, sayings— in brief, proverbs. These commonly offer pointed descriptions and comparisons, and generally constitute advice or admonitions as to attitudes and conduct. There are also longer collections or ruminations on such topics as the perils of association with "loose women" (7:5–27; 9:13–18), the merits of wisdom (8:1–36), the undesirable aspects of experiencing inebriation (23:29–35), the futility of dealing with fools (26:1–12), and the surpassing worth of a good wife (31:10–31).

Commonly the writer assumes the role of a father addressing his son; but one exception is Prov. 6:20, which commends adherence to one's mother's teaching. Chapter 31 is attributed to the mother of King Lemuel (31:1). Wisdom—a feminine being, *Hochmah*—herself also speaks occasionally (1:20–33; 8:1—9:6). Much of the book is ascribed to Solomon (1:1; 10:1; 25:1), but other persons also are credited with many of the sayings (24:23; 30:1; 31:1). A number of different concerns or foci appear in Proverbs.

Several proverbs, particularly in the final chapters, show a kind of prescientific interest in observing and classifying phenomena on some principle of similarity (e.g., 30:15–16, 24–28, 29–30). Most refer to human characteristics (e.g., 25:20; 26:20–21; 30:21–23, 33).

Quite a few sayings advise youths who aspire to associate with rulers and kings as to how to make a favorable impression (18:16; 22:11), or avoid doing otherwise (17:18; 25:6–7; 26:17–19; 27:2). Some advise rulers or kings themselves how best to proceed (15:22; 20:18; 29:4, 12, 14; 31:4–5).

The majority of the sayings appear to be addressed to general readers, and concern what we might call etiquette and morality. Prudence is particularly commended. Thus readers are urged to avoid contention (3:30; 26:17), evil companions (1:10–19), angry men (22:24–25), fools (14:7), and gossips (20:19). They are admonished to shun harlots and adulteresses (5:1–23; 6:23–35; 7:6–27; 23:26–28). One should stay clear of danger (22:3 or 27:12), act with caution and discretion (14:15–17), be slow to anger (14:29; 19:11; 29:11), answer softly (15:1), ignore insults (12:16), maintain discreet silence (17:27–28), not waste words on scoffers and fools (9:7–8; 23:9), abjure excessive indulgence in pleasures (12:11; 21:17), avoid imbibing wine (20:1; 23:20–21), and refrain from oppressing the poor and afflicted (22:16, 22–23) and from moving ancient landmarks (22:28; 23:10). Diligence and work are recommended repeatedly, in contrast to the way of the "sluggard" or lazy bones (24:30–34; 26:14–15). Yet one ought not strive to gain wealth (23:30–34; 28:20). There are also positive admonitions to be responsive to the needs of the poor (14:31; 19:17; 28:27; 29:7; 31:8–9) and kind to one's animals (12:10).

Some sayings primarily offer practical advice, such as how to get along with one's neighbors (3:28–29; 25:17; 27:14), and ideas about agriculture (12:11; 14:4; 27:23–27), diet (eating honey, but not too much, 24:13; 25:16), and building construction (24:27). The writer recurrently bemoans the fate of those who dwell with a contentious woman or wife, thereby, perhaps, revealing his own unhappy experience (21:9, 19; 25:24; 27:15–16). One saying suggests the writer's exasperation at having to try to teach wisdom to inattentive or slow learners: "Why should a fool have a price in his hand to buy wisdom, when he has no mind?" (17:16). Throughout Proverbs the reader is urged to listen to instruction ("my commandments"), love wisdom, and bring up children accordingly, not sparing the rod (13:24; 22:15; 23:13–14; 29:15).

Numerous sayings affirm that in this life the righteous are rewarded and the wicked punished (11:17–21; 12:21; 22:8–9). This understanding is commonly designated the orthodox wisdom theology. It surfaces elsewhere, for example, in Sirach (Ecclesiasticus) and Psalm 37, but is questioned in Job and Ecclesiastes. The orthodox wisdom theology is similar to the prophetic and Deuteronomic theologies of history, which held that if or when Israel (or Judah) broke covenant with Yahweh, he would or did punish the nation with disaster. An important difference, however, is that the orthodox wisdom theology focuses on the situation of individuals, not that of nations as a whole. Like many of the prophets, the writer of Proverbs urges that justice and righteousness are more acceptable to Yahweh than sacrifices (21:3).

Though wisdom as such is frequently personified and praised, the insistence that wisdom comes from God and that the beginning of wisdom is fear of (i.e., reverence for) him pervades Proverbs. Several sayings affirm God's providence or sovereignty over human affairs (16:9; 19:21; 20:24). Basic themes in the legal tradition are reiterated: the law and commandments are to be kept (10:8; 19:16; 28:7; 29:18); the rights of the poor and the orphan are to be protected (14:31; 22:22–23; 23:10–11); just weights are to be used (11:1; 20:10, 23); father and mother are to be honored (19:26; 20:20; 23:22); true witness or testimony given (12:17; 19:5, 9); and impartial justice rendered (24:23–25). Generally, righteousness is equated with wisdom, and wickedness with foolishness.

ECCLESIASTES

The anonymous author calls himself Qoheleth, meaning one who holds forth, probably as teacher, in a *qahal* or assembly. Like other wisdom writings, Ecclesiastes consists largely of short, detached sayings, with occasionally longer passages (e.g., 2:1–11 on the quest for pleasure, and 12:1–7 with its imaginative images of aging and death). Several sayings reflect interests common to the wisdom tradition, such as those in Proverbs: scientific observations and comparisons (4:9–12; 11:3); advice to those aspiring to royal favor (8:2–5; 10:4, 20); and other prudential or practical advice (7:9; 10:10; 11:4, 6). Sloth is deplored (10:18), work is commended (9:10), wisdom praised (7:11–12, 19), and the way of fools condemned (7:6; 10:3, 12–15).

Yet Qoheleth (or "the Preacher," RSV; "Speaker," NEB) repeatedly questions traditional wisdom. He disputes the value of work (1:3; 2:18–23), and even doubts the worth of wisdom: "In much wisdom is much vexation, and he who increases knowledge increases sorrow" (1:17–18). Qoheleth particularly challenges the claim of orthodox wisdom theology that the righteous are rewarded and the wicked punished in this life (7:15; 8:14).

Moreover, contrary to common biblical affirmations and assumptions, the Preacher's key theme is the proposition that all is vanity ("emptiness," NEB), that is, futile, senseless, without meaning (1:2, 14). Like the ancient Greeks, he holds that time and chance happen to all (9:11) and that history, like nature, is doomed to repeat meaningless cycles (1:4–10; 3:15). His appraisal of humanity is pessimistic: though God made man upright (7:29), none is so righteous as to do good and never sin (7:20). Indeed, men's hearts are full of evil and madness (9:3). Even human creativity is inspired by men's envy of their neighbors (4:4). Man's desire for money is insatiable (5:10; cf. the sardonic comment at 10:19; "Money answers everything"). The human scene is characterized by oppression and injustice (4:1; 8:9).

The writer frequently takes an agnostic stance as to ultimate questions: "Who knows" what is good for man during his lifetime, or what will happen after his death (3:21; 6:12)? God has "put eternity into man's mind," but man cannot know the ways of God—not even "the wise" who claim to know the answers (3:11; 8:16–17). Evidently Qoheleth agrees with the author of Job (see Job 42:1–6) that the answers to life's ultimate questions are unknowable. Thus he concludes—corroborating the experience of all students everywhere—"Of making many books there is no end, and much study is a weariness of the flesh" (12:12).

The shadow of death falls across all human activity. Wise and foolish, righteous and wicked alike come to the same end (2:15–16; 9:1–3). The fate of men is the same as the fate of beasts: all are from the dust, and all will turn to dust again (3:19–20; cf. Gen. 3:19). The dead are more fortunate than the living, and those unborn even more so, since they have not seen the injustices committed under the sun (4:2–3). The Preacher does not look for any life beyond death; moreover, he holds that after people die, they and their deeds, whether wise or foolish, good or evil, will be forgotten by those who come after; their love, hate, and envy will have perished with them and they will have no more share in all that is done under the sun (2:16; 9:5–6). The phrase "under the sun" recurs thematically throughout the book, generally in texts that point to the fewness of a person's days or to the folly and injustice that characterize human existence. Like Tobit (e.g., Tob. 2:3–9), the Preacher considers burial a matter of great importance (6:3).

Taking the role of Solomon in chaps. 1 and 2, the author reports that he has tried to find meaning in pleasure (2:1–10), but has discovered that this is merely "vanity and a striving after wind" (2:11). Work too proves pointless and futile (2:18–23). Nevertheless, though all are doomed to die, Qoheleth recommends that a man seek enjoyment in eating, drinking, toil (2:24–25; 3:12–13; 8:15), and companionship with his wife whom he loves (9:9). Such at least will distract him from considering the brevity of his life (5:18–20). Offering sacrifices may be foolish and futile (5:1; 9:2), but Qoheleth—or a later editor—commends keeping God's other commandments (12:13).

Certain passages seem to run counter to the book's usual agnosticism and gloom. The excellence of wisdom is affirmed, after all (2:13–14a; 9:13–18a); the righteous and wicked do receive fitting recompense (2:26; 8:12–13); men will be judged for their deeds (3:17; 11:9b; 12:14). These may be later editorial "corrections," or part of the author's original, perhaps paradoxical, perspective. Throughout, readers are admonished to fear (i.e., have reverence for) God, even if his ways are unknowable (3:14; 5:7; 7:18; 12:13).

SONG OF SOLOMON
(or CANTICLES)

Traditional Judaism and traditional Christianity have seen in this book an allegorical statement of God's love for Israel and of Christ's love for the church ("the bride of Christ"), respectively. As it stands, the book contains one or more poems concerning the love of a man and a woman for each other. Alternately, female and male speakers address their lover, with occasional comments by companions or a chorus (NEB supplies captions). Some or all of the poems may originally derive from wedding songs. Solomon is mentioned from time to time (1:1; 3:7, 9–11; 8:12; perhaps 6:13 where *Shulammite* may mean "bride of Solomon"). In 6:8–9, the male tells his beloved that she is the fairest of sixty queens and eighty concubines. This also suggests Solomon, the famous lover (or owner) of even more wives and concubines than that (1 Kings 11:3). Though scholars generally doubt that Solomon wrote it, most think that the book was included in Scripture because the Jewish authorities who decided which writings were to be regarded as such believed that Solomon was its author.

Periodically the female adjures the daughters of Jerusalem not to waken love (or her lover) until it (or he) is ready (2:7; 3:5; 8:4; cf. 5:8). Thematically, the man tells the woman, "you are beautiful, my love," and proceeds to picture her attributes through various images and comparisons (1:15; 4:1–8; 6:4–7). In the many descriptions of the lovers and their visits to gardens, orchards, and fields, we find numerous comparisons and allusions to trees, flowers, fruit, scents, birds, and animals, as well as to gold, ivory, and jewels. The male occasionally calls his beloved "my sister" (4:9–10; 5:1–2), an idiomatic term of endearment found also in Tobit (e.g., Tob. 7:16; 8:4, 7). Twice he goes off and must be sought by his would-be lover (3:1–4; 5:2–8). His later disappearance provides the woman occasion to describe her lover to the "daughters of Jerusalem" (5:9–16). Again, thematically, love and the lovers' kisses are compared favorably to wine (1:2; 4:10; 7:9). Lovers generally—or perhaps guests at a wedding party—are encouraged to "eat . . . and drink: drink deeply" (5:1). A notable poem in praise of love is included at 8:6–7.

As with other biblical traditions, physical love between man and woman is valued highly among the blessings of life in the created world (see, e.g., Gen. 2:23–24; 29:10–11; Deut. 24:5; Tob. 8:4–8). Only the corruption of this relation through adultery, exploitation, or promiscuity is deplored in the law and by the prophets and wisdom writers.

ISAIAH

This book contains traditions from several different periods. Isaiah is named only rarely, and not at all after chap. 39. Nevertheless, most of the sixty-six chapters are attributed either to the Isaiah who prophesied in Jerusalem ca. 742–690 B.C., or to his disciples (see 8:16) or "school." Chapters in the book from later times reiterate basic Isaianic themes, such as God's holiness and sovereignty over nations, and the assurance that those who look to him as their Maker and King need not fear. Some other prophets, like Micah and Habakkuk, also echo some of these themes and may well have been influenced by Isaiah. The present Book of Isaiah may include writings from as many as four different prophets and span a period of some five hundred years.

Most of chaps. 1—23; 28—33; 36—39 relate to Isaiah of Jerusalem, but some of the "oracles against foreign nations" (e.g., chaps. 13; 21; 23) evidently presuppose later circumstances and probably come from later hands. Chapters 36—39 essentially duplicate 2 Kings 18—20, from which they may derive. A psalm (of lament) attributed to King Hezekiah is included at 38:10–20.

Several major events occur during Isaiah's career. In 738 B.C., Assyria invades Israel, which purchases its survival by paying tribute to the Assyrian king, Tiglath-pileser, known as "Pul" in 2 Kings 15:19–20. A few years later, kings Rezin of Syria and Pekah of Israel try to induce Ahaz, king of Judah, to join them in an alliance against

Assyria. When Ahaz declines, Syria and Israel besiege Jerusalem, the capital of Judah, hoping to force that country to join. Ahaz, however, asks help from Tiglath-pileser—of all people (2 Kings 16:5–9). These events, ca. 735–34 B.C., prompt Isaiah's famous Immanuel and Mahershalalhashbaz prophecies (Isa. 7:1—8:8), in which he warns Ahaz that Yahweh will be with Judah in the form of devastation wrought by Assyrian armies before the newborn child grows beyond infancy (7:15–20; 8:3–4). In 721, Assyria overruns Israel, bringing that kingdom to its end (1 Kings 17:1–8). Judah survives, sometimes paying massive tribute. Twenty years later (701 B.C.), Assyria lays siege to Jerusalem, but then, for one reason or another, withdraws (Isa. 36—37).

Isaiah is the first prophet—so far as we know—in Judah. Like his contemporaries Amos and Hosea (ca. 740 B.C.) who prophesy against Israel in the North, Isaiah proclaims the word of Yahweh against Judah, the Southern Kingdom, for its faithlessness, injustice, and oppression. Isaiah especially emphasizes the rule of God over history. Because of her injustice, luxury, pride, and indifference to Yahweh, Judah will experience his rule as judgment in the form of invasion by Assyria (chaps. 5; 7; 8; 10). Yet at times Isaiah promises that Yahweh will protect Jerusalem (33:20–22; 37:33–35). In time, Yahweh also will punish Assyria for its pride (10:12–19). Moreover, he will bring back a remnant of his people and establish his rule over all the earth. That will be the "peaceable kingdom," the time when the wolf and the lamb, the leopard and the kid, the calf and the lion, the cow and the bear, the serpent and the little child shall all dwell together: "They shall not hurt or destroy . . . for the earth shall be full of the knowledge of Yahweh as the waters cover the sea" (11:6–9). Some passages tell of a new king from the family of David (9:2–7; 11:1–5); others look for the transformation of history and creation without mention of a messiah or king (e.g., 2:2–4; 29:17–21). All nations will then worship Yahweh and be his people (2:2; 11:10; 19:19–25). In the meantime, Yahweh does not desire animal sacrifices or pious ceremonies; instead, he asks that his people "cease to do evil, learn to do good, seek justice, correct oppression, defend the fatherless, [and] plead for the widow" (1:10–17). Because Yahweh is holy and lifted up, he is against all that is proud and lofty, especially the pride of men (2:11–17). Those who trust him may look for deliverance (7:4; 10:24–27), but those who seek foreign alliances lack faith and will perish along with such helpers (31:1–3). Isaiah offers several "signs" to reinforce his message (7:10, 14; 20:2–6; 37:30; 38:7–8), and gives at least two of his sons symbolic names: Shearjashub (7:3) and Mahershalalhashbaz (8:1–4; cf. Immanuel, 7:14–17; 8:5–8).

An anonymous prophet commonly designated Second Isaiah is credited with chaps. 34—35 and 40—55, which seem to come out of the latter years of the exile, perhaps as late as ca. 540 B.C., slightly after the time of the Deuteronomic historian. Animus directed against Edom in chap. 34 probably reflects the prophet's recollection of that nation's role in assisting Babylon to destroy Jerusalem in 586 B.C. (see Obadiah). Only wildlife will possess the land of Edom in years to come and they shall possess it forever because Yahweh has cast his lot for them (34:11–17; cf. Isa. 11:6–9; Hos. 2:18). Second Isaiah is mainly concerned to assure the exiles, who are still in Babylon, that the time for punishment is past (40:2), that Yahweh is preparing a highway in the wilderness (35:1–10; 40:3–4) for their return to Zion (Jerusalem), and that the time for them to go forth is at hand (48:20; 49:9; 52:11–12; 55:12). Like Isaiah of Jerusalem, Second Isaiah affirms the holiness, majesty, and sovereignty of God. But now Yahweh is going to do a "new thing" (43:19), that is, deliver his people, rather than punish them (cf. Jer. 28:8–9). Thus, speaking for Yahweh, Second Isaiah repeatedly assures the exiles, "Fear not, I am with you" (41:10, 13; 43:5). Like Isaiah of Jerusalem (6:5; 17:7), Second Isaiah hails Yahweh as Israel's Maker and King, but now also as her Redeemer (43:15; 44:6; 54:5). Yahweh appoints the Persian emperor Cyrus as his messiah (anointed) to overthrow Babylon and release the exiles (45:1–6). Creation and exodus imagery give promise of a new beginning and deliverance (43:15–17; 44:24, 27). Like Hosea, Second Isaiah declares that Yahweh is prompted to act because he loves his people (43:4; 49:15; 54:8, 10 [cf. Deut. 7:7; 10:15]). He proclaims that Yahweh has created all that is and alone is God (40:12–28; 44:6–8); thus some modern interpreters view Second Isaiah as the first biblical proponent of theoretical monotheism. Since only Yahweh is God, all other "deities" are bogus, and worship of manmade gods or idols is necessarily pathetic and futile (40:18–20; 44:9–20), a theme developed in later times (e.g., Wisd. of Sol. 13:1—15:17; Letter of Jeremiah; Bel and the Dragon). The several "servant of Yahweh" passages present a problem for interpretation. Is Cyrus, the liberator of the exiles, who is named Yahweh's shepherd and anointed the one so designated (44:28; 45:1)? Or does the prophet mean that the servant is Jacob (Israel), or perhaps the exiles (42:18—43:7; 43:8–13; 49:1–6)? Or is the servant some other person (see esp. 52:13—53:12), possibly the prophet himself (50:4–11)?

Chapters 56—66 may come from a later Isaianic prophet who lived in Jerusalem after the exile, but before the temple was rebuilt, perhaps ca. 520 B.C.—the time also of Haggai and Zechariah (chaps. 1—8)—and also afterward, for a decade or two. This Third Isaiah likewise emphasizes Yahweh's transcendence and holiness (57:15) and names him Israel's Redeemer (60:16b). He tells that Jerusalem will be restored, that Yahweh's glory will come upon the Jewish people, and that all will enjoy permanent prosperity and possession of the land (chaps. 60—61). There is no mention of a Davidic king, but a radically transformed era is expected—indeed, a new heaven and a new earth that will incorporate the "peaceable kingdom" in which all kinds of creatures will dwell together in harmony (65:17–25; cf. 11:1–9). Like Haggai and Zechariah, Third Isaiah anticipates that the wealth of other nations will then flow into Zion (60:5; 61:6; cf. Hag. 2:6–7; Zech. 14:14). Christian Christmas tradition later would draw on passages such as 60:1–7 (see also Isa. 1:3; 7:14; 9:1–7) for inspiration in reconstructing some of the circumstances of Jesus' birth. The "grapes of wrath" imagery in 63:1–6 refers to Yahweh's future trampling down of Judah's oppressors. Yet when Yahweh transforms heaven and earth, "all flesh" will worship him in Jerusalem (56:3–8; 66:23; cf. 19:19–25).

In the meantime, Sabbath observance is important, but Third Isaiah repudiates sacrificial offerings in favor of doing justice and caring for the needy (58:6–9; cf. 56:7). Yahweh has made all things; they are already his; so he has no need for animal sacrifices (66:1–4; cf. Ps. 50:9–15). Like earlier prophets, Third Isaiah proclaims Yahweh's judgment against the Jewish people for their apostasy and covenant violations (57:1–13; 59:1–15). Here we encounter the first biblical text to look for the eternal torment of the wicked (66:24; cf. Jth.16:17; Mark 9:43–49).

Chapters 24—27 generally are attributed to a later prophet, sometimes designated Fourth Isaiah, who may have lived in the third or second centuries B.C. This prophet looks for God's deliverance not only from foreign nations, but from cosmic or supernatural powers (24:21–23; 27:1). Yahweh will punish the whole earth (chap. 24), but then will establish a new age "for all peoples"; there will be feasting and wine, the dead will be raised, death itself will be swallowed up forever, and, at the sound of a great trumpet, the people of Israel will gather to worship Yahweh in Jerusalem (25:6–8; 26:19; 27:12–13; cf. 1 Cor. 15:52–54). The sayings in Fourth Isaiah are eschatological, in that they refer to events expected at the end of history and to the

conditions of life in the expected new age. As in Third Isaiah, however, there is no mention of a coming messiah or king from the line of
David.

JEREMIAH

Like Isaiah—but a hundred years later—Jeremiah prophesies in
Judah, especially Jerusalem, for several decades. Some narratives and
oracles refer to identifiable settings, but they are not all in chronological order. Jeremiah's career begins during the reign of Josiah, ca. 626
B.C. (1:2), shortly before the Deuteronomic reform, and extends
through the initial conquest of Judah by Babylon in 598 and its final
defeat in 586 B.C., when the Babylonians destroy the temple, the
palaces, larger houses, and walls of Jerusalem (chap. 52; cf. 2 Kings
24:18—25:30), and into the first years of the exile. He is last seen in
Egypt, condemning those Jews (Judahites) who have fled there and
have not only failed to repent for their past wickedness, but continue
to ignore Yahweh's law and statutes, while idolatrously worshiping
the "queen of heaven," perhaps the goddess Ishtar (chaps. 43—44).

In the years before 598, and down to 586, Jeremiah generally
prophesies that Yahweh will bring doom and destruction upon Judah
because of its many offenses (e.g., chap. 6). But, especially after 586,
he begins to proclaim that Yahweh will restore the fortunes of his
people (e.g., 30:18–22). Throughout the book, Jeremiah declares that
Yahweh intends both "to pluck up and break down," and "to build and
to plant" (1:10; 31:28; 45:4).

Yahweh will punish the people of Judah, Jeremiah repeatedly
warns, because of their apostasy, disobedience (7:21–26), compla-
cency (5:11–17), corruption (5:25–29), injustice (8:10), pride (13:9),
and other forms of wickedness and iniquity. All have acted wrongly:
kings, prophets, priests, and common people (2:4–8; 5:1–5, 30–31).
Because they do not wish to hear about their wickedness or Yahweh's
pending judgment, they ridicule, beat, and imprison Jeremiah from
time to time, and more than once threaten his life. He is nearly
lynched when he announces that Yahweh will destroy the temple, in
which people have put so much trust (chaps. 7; 26). His advice to
submit to Nebuchadnezzar as agent of Yahweh's judgment is viewed
by many as treason (38:1–28). In turn, Jeremiah frequently berates
both the false prophets and priests who tell people what they want to
hear by proclaiming peace when there is no peace (6:13–14; 8:10–11;
23:9–32).

Jeremiah suffers in his role as spokesman for Yahweh's judgment against his people. Though commanded otherwise by Yahweh (7:16; 11:14), he persists in praying for the nation (14:7–9, 19–22); moreover, in his "confessions" or complaints, Jeremiah unfolds his intimate feelings of grief and anger at his lot and that of his people, while also giving vent to his desire for vengeance against his persecutors (11:18–20; 18:19–23; 20:7–12). Yet Yahweh repeatedly assures Jeremiah that he will make him "a fortified city" and admonishes him to stop feeling sorry for himself and get on with his task as prophet (1:4–19; 12:1–6; 15:10–21). Notwithstanding his complaining, Jeremiah stands his ground in crisis after crisis, effectively declaring Yahweh's word despite opposition. Thus after being beaten and put in stocks by Pashur, the chief priest, Jeremiah declares that Yahweh will especially punish Pashur and his friends (20:1–6). After the prophet Hananiah breaks the yoke bars that Jeremiah has worn to symbolize Judah's pending subjugation to Babylon, Jeremiah comes back with the word that Yahweh has not authorized Hananiah, and will cause the latter to die within the year (28:1–17). After being banished from the temple, Jeremiah dictates the words of Yahweh, and sends his secretary Baruch to read them there; and when King Jehoiakim destroys that scroll (after it was confiscated by the temple authorities), Jeremiah dictates another, this time pronouncing further doom, specifically on Jehoiakim, his friends, and his associates (36:1–36).

Once the Babylonian ax fell in 586, Jeremiah declares that Yahweh will restore his people, both Israel and Judah. He will bring them back (16:14–15), make a new covenant with them, one written in their hearts (31:31–33), an everlasting covenant (32:40; 50:4–5). A few passages refer to a new king of "branch" (cf. Isa. 11:1) that will spring up from the house of David. This new king's reign will be marked by peace and justice (23:5–6; 33:14–16). Most of Jeremiah's oracles of hope for the future, however, make no mention of a future messiah or king. Chapter 29 reports the substance of a letter that Jeremiah wrote to the people of Judah who have been deported to Babylon in 598 B.C. In it, he urges them to recognize what has happened as Yahweh's doing, and to settle down there and seek the welfare of that city, assuring them that in due time Yahweh will give them "a future and a hope" (29:4–14). Jeremiah particularly emphasizes Yahweh's love for his people (31:3). Like Hosea, Jeremiah compares Yahweh's intended relationship with the people of Israel and Judah both to that of a husband and wife (2:2; 3:20; 31:32) and father and son (3:19; 31:9, 20), a relation which, though violated by these people, Yahweh means to restore in order to fulfill his own purposes.

Some later chapters (e.g., 36—45) may have been composed by

Baruch. Also, some material may come from later times. Certain passages suggest that Jeremiah was a proponent of the Deuteronomic reform, which established the Jerusalem temple as the sole place for sacrificial worship (2:20–28; 17:12–13, 26; 19:4–5). He may well have been, though sometimes he seems to say that Yahweh is opposed to all sacrificial offerings (e.g., 7:21–23; but see 33:18–22—possibly a later addition—which endorses sacrificial offerings by "the Levitical priests"). Like Second Isaiah, but unlike earlier prophets, Jeremiah may have commended Sabbath observance, though it could be that the principal text so indicating, 17:19–27, was added by a later proponent of such observance (cf. Neh. 13:15–22). The oracles against Babylon (chaps. 50—51) appear contrary to both Jeremiah's view that the Babylonians were God's instrument of judgment against Judah and his advice that the exiles in Babylon seek that city's welfare (chap. 29).

It may be that Jeremiah was in the "school" of Isaiah (cf. Isa. 8:16, which orders that the prophet's testimony be preserved among his "disciples"). Numerous passages echo Isaianic themes and terms, such as Yahweh's sovereignty over the nations, the assurance that a remnant, blind and lame included, will return with singing to Zion (31: 7–13), and Isaiah's characterization of Yahweh as Redeemer (Jer. 50:34) and the Holy One of Israel (Jer. 51:5). In any event, Jeremiah was a major figure in his own right, as was his contemporary, the prophet Ezekiel.

LAMENTATIONS

Traditionally, the book is ascribed to Jeremiah. Several passages do recall, and some may incorporate, that prophet's words (e.g., 1:13; 2:14, 22; 3:14, 48). Scholars commonly assign the writing to other hands, however, partly because after 586 B.C. Jeremiah's message clearly and consistently was one of hope for the future that Yahweh would surely bring.

Lamentations consists of a series of poems or psalms which express and commemorate the anguish of the Jewish people who remain in Jerusalem (Zion) after the Babylonians overran it in 586 B.C. The Jewish exiles who were deported to Babylon long bitterly for Zion (Psalm 137). But things are hardly better for the captive Jews who continue to dwell amid Jerusalem's ruins. The siege was terrible: people starved or killed their own children for food (2:20; 4:9–10); the city was burned (4:11) and the temple destroyed (see 2 Kings 25:1–12). Famine is still severe, and the humiliated survivors are subjected to physical abuse and hard labor (5:1–13). The vividness of these recollections suggests that the poems were written not long after the events of 586, perhaps within a decade or two.

Remarkably, the catastrophes experienced by these survivors are perceived as Yahweh's judgment against the Jewish people because of their transgressions (1:5; 2:17). This perception contrasts markedly with that of Obadiah, who devotes his entire book to the condemnation of Edom, which had aided Babylon as it pillaged and devastated Jerusalem, and even more with Psalm 137, in which Jewish exiles in Babylon call for Yahweh's vengeance upon Edom and pronounce blessings on anyone who would massacre Babylonian children. Neither Obadiah nor the author of Psalm 137 acknowledges the hand of Yahweh in the disasters of 586 B.C. The understanding found in Lamentations, on the other hand, reflects the warnings of the prophets to the effect that Yahweh would punish—indeed, destroy—this people if they continued to forsake him and his covenant (e.g., Isa. 10:1–11; Jer. 5:1—6:26; 9:1–11; Ezek. 5:1—6:27). The Deuteronomic historian, writing a few decades later, likewise recognizes the exile as Yahweh's judgment against Judah and its people for breaking covenant (Deut. 8:11–20; 2 Kings 24:1–4, 20).

Nevertheless, the writer cries out for Yahweh to avenge and help the Jewish people (1:21–22; 5:21; cf. Psalms 74, 79). Like Second Isaiah, who also writes after 586 B.C., the author of Lamentations declares that the time of punishment is over, and that the exile must soon end (4:22a; cf. Isa. 40:2). Trusting in Yahweh's steadfast love, the poet dares to hope that he will not forever cast them off (3:22–33). But that hope is by no means a certainty: the book closes with the haunting question to Yahweh: "Or hast thou utterly rejected us?" (5:22).

EZEKIEL

Ezekiel's career as prophet begins in the final years of Judah's existence as an independent nation, and continues a decade or more, into the period of the exile. The earliest date indicated is ca. 593 B.C., five years after the first deportation (1:2); the latest, perhaps, is ca. 573 (40:1). Most of his time is spent among fellow exiles in Babylon by the river Chebar, though occasionally he visits Jerusalem, at least in visions (8:3—11:25). A few chapters (e.g., 3—7; 12; 16) possibly report somewhat earlier activity in Jerusalem. The account of Ezekiel's call to be a prophet is characteristically vivid: the voice of Yah-

weh tells him to eat a scroll and then speak the words written on it to
"the house of Israel" (2:1—3:11; cf. the calls of Isaiah and Jeremiah,
Isa. 6:1–13; Jer. 1:1–10). In Ezekiel, as in much other biblical tradition written after the fall of the Northern Kingdom, "Israel" generally
refers to the surviving Southern Kingdom, Judah. Throughout the
book, Yahweh typically addresses the prophet as "son of man," a term
equivalent to "man" (see Ps. 8:4), connoting his lowly condition
before God.

Like Jeremiah, his contemporary, Ezekiel proclaims not only doom
and destruction, but also hope for the future. Before the end came in
586, Ezekiel declares that Yahweh will punish Judah and Jerusalem
for their various offenses. Like the other classical prophets, Ezekiel
focuses on two dimensions of transgressions: those against Yahweh,
and those that take the form of injustice, oppression, and unrespon-
siveness to the needs of others in the community. Like Hosea and
Jeremiah, Ezekiel characterizes the people's persistent worship of
other gods as harlotry (chaps. 16; 23). Israel and Judah always have
been nations of rebels, a stubborn people (2:3–4), but Judah is even
worse than her late sister (16:51; 23:11): she continually fails to keep
Yahweh's ordinances and statutes, and worships other gods at pagan
shrines (5:6; 6:13; 11:12; 20:28). Such passages resemble Deuteronomic language and suggest that Ezekiel may have been influenced by
the Deuteronomic reform of 622 B.C. which had instituted the requirement that sacrifices be offered only in one place, Jerusalem (see
Deuteronomy 12—19; 2 Kings 22—23). Ezekiel also condemns his
contemporaries for violating the horizontal dimension of the covenant:
they have shed innocent blood, dishonored their parents, wronged the
poor, sojourners, orphans, and widows, committed adultery and
incest, taken interest, and practiced extortion (22:6–12). Everyone—princes, priests, prophets, and ordinary people alike—has done
wrong in these ways (22:23–29). Not a single righteous man—for
whose sake the nation might be spared—is to be found (22:30; cf. Jer.
5:1–5; Gen. 18:17–33). Because of these offenses, Ezekiel declares
that Yahweh will send pestilence, famine, and the sword against
Jerusalem and the whole nation of Judah or "Israel" (chaps. 5—7).
When disaster befalls them, his people will know that he is Yahweh
(7:27).

Yet once the Babylonians captured and demolished Jerusalem and
took most of its remaining citizens into exile, Ezekiel declares that
Yahweh would gather his people and bring them back to their own
land (28:25; 36:24), give them a new heart and a new spirit, so that

they will "walk in his statutes," that is, willingly and gladly obey his laws (11:19–20; 36:26–27), and make an everlasting covenant of peace with them (37:26). Wild beasts will be banished from the "prosperous plantations" that Yahweh will give to his people, who will then be the sheep of his pasture (34:25–31). The most famous of Ezekiel's images of hope for the future is his vision of the valley of dry bones (37:1–14). Just as the bones come together again and are brought to life, so "the whole house of Israel" will be restored to nationhood. When their fortunes are restored, they shall once more know that Yahweh is their God (39:25–28). Like Isaiah and Jeremiah, Ezekiel looks for a king from the house of David who will then rule in righteousness (34:23–24; 37:24–25; Ezekiel may even have meant that David himself would return; cf. Mal. 4:5). Moreover, through his demonstration with the two sticks, Ezekiel gives assurance that this king will rule over a reconstituted Israel that will be united with Judah into one nation, as in the golden days of yore (37:15–23).

More frequently than other prophets, Ezekiel reports complex visions and allegories (e.g., chaps. 16; 17; 24), and acts out symbolically the disasters Yahweh is going to inflict as judgment upon the people of Jerusalem and Judah—thereby engaging the attention of passers-by, after the fashion of modern guerrilla theater performers (e.g., chaps. 4—5; 12; 24). Lest any of his hearers or readers suppose that his prophecies are for "times far off," Ezekiel insists that Yahweh means them for those alive at the time, and that the prophesied events will occur without delay (12:21–28; cf. Rev. 22:10, 12, 18–20). Another of his memorable visions describes a representation of Yahweh's transcendent but all-seeing presence among the exiles in Babylon, the mobile "chariot" with wheels within wheels (chaps. 1; 10). Jeremiah, too, assured the exiles that Yahweh was with them (Jeremiah 29; cf. Psalm 137, whose author did not believe that the Babylonian exiles could worship Yahweh in a foreign land, and Jonah, who tried to escape Yahweh's presence by sailing to Tarshish, Jonah 1—4).

Earlier prophets sometimes emphasized individual responsibility for keeping the covenant, but Ezekiel does so systematically: the old proverb "The fathers have eaten sour grapes, and the children's teeth are set on edge" will no longer apply; instead, each person is to be accountable for his own offenses (18:1–24; cf. Lam. 5:7). Even prophets are liable if they fail to warn the wicked (3:16–21; 31:1–9). The righteous shall live, while the sinner shall surely die, but the righteous can lapse, and sinners can change their ways; therefore the prophet calls the wicked to repent, for Yahweh takes no pleasure in the death of anyone (18:30–32). We find a similar emphasis on individual rewards and punishments in this life in the wisdom writings (e.g., Prov. 10:2–3, 27–30).

Like many other prophetic books, Ezekiel contains several "oracles against foreign nations" (chaps. 25—32; 35), some of which may have been added after Ezekiel's time. Like such oracles in other prophetic writings, these point to Yahweh's sovereignty over all nations, promising or warning that he will judge them (and not only Israel or Judah) for their pretension and wickedness (e.g., Isa. 10:12–19; Amos 1:3—2:3). Some also may be tinged by a spirit of xenophobia or desire for national revenge (e.g., Joel 3:1–17, 19; Obadiah; Nahum).

The book closes (chaps. 40—48) with a detailed description of an ideal temple and various laws concerning sacrifices, priests, and Levites. Since these interests appear to reflect the influence of emerging Priestly (P) tradition recorded, perhaps, ca. 450–400 B.C., some interpreters suggest that these chapters are the work of a later prophet, apocalyptic seer, or priest. Here the sons of Zadok are distinguished from the other sons of Levi, and only the former may minister at Yahweh's altar (40:46–47; 43:18–19; 44:15–16). Earlier traditions make no distinction between priests and Levites; but P tradition and Chronicles insist that only the "sons of Aaron" may be priests, while Levites may serve only in lesser sacerdotal capacities. It may be significant that chaps. 40—48 make no mention of David or a king or messiah descended from him, even though these chapters, broadly speaking, depict conditions of life in the "messianic" or new age to come. Instead, the priestly sons of Zadok are the central leadership figures. Their task would be to preside over the offering of sacrifices in the temple of the new age. Later prophets, notably Haggai, Zechariah, and Malachi, would continue to accentuate the importance of the temple and ritual observances there, especially the offering of proper sacrifices.

In chap. 47, the prophet—or a later apocalyptic editor—looks for the preternatural abundance of fish and fruit in the new era: then all kinds of trees will bear fresh fruit every month (47:7–12; cf. the tree[s] of life in Rev. 22:1–2). Other postexilic and intertestamental texts likewise look for superabundant harvests or food in the coming age (e.g., Isa. 25:6; Joel 3:18; Amos 9:13; 2 Bar. 29:4–5; *Shabbat* 30b). Various NT texts also anticipate that the righteous will eat and drink together in the coming age (e.g., Matt. 26:29; Luke 13:29; Rev. 2:7).

Some prophets looked only for the glorification of Israel, Judah, or the Jewish people in the coming age. Ezekiel, on the other hand, seems to be among those others who declared that Gentiles (other nations or peoples) would have a share in the blessings of life in that new era (37:28; 47:22–23). Other prophetic texts to the same effect include Isa. 11:10; 19:19–25; 25:6–7; 49:6; Jer. 48:47; 49:6; Mic. 4:1–4; and Zech. 14:16–19.

DANIEL

The ostensible setting is the period from the beginning of the exile— dated, oddly, in the third year of Jehoiakim, 606 B.C. (1:1)—and extending into the reign of the Persian king Cyrus (ca. 530 B.C.), who had conquered the Babylonians and issued his famous decree in 538 B.C. allowing Jewish exiles to return to their former homeland. As the story is told, Daniel and some of his friends are chosen by the Babylonian king Nebuchadnezzar to serve in his court. The king renames Daniel Belteshazzar (not to be confused with Belshazzar), and soon Daniel is interpreting the king's dreams (chaps. 2—4). Daniel also interprets King Belshazzar's famous vision of the handwriting on the wall (chap. 5), and later, during the reign of the Medes and the Persians, his own dreams and visions (chaps. 7—12). Like Joseph, whom Pharaoh honored for interpreting his dreams, Daniel serves these kings in various high official capacities (when he is not being persecuted for refusing to abandon Jewish tradition). Several dreams and visions refer to developments in later centuries, particularly the rise and breakup of the Greek empire (chap. 11), and finally, the oppressive reign of a later king who seems to fit the description of the Syrian tyrant Antiochus IV ("Epiphanes"), known to us from 1 Maccabees (see, e.g., Dan. 7:19–21; 8:11–13; 12:11; cf. 1 Macc. 1:20–23, 41–50, 54–64). The resemblance is so considerable that many interpreters have concluded that Daniel was written during the reign of Antiochus IV or in the early Maccabean years (ca. 170–160 B.C.). The book is concerned with religious persecution of the sort first experienced—so far as we know—at that time. Much of it is explicitly apocalyptic in form: the words and visions purport to have been revealed to persons living in earlier times, but to have been "shut up and sealed" (8:17, 26; 12:4, 9) until the proper time, evidently that of the persecution under Antiochus IV. Intervening history is represented by a variety of symbolic figures, beasts, and horns. Second-century Jews, looking back to the time of Daniel and taking his interpretations as prophecies of things to come, could see that history had unfolded in accordance with this now unsealed or revealed plan, and so be encouraged to believe that the time of deliverance promised in the book would soon come to pass as well, since God had long known, if not also ordained, everything that was to happen.

The stories about Daniel and his friends all have the same point: God will deliver those who continue to trust him, refuse to worship other gods, and keep Jewish tradition despite persecution. Thus Shadrach, Meshach, and Abednego, Daniel's three friends who refuse to worship the golden image, are rescued from the fiery furnace by god's angel (chap. 30). Likewise, Daniel, who persists in praying to his God despite Darius's decree, is saved from the lions, again by the angel (chap. 6). Moreover, the several dreams, visions, and the supernatural handwriting on the wall all reveal that Daniel's God (identified as Yahweh only in chap. 9) rules over the kingdoms of men, notwithstanding the arrogant presumptions of certain kings (4:3, 17, 25–26; 5:18–28), and that these kingdoms will endure only for a time, after which God will establish his rule on earth through his saints (faithful Jews) forevermore (2:31–44; 7:14, 18–27; 8:3–25). The mysterious power of God is expressed in a particularly dramatic way in two instances. A stone "cut out by no human hand" smashes the great image representing the four kingdoms (2:23; see also 8:25). Only the fingers of a man's hand appear and write on the wall—the eerie effect of which is not lost upon Belshazzar (5:5–6). The latter scene, one of the most vivid in the Bible, gives Daniel occasion to interpret the ominous words, "MENE, MENE, TEKEL and PARSIN," thereby demonstrating again that God is in control of history, and that he puts down those who exalt themselves, lord it over the Jewish people, and fail to honor him (6:13–30).

The "son of man" dream or vision of Daniel's in chap. 7 has several distinctive features. Biblical tradition generally is reluctant to describe God, perhaps to avoid transgressing the prohibition against making likenesses of him (Exod. 20:4; Deut. 5:8). Ezekiel, for instance, cautiously characterizes Yahweh's enthroned presence: "Such was the appearance of the likeness of the glory of Yahweh" (Ezek. 1:28b). Daniel 7:9 not only describes the throne (which, as in Ezekiel 1, has fire as well as wheels), but also "one that was ancient of days," namely, God, along with his raiment. Here "Ancient of Days" and "the Most High" are circumlocutions, that is, ways of referring to God without using his name. Beginning in the third or second centuries B.C., Jewish tradition increasingly tended to avoid naming God, perhaps to avoid inadvertent contravention of the Third Commandment (Exod. 20:7; Deut. 5:11). The implication of 7:10c is that at the last judgment, individuals will be judged on the basis of their deeds (cf. 12:1–3). The term "son of man" as such does not appear here; instead, 7:13 refers to "one like a son of man" who is pictured ascending to the Ancient of Days on or with the clouds of heaven. As the vision goes on, this "person" is to be given "dominion and glory and kingdom" forever (7:14). Later, the report tells that "the saints of the Most High," that is, Jews who remain faithful despite persecution, will receive the kingdom and dominion forever (7:18, 22, 27). Many scholars conclude from these texts that Daniel (or the apocalyptic seer who wrote in his name) used the expression "one like a son of man" to stand for those righteous Jews who would receive dominion over the kingdoms of the earth once their persecutors were overcome. There is no mention of a messiah or Davidic king in the Book of Daniel.

The basic message of the Book of Daniel, as of most apocalyptic writings, is this: keep the faith, and endure to the end, for God will deliver those who do so. A time of unprecedented tribulation or persecution is expected just before the final deliverance (12:1). This expectation is shared by other Jewish and early Christian writers, who sometimes look for accompanying cosmic manifestations as well (Joel 2:30–31; Zech. 14:1–5; Add. to Esther 11:5–9; Mark 13:8, 14–19). One of the few OT passages that mentions resurrection, Dan. 12:2–3 offers hope for those who have perished, perhaps in the course of persecution.

The earliest known versions of other OT books were written in Hebrew; however, Daniel 2:4b — 7:28 is first known in Aramaic. The writer uses the term Chaldeans in a special sense, as "wise men," in company with magicians, enchanters, sorcerers, and astrologers (2:2; 5:7). Elsewhere in the OT, Chaldeans means simply Babylonians. Further traditions about Daniel and his friends are included in the Greek Bible, or Septuagint, and in later Catholic Bibles. In Protestant editions, these other traditions are placed in the Apocrypha under the heading of Additions to Daniel and include the Prayer of Azariah and the Song of the Three Young Men, Susanna, and the stories of Bel and the Dragon.

HOSEA

One of the first major prophets whose sayings or writings have been preserved in a separate book, Hosea prophesied in Israel (Ephraim, Samaria, or the Northern Kingdom) ca. 750–725 B.C., about the same time as Amos. Despite numerous textual problems (see footnotes in RSV and NEB), his message is clear: Because the people of Israel have forgotten Yahweh and his law or covenant, Yahweh will reject, indeed destroy them. And yet, in various ways, Hosea declares that Yahweh nevertheless loves his faithless and degraded people, Israel, and means to restore them.

Israel's fundamental offense is infidelity or apostasy. Forgetting Yahweh who brought them from Egypt (2:13; 8:14; 13:46), the people of Israel commit harlotry (5:3–4; 9:1) by worshiping other gods, such as the fertility gods (Baalim or Baals) of Canaan, or various manmade idols (8:4–5; 11:2; 13:2). This pattern is expressed memorably in Hosea's comparison of Israel with his faithless wife, Gomer (chaps. 1—3). Moreover, worship of the fertility gods entails recourse to cult prostitutes (4:13–14), making the characterization of Israel's apostasy as harlotry especially apt. In addition, Israel has turned to foreign alliances instead of to Yahweh (5:13; 8:9–10), and, forgetting Yahweh, pretended to self-sufficiency (10:13–14; 12:8; 13:5–6). Israel's history, Hosea declares, shows this pattern to be chronic: "as in the days of Gibeah" (9:9; 10:9; cf. Judges 19—20), or Baal-peor (9:10; cf. Numbers 25). Hosea also objects that Israel's having a human king is contrary to Yahweh's purposes (8:4; 13:10–11). Evidently Hosea, himself a Northerner, shares the Northern belief that kings or would-be kings of Israel usurped Yahweh's role as King of Israel (see Judg. 8:22–23; 1 Sam. 8:4–7). In these several ways, Hosea says, Israel has turned from Yahweh to other gods, thereby violating the vertical dimension of the covenantal requirement: "no other gods besides me" (Exod. 20:3 or Deut. 5:7). In a sweeping indictment, Hosea declares that there is no knowledge of Yahweh in the land, and also no faithfulness or kindness (4:1; 5:4).

The horizontal dimension of the covenant—the basic commandments governing conduct within the human community—also have been violated. Israel is condemned for its bloody deeds (1:4; 6:8–9), evil works (7:2), false balances, and oppression (12:7). The people of Israel love to offer sacrifices, but what Yahweh desires is steadfast love (6:6; 8:13).

Because of her several offenses, Israel will experience Yahweh's judgment in the form of Assyrian oppression; literally or symbolically, she will go back to Egypt, the land of bondage (8:13b; 9:3, 6; 11:5). Yahweh's repudiation of Israel is symbolized in the names the prophet gives the children of Gomer, his harlotrous wife: *Lo Ruchamah* (" Not pitied," 1:6) and *Lo Ammi* ("Not my people," 1:8). The name of another son, Jezreel, represents Yahweh's condemnation of Jehu's murderous revolution instigated by the prophet Elisha a century earlier (2:4; 2 Kings 9:1—10:36). Though the prophet often says that Yahweh will punish Israel (3:13; 4:9; 8:13b; 9:7, 9; 12:2), he also frequently declares that Yahweh intends to destroy the nation and its people, to bring them to an end (1:4; 9:12–16; 13:1–9, 14, 16).

Yet elsewhere Hosea speaks as if Israel might yet repent and return to Yahweh (5:15—6:3; 14:1–3), seek him, and practice righteousness and steadfast love (10:12), and—as if to summarize the burden of the Law and the Prophets—at last hold fast to "love and justice" (12:6). To be sure, Yahweh will hedge faithless Israel about and punish her (2:6–13), but afterwards will restore her and again treat her as his bride (2:14–16), making a new covenant with her, and also with "the beasts of the field, the birds of the air, and the creeping things of the ground"—establishing or reestablishing the peaceable kingdom of all creation (2:28; cf. Gen. 9:8–17; Isa. 11:6–9; 65:20–25). Life in this new era will be marked by six central biblical norms: righteousness, justice, steadfast love, mercy, faithfulness, and, perhaps all-inclusively, knowledge of Yahweh (2:19–20). Hosea also pictures Yahweh's love for Israel as that of a father for a wayward son: "It was I who taught Ephraim to walk. . . . How can I give you up, O Ephraim! . . . My compassion grows warm and tender. . . . I will not again destroy Ephraim" (11:3–9).

As the text stands, the issue is unresolved: Will Yahweh destroy his people, or will he sustain them with his love despite all that they have done? In one passage, it is a matter of justice and condemnation (11:5–7); in the next, of compassion (11:8–9). Both moods recur throughout the book, which concludes with further oracles of doom (13:3–16), followed by assurances of Yahweh's love and support (14:4–7). In fact, not long after Hosea's time, Israel was destroyed by Assyria (722 B.C.).

JOEL

This book consists entirely of prophetic sayings or oracles, and offers no particular evidence as to the prophet or his time. Its numerous references to Zion (i.e., Jerusalem) and Judah suggest that he lived in or near Jerusalem. The oracle against Edom (3:19) points to a date after 586 B.C., when the Edomites helped Babylon destroy Jerusalem and capture its people (see Ps. 137:7; Obad. 10–14). Evidently the temple ("house of God") has been rebuilt (1:14; 2:17), which indicates a date after 515 B.C. However, because of locusts, drought, fire, and/or devastation by foreign armies, crops have failed to such an extent that sacrificial offerings are suspended (1:13–16). From Haggai (ca. 520 B.C.) and Malachi (ca. 450 B.C.) we learn that crop failure became a serious problem after the exile. Possible echoes of Malachi hint that Joel was set down after 450 (2:11b, 31b; cf. Mal. 3:2; 4:5b). Mention of Greeks (3:6) may suggest a date no earlier than the fourth century, while the book's eschatological sections (2:28–32; 3:14–15, 18) accord with Jewish sources dating from the third and second centuries B.C.

Joel's message contains four motifs. The first is that Yahweh's judgment will come upon the Jewish people in the form of catastrophe (1:1—2:11). Already fields, orchards, and pastures are in ruins, meaning, evidently, that Yahweh has begun to punish the Jewish people. There is little or no food for persons, domestic cattle, and sheep, or water for wildlife (1:16–20). Earlier traditions also saw that other creatures suffered as a result of human depravity: Gen. 6:5–7; Hos. 4:1–3. And more catastrophes will soon follow: the day of Yahweh is near. It will be a day of darkness, gloom, and destruction from the Almighty (1:15; 2:1–2, 11; cf. Amos 5:18–20). The demonic army pictured in 1:4–7 and 2:2–10, whether locusts, foreign troops, or both, is sent by Yahweh to execute his word (2:11).

"Yet even now," Joel declares, Yahweh calls his people to return: "Rend your hearts and not your garments" (2:12–13). This is Joel's second motif: because Yahweh "is gracious and merciful, slow to anger, and abounding in steadfast love, and repents of evil" (2:13; cf. Exod. 34:6; Neh. 9:17), he may yet bless them if they repent. Thus the prophet's declarations about catastrophes already experienced and those that are near seem to be meant as warnings to prompt his Jewish contemporaries to repent (shub, literally, "to return" or "turn around").

The third motif is the prophet's message of hope. As if in response to their petition, Yahweh then assures his people that he will indeed restore their fortunes and never again put them to shame (2:18–27). Wildlife, wilderness pastures, fruit trees, and vines also will take part in this great restoration (2:22; cf. 3:18). In addition, he will bestow his spirit, the gift of prophecy, upon them and warn them through apocalyptic portents so that they may repent "before the great and terrible day of the Lord comes" (2:28–32). Judah will then enjoy abundant wine, milk, and water, and be inhabited forever (2:19, 21–26; 3:18).

The final motif concerns foreigners or Gentiles. In the coming era of restoration, foreigners will have no place in Jerusalem (3:17b; cf. Isa. 11:10; 25:6; Ezek. 47:22–23; Zech. 14:16–19). Moreover, Joel promises that "in those days" Yahweh will gather all nations for judgment and wreak vengeance on them for the acts of violence they have committed against the people of Judah (3:1–21; cf. Matt. 25: 31–46, where nations will be gathered for judgment, but the fate of individuals will depend on what each has done or failed to do).

AMOS

Several prophetic books are placed before his, but Amos may have been the earliest of the classical prophets—although Hosea and Isaiah may have been near contemporaries. Though a Southerner, he delivered his oracles in Israel sometime in the middle of the eighth century B.C. (1:1). (Israel here means the Northern Kingdom, also referred to in Amos as Samaria, Joseph, Isaac, and Jacob.) Much or all of Amos's message may have been spoken at Bethel.

Amaziah, the priest in charge of the Northern sanctuary at Bethel, is not pleased to see Amos there, and tries to disparage and dismiss him as a two-bit "seer" or fortuneteller and a carpetbagger (7:12; cf. 1 Sam. 9:6–9). Amos insists that he is not a professional prophet; rather, he is a shepherd from Judah who has experienced Yahweh's call to go and prophesy to Israel (7:14–15). Moreover, he adds some further words from Yahweh as to the miserable fate in store for Amaziah and his family (7:16–17).

He begins by announcing Yahweh's intention to punish a series of foreign nations for their crimes (1:3—2:3). Very likely a gathering crowd of Israelites cheers him on as he proclaims Yahweh's judgment against Syria, certain Philistine cities, Tyre, Edom, Ammon, and Moab for their various acts of cruelty not only against Israel but against each other. But then, using the same formula, he abruptly declares that Yahweh will punish Israel for its own offenses (2:6–16). Now the special relation Yahweh has had with Israel in the past becomes the basis for special condemnation: "You only have I known of all the families of the earth; therefore I will punish you for all your iniquities" (3:1–2). No wonder Amaziah views Amos as a troublemaker and orders him to leave "the king's sanctuary" (7:10–12).

In particular, Amos declares that the people of Israel have violated the horizontal dimension of the covenant. They have failed to provide justice in the local courts ("the gate"); instead, the wealthy and powerful have been exploiting the righteous, poor, and needy, the very people whose interests the covenant required them to protect (2:6; 5:11a; 8:4–6). They have also committed other offenses against persons in the covenant community (2:7–8, 12). Moreover, both the men and women of Israel have been living in ease and luxury without regard to the plight of the poor and needy, or to the future of the nation, against which Yahweh, who is just, will surely bring judgment (3:15—4:1; 6:1–6). The people of Israel think they can multiply their transgressions, but then make everything all right by offering sacrifices. They love to offer sacrifices, but Yahweh will not be bought off by religious services and offerings (4:4–5; 5:21–23); what he does require is justice and righteousness (5:15, 24). Amos, like Jeremiah after him, implies that Yahweh never asked for sacrifices in the wilderness, the time when the Law was given to Moses, and hints, perhaps, that Yahweh never did ordain sacrificial offerings (Amos 5:25; Jer. 7:21–23; cf. Isa. 1:12–17). The term classical prophets generally is used to designate those prophets who, beginning with Amos, emphasize this horizontal dimension, that is, Yahweh's requirements of justice, righteousness, and mercy, and especially, concern for the poor, the fatherless, the widow, and the orphan. Yahweh repeatedly has tried to warn Israel, Amos says, by bringing famine, drought, blight, mildew, locusts, pestilence, and conquering enemies upon them. "'Yet you did not return to me,' says Yahweh" (4:6, 8, 9, 10, 11). Now time has run out; doom is nigh: "Prepare to meet your God, O Israel" (4:12).

Like Jeremiah after him, Amos pleads with Yahweh for the nation (7:1–6), but ultimately to no avail. Amos depicts not only devastation and decimation (3:12; 5:3) but the total destruction of Israel and the Israelites (5:2; 8:1–2; 9:1–4, 8a–b). A few passages hint that it still may not be too late: that Israel may yet seek Yahweh and live (5:4, 6, 14–15). But otherwise Amos's message is one of certain and impending doom. Because Israel has violated the covenant, particularly the covenant obligation of the rich and powerful to look out for the well-being of the poor and needy, Yahweh will bring the whole nation to judgment.

Interpreters generally regard most of the present ending (9:9c–15) of the book as a supplement appended after the tragic events of 586 B.C. to give hope to the exiles of Judah or their later Jewish descendants. The transition from 9:8b to 9:8c seems abrupt and even contradictory: "I will destroy it from the surface of the ground; except that I will not utterly destroy" it. The declaration that sinners will die (9:10) is more like Ezekiel's and the orthodox wisdom theology's emphasis on individual retribution than Amos's characteristic focus on Yahweh's pending judgment on the nation Israel as a whole. David's "booth" (9:11), that is, the line of Southern or Judahite kings, had not yet fallen in the time of Amos—nor was Amos generally concerned with Judah. That Yahweh was going to restore the Davidic line would, of course, have been good news to Jews living under the dominion of foreign empires following 586 B.C. (cf. Jer. 33:14–16; Ezek. 37:24–25). As in other late prophetic and apocalyptic writings, we see in 9:13 the prospect of a restored or transformed fertility of the ground (cf. Joel 3:18). Yahweh's promise to restore the fortunes of his people Israel and make them forever secure in their land (9:14–15) is congruent with assurances found in the other classical prophets: Hosea, Isaiah, Jeremiah, Micah, and Ezekiel. It may be that Amos, like these other classical prophets, believed that after Yahweh had punished his special people, he would make a new beginning with them. If he did not so believe, a later prophet or editor did, and added these oracles to complete our present book of Amos.

OBADIAH

This is the briefest writing in the Book of the Twelve, the collection of relatively short prophetic books, Hosea through Malachi, that follows the longer prophets, Isaiah, Jeremiah, and Ezekiel. Obadiah either lived through or otherwise knew of the destruction of Jerusalem by Babylon in 586 B.C. His book consists largely of a declamation against Edom, which not only had gloated over Judah's "day of distress," but actively joined in plundering Jerusalem and rounding up Jewish fugitives (vv. 10–14). For this, Obadiah proclaims, Yahweh will destroy Edom and its people. Not a survivor of them will remain (vv. 9–10, 18). Other writings from this period and afterward express similar hatred for Edom (e.g., Ps. 137:7; Jer. 49:7–22; Lam. 4:21–22; Ezek. 25:12–14; Joel 3:19). Obadiah also condemns Edom for its pride (vv. 3–4).

Edom was the small nation south of Judah and the Dead Sea. There had been little interaction between Edom and Judah in previous centuries, probably because the Negeb desert made travel difficult between the two. That Edom should have turned against Judah was especially bitter, since according to ancient tradition (Gen. 25:36), the Edomites were descendants of Esau, Jacob's brother (see Obad. vv. 10–12).

Like Amos, Obadiah affirms Yahweh's universal justice: all nations soon will be punished according to their deeds (vv. 15–16). The "Day of Yahweh" (v. 15), a term used by many prophets, refers to the time when Yahweh will punish Israel, Judah, or other nations for their wickedness; it also often designates the time when Yahweh will act to restore Israel, Judah, and, sometimes, other nations. Here, like other prophets, Obadiah expresses the belief that this day is near: it will not be long before Yahweh acts to requite the nations for their evil deeds. Unlike Jeremiah, Ezekiel, the author(s) of Lamentations, and the Deuteronomic historian, Obadiah does not characterize the catastrophic events of 586 as Yahweh's judgment against the people of Judah for breaking covenant. But like Jeremiah, Ezekiel, and Second Isaiah, he holds out hope that the Jewish exiles will be restored. In fact, he seems to say that only "the house of Jacob" (the exiled people of Judah, if not also of Israel) will survive the time of judgment; other nations will "be as though they had not been" (vv. 16–17). The exiles will repossess not only their own land (v. 17b) but also the land that belongs to other nearby nations (vv. 19–20). The newly constituted kingdom will be Yahweh's (v. 21). The idea here is similar to that expressed in Daniel 7: in the coming era, the Jewish people will have dominion, if not over all the earth (cf. Zech. 14:9), at least over their own and several neighboring lands. As in Daniel, Joel, and many other apocalyptic and prophetic texts, there is no reference to a future Davidic king or messiah. Obadiah, v. 17 is the first of the very few biblical passages that designate Jerusalem or Judah a holy place (see also Ezra 9:8; Zech. 2:12; Wisd. of Sol. 12:3; 2 Macc. 1:7). Obadiah's nationalistic vision of the future era is somewhat similar to Joel's (Joel 3:1–17, 19) and Nahum's, but contrasts sharply with the declarations of several other prophets, such as Isaiah (11:10; 19:19–25; 25:6–7; 49:6), Jeremiah (e.g., 48:47; 49:39), Ezekiel (47:22–23), Micah (4:1–4), and Zechariah (2:11; 14:16–17), to the effect that some or all other nations will also have a share in the blessings of life in the coming age.

JONAH

This is a parable about a man whose God is too great and too merciful to suit him. Summoned by Yahweh to go to Nineveh (the capital of hated Assyria) and "cry against it," Jonah boards a ship bound in the opposite direction, hoping desperately to escape Yahweh's presence—as the narrator states three times in the opening verses (1:3a, 3b, 10b) lest readers miss this significant point. But Yahweh is lord of wind and sea, and stirs up a great storm. The pagan sailors pray to their gods while Jonah sleeps in the ship's hold. Finding him there, the pagan captain orders Jonah to get up and pray to his own god (Yahweh). (The storyteller does not say that Jonah does so.) The sailors then cast lots to see who is responsible for their trouble. When it turns out to be Jonah, he admits that he fears Yahweh "who made the sea and the dry land" (1:9). One might suppose that, knowing this, Jonah should have realized that trying to escape Yahweh's presence would prove futile, but evidently he was desperate enough to try anyway. The narrator does not yet reveal why Jonah wants to escape the presence of Yahweh. The pagan sailors, decent men that they are, hesitate to throw Jonah overboard, yet since this obviously is what Yahweh desires, they finally go ahead and do so. They even proceed to worship Yahweh with vows and sacrifices when the sea ceases to rage. Jonah is now swallowed by the great fish appointed by Yahweh for this purpose (1:17). Jonah at last prays to Yahweh from the belly of the fish—surely a strange place—thereby tacitly acknowledging that there is no escape from the presence of Yahweh. (Cf. Ps. 137:4: "How shall we sing the Lord's song in a foreign land?") Yahweh now speaks to the fish, which obediently deposits Jonah safely on dry land.

Again the "word of Yahweh" summons Jonah to go to Nineveh. This time he goes, though very grudgingly. His message is this: "Yet forty days and Nineveh shall be overthrown!" (3:4b). In response to this terse and unpromising announcement, "the people of Nineveh believed God," one and all. Moreover, its king now decrees that not only man, but also beast, herd, and flock should fast, put on sackcloth, and pray urgently to God (cf. Ps. 150:6), just in case he might be persuaded to spare them—even though Jonah has not mentioned this possibility. And then God changes his mind and does not destroy them after all.

This is too much for Jonah, who now, in his complaint to Yahweh, clearly explains why he tried to avoid this mission to Nineveh in the first place: "for I knew that thou art a gracious God and merciful, slow to anger and abounding in steadfast love, and repentest of evil" (4:2; cf. Exod. 34:6; Neh. 9:17; Joel 2:13). In short, Jonah did not want Yahweh to spare Nineveh at all, and feared from the first that Yahweh would do so. Jonah is particularly outraged to have been appointed the agent of that hated city's deliverance. Jonah wants Yahweh to be a tribal deity, concerned only with the well-being of Israelites, Judah-ites, or Jews. Rather than go on living in a world ruled by a gracious and merciful God who spares Ninevites, Jonah now prays to die. Still sulking, he clings to the hope that Yahweh may yet destroy the city, and sets up camp overlooking it—but at a safe distance—"till he should see what would become of the city" (4:5).

Again Yahweh shows his rule over all creation: he appoints a large-leaved plant to give Jonah shade, a worm to attack the plant, and a hot wind and sun to make Jonah uncomfortable, all in order to get through to him. Jonah sorely misses the plant in his self-pity, but how much more should he, like Yahweh who sent him there, care about Nineveh with its one hundred twenty thousand innocent children "and also much cattle" (4:11)! The story does not say whether Jonah finally gets the point or remains in the shell of his narrow tribal religion. But the book's author clearly wished the reader to see that the God who made and presides over the sea and dry land is concerned for the well-being of "all creatures that on earth do dwell"—human and otherwise. This understanding is one with that of the prophet Isaiah, who looked for that time when Yahweh would bring peace among nations and within all creation (Isa. 2:2–4; 11:6–9; 19:19–25). Reference to "much cattle" in 4:11 is consistent with 3:6–9, which tells that both man and beast, herd and flock, had fasted, put on sackcloth, and prayed to God! Yahweh's concern for "cattle" (probably meaning all kinds of domestic or farm animals) and wildlife appears in numerous other biblical texts (e.g., Gen. 6:19–20; 8:1, 15–19; 9:8–17; Exod. 20:10 or Deut. 5:14; Exod. 23:4–5; cf. Deut. 22:1–4; Lev. 25:6–7; Job 39:5–6; Pss. 50:9–12; 104:10–14, 16–18, 26; Isa. 65:25; Hos. 2:18).

Jonah, the parable's protagonist—or antihero—is presented as a somewhat ridiculous figure. He knows all along that Yahweh is the God of heaven who made both sea and dry land, but he tries to escape Yahweh's jurisdiction by sea anyway. Because he also knows that Yahweh is gracious and merciful—and therefore not likely to destroy Nineveh—he tries to ignore Yahweh's summons to preach there. And when Yahweh does spare the city because the Ninevites repent after hearing Jonah preach, Jonah prays that he might die. It is probable that the narrator drew Jonah as a caricature of the xenophobic tendencies in Judaism, represented, perhaps in milder form, in Deut. 23:3; Ezra 9—10; Nehemiah 13; Esther 9:5–16; Joel 3:1–17; Obadiah; Nahum; and Add. to Esther 14:15.

MICAH

Micah lived in the Southern Kingdom, Judah, about the same time as Isaiah (ca. 735–700 B.C.). Like other Southern prophets, he took up certain Isaianic themes, and may have been one of that prophet's early disciples (cf. Isa. 8:16). But while Isaiah remained in Jerusalem, Micah seems to have lived in the countryside west of the city. Little is known about Micah, but a few passages reveal his personal commitment and feelings, namely, 1:8; 3:8; 7:7. Micah's precise meaning often is obscure, a number of passages present textual problems, and several evidently are later additions, as can be seen by the number of footnotes (in the RSV and NEB) indicating translators' recourse to conjecture or alternate readings, such as Greek and Syriac versions. Some verses seem to presuppose the exile (e.g., 2:12–13; 4:6–10; 5:2–4; and possibly 7:8–20), and may have been added after 586 b.c. by later hands.

Despite textual uncertainties, Micah's overall message is clear. The rich and powerful have been oppressing and exploiting the poor and helpless, a point most vividly stated at 3:1–3 (cf. Isa. 3:14–15). Like most prophets, Micah addresses the power structure, here the heads and rulers of Judah (3:1, 9–11). Instead of giving justice and equity in the courts, they "give judgment for a bribe" (3:9–11). Some covet and seize fields and houses (2:1–2), driving women and children into the streets (2:9). Some cheat in the marketplace with false weights and measures (6:10–11; cf. Deut. 25:13–16). Children treat parents with contempt (7:6a; cf. Exod. 20:12 or Deut. 5:16). None of the men is upright (7:2; cf. Jer. 5:1–5; Ezek. 22:30), all prey upon each other, and neither friends nor family can be trusted (7:2–6). Micah rebukes the false prophets who prophesy for hire and tell people only what they want to hear (3:5, 11; cf. 2 Kings 22:6, 11–12; Jer. 28:1– 17)—and the people who wish to hear only comforting lies (2:6). Such people would like religion to be an opiate: "If a man should go about and utter wind and lies, saying 'I will preach to you of wine and strong drink,' he would be the preacher for this people!" (2:11). In the manner of other classical prophets who stressed the central importance of the covenant's horizontal obligations, Micah resoundingly declares that Yahweh requires not sacrifice, but justice, kindness, and walking humbly with God (6:6–8; cf. Isa. 1:11–17; Amos 5:21–24). Like Isaiah, he proposes to walk about Jerusalem "stripped and naked" to bring home to the people of that city his message that it is doomed (1:8; Isaiah 20). Because of their several offenses, Yahweh will bring catastrophe upon Samaria (the capital of Israel) and Jerusalem (the capital of Judah): "I will make Samaria a heap in the open country" (1:6); "Zion shall be plowed as a field" (3:12). (A hundred years later, Jeremiah's life will be spared when, during his trial as a traitor or security risk for so preaching, someone remembers that Micah preached earlier to the same effect [Jeremiah 26].) Micah warns his contemporaries that Yahweh will cause them to suffer hunger and privation (6:13, 15) and domination by foreign nations (1:3–16; 2:3–4).

Like most other classical prophets, Micah also promises a brighter future. In the famous "floating oracle" (4:1–3), so called because it also appears in Isa. 2:2–4, Micah looks for an era of international peace, when many nations will come to Jerusalem to be taught the ways of God. Then "they shall beat their swords into plowshares, and their spears into pruning hooks," and every man shall sit "under his vine and under his fig tree" in peace and security (4:3–4; cf. Zech. 3:2).

Some oracles, probably added following the catastrophic events of 586 B.C. that marked the beginning of the exile (see 2 Kings 25), emphasize further hopes. Echoing Isaiah, 2:12 and 4:7 promise that Yahweh will bring back a remnant. Like Second Isaiah (Isa. 35:3–10), Micah 4:6–7 looks for Yahweh to bring the lame and those otherwise afflicted and "cast off" back to Zion, where he will reign forevermore. The messianic oracle in 5:2–4 promises the appearance of a ruler from the tribe of Judah (cf. Gen. 49:10), evidently a Davidic king—an expectation implicit also, perhaps, in 2:13, but absent from traditions more likely attributable to Micah, the eighth-century prophet. The later traditions also anticipate Israel's crushing victory over other nations (4:11–13; 5:7–9; 7:8–10, 15–17), a scenario that contrasts sharply with the prospect of international peace and goodwill pictured in 4:1–4. The expected expropriation of the wealth of nations for the glory of Yahweh and Jerusalem (4:13) accords with hopes expressed in various other postexilic texts, such as Isa. 61:6; Hag. 2:6–9; Zech. 14:14.

NAHUM

Here we have another of the twelve shorter prophetic writings that constitute the Book of the Twelve. Nahum is concerned with a single theme: the impending defeat of Nineveh and the prospect of Judah's deliverance from Assyrian domination. Nineveh was the capital of Assyria. From the latter third of the eighth century B.C., Judah had been under the weight of Assyrian power in the Near East. Nineveh fell to Babylonian forces in 612 B.C.

Nahum rejoices at the prospect of Nineveh's overthrow, which he views as Yahweh's judgment against it for its idolatry, wickedness, and oppression. He seems to share Isaiah's understanding that Assyria has been the rod of Yahweh's anger against Judah (1:12; cf. Isa. 10:5–11), but now Yahweh is about to liberate his people by breaking the Assyrian yoke "from off" their necks (1:13). Not only will Yahweh punish Nineveh; he will completely destroy that hated city (1:8–9, 14–15). The prophet confidently proclaims the imminent arrival of an era of peace and glory for Judah, and perhaps for all Israel (1:15; 2:2). Evidently he believes that Judah's troubles will be over for good: "For never again shall the wicked come against you" (1:15c).

But Nahum's hopes proved premature. Soon the bell would toll for Judah, too. Three years later, in 609, Josiah, the great reformer king of Judah, perhaps inspired by hopes like Nahum's, leads his troops against an Egyptian contingent on its way to reinforce the beleaguered Assyrians. Josiah is killed in battle, and the Egyptian Pharaoh makes Judah a vassal tributary (2 Kings 23:29–35). Soon afterward, the Babylonians come on, not as Judah's liberators, but as overlords and conquerors (2 Kings 24—25).

As with other prophetic oracles against foreign nations, Nahum testifies to the universal sovereignty of Yahweh. His message of hatred for Nineveh, however, contrasts with the outlook of the author of the book of Jonah, who understands that Yahweh is concerned for the well-being of the people of that city—with their one hundred twenty thousand young children who do not know their right hand from their left—and also their "much cattle" (Jon. 4:11). Nahum's nationalistic vision of the future also differs notably from that of Isaiah, who prophesied that in the coming age Assyria, together with Egypt and Israel, would be Yahweh's people and enjoy his blessings (Isa. 19:23–25).

HABAKKUK

As at the beginning of Amos and Micah, the caption at 1:1 states that the words which follow are what the prophet "saw." The book gives no information about the prophet or his times. The prophet Habakkuk who appears in the fictional story of Bel and the Dragon was supposedly a contemporary of Daniel's, but is not connected with the writer of this book. Reference to "the Chaldeans" at 1:6 hints that this book's author lived before 586 B.C., while Jeremiah and Ezekiel proclaimed that Yahweh was bringing the Babylonians (or Chaldeans) against Jerusalem and Judah in judgment for their breaking covenant.

Nothing else in the book, however, indicates this period; references to the past or present activities of an enemy nation are vague, and seem to symbolize sometimes an oppressive nation, sometimes a wicked and oppressive individual within the community. Later writings, like Judith and Revelation, use Babylon as a symbol for mythic or latter-day enemy nations. Habakkuk's preoccupation with the problem of theodicy seems more at home in the time of Job, Ecclesiastes, or the Wisdom of Solomon, which likewise address the question why God, who is believed to be both righteous and all-powerful, permits the wicked to go unpunished while they exploit or "swallow up" the righteous (1:4, 13).

The book consists of four distinguishable sections: a dialogue with Yahweh (1:2—2:5); a list of woes in store for an unrighteous man or nation (2:6–17); a short polemic against belief in idols (2:18–20); and a psalm (chap. 3).

The first section is structured in the form of questions and answers (cf. Malachi, 2 Esdras, and James). Habakkuk complains about the violence and injustice he sees in the land (1:2–4). Yahweh replies that he is sending the Chaldeans as a judgment against the people of Judah (or the Jewish people)—although the Chaldeans do not know this (1:5–11; cf. Isa. 10:5–14), supposing their own might to be god (cf. Wisd. of Sol. 2:11). Habakkuk replies that Yahweh, who is everlasting, may well send them as a judgment, but he questions whether it is right for faithless and wicked men to keep on swallowing the righteous, "mercilessly slaying nations for ever" (1:12—2:1). Yahweh answers by instructing the prophet to write the words set forth in a vision on a tablet for all to read (2:2; cf. Isa. 8:1; Dan. 12:4). It is unclear which of the following verses, if any, record the words revealed in that vision. The next verse (2:3) says that the time when the vision will be fulfilled "hastens to the end," and that though it may seem to move slowly, "it will not delay" (cf. Ezek. 12:21–28; 2 Esd. 4:26–52). Perhaps the gist of the vision is the assurance implicit in 2:4: the righteous who remain faithful (despite oppression or persecution) shall live, or, alternately, the righteous who aspire to enjoy the time of vindication must live faithfully in the meantime.

Next follows a series of "woes" against a man (or men) or nations who act unjustly (2:6–17; cf. Isa. 5:8–23; Luke 6:24–26). Taking and keeping pledges is contrary to the covenant requirement that they be returned (Exod. 20:26–27; Deut. 24:10–13); but most of the other offenses enumerated here are more the sort that nations commit. The third section (which also includes a "Woe to him who . . ." saying) briefly ridicules the futility of trusting in manmade idols. This theme, enunciated earlier by Second Isaiah (Isa. 40:18–20), recurs especially in the OT Apocrypha (Wisdom of Solomon 13—15, Letter of Jeremiah; Bel and the Dragon).

Chapter 3 is in the form of a psalm. The term *selah* (3:3, 9, 13) commonly appears in psalms to mark a "pause" in the singing or recital. *Shigionoth* (3:1) means hymns, as in the caption to Psalm 7 (*Shiggaion* means hymn); but the phrase "according to" usually precedes a specific hymn tune (e.g., before Psalms 6 and 46, RSV) instead. Placing instructions "to the choirmaster" after Hab. 3:19, RSV, also is unusual. Ordinarily this sort of notation comes first (e.g., Psalms 75; 76; 88, RSV). The psalm praises Yahweh, who in the past has used his terrible power to save his people. The prophet's final answer is then stated: He will quietly wait for Yahweh to bring the invaders to judgment; even though fruit and flock may fail, he will trust Yahweh and rejoice in him (3:16–19; cf. Job 1:13–21).

ZEPHANIAH

The book begins, like Hosea, Amos, and Micah, with an editorial description of the prophet and his period (1:1). Much of the text may come from the time of Josiah (640–609 B.C.). Like that king and the Deuteronomic reformers, Zephaniah undertakes to oppose the Judahites' continuing worship of Baal and other foreign gods (1:4–6).

He proclaims that Yahweh will punish the people of Jerusalem and Judah for their offenses, which include apostasy, adopting foreign attire, violence, and fraud (1:4–9); supposing that Yahweh will not act justly (1:12); and oppression, exploitation, corruption, and faithlessness, particularly on the part of the community's leaders and officials (3:1–4, 7). A number of verses seem to echo passages in Amos. Like Joel and Amos, Zephaniah refers to the "day of Yahweh": it is near, this day of wrath, ruin, devastation, and darkness (1:7, 14–15). It will not merely be punishment, nor will Judah alone bear it; Yahweh "will be terrible" against many nations, including Assyria (2:11–15; cf. Nahum). Indeed, Zephaniah looks for Yahweh's judgment against the whole earth: man and beast, bird and fish, everything will be swept away, the earth and all its inhabitants (1:2–3, 18; 3:8; cf. Gen. 8:8–17).

And yet the nation may still repent (2:1–3). Several passages—some containing typical Isaianic terms and tones—look for Yahweh to restore the fortunes of his people (e.g., 2:7; 3:11–20). Zephaniah's message of assurance for the future is distinctive in that it implies an intervening judgment of individuals: the "proudly exultant" will be removed; those who are "humble and lowly" will remain, so that the restored Israel might constitute a righteous remnant: there will be none left who will do wrong (3:11–13). By contrast, Jeremiah expected Yahweh to transform the hearts of all his people so that they would keep the new covenant that he would make with them (Jer. 31:31–34). Like Joel and several other prophetic books, Zephaniah includes oracles against certain foreign nations (2:4–15), but looks forward to the time when all nations "may call on the name of Yahweh and serve him with one accord" (3:9). The author promises that in the coming time of restoration, Judah will be "renowned and praised" by "all peoples of the earth" (3:20; cf. Gen. 12:2–3). Some scholars think it likely that certain of these beliefs and expectations for the future were added by a later postexilic writer or writers. On the other hand, most scholars recognize that some prophets who proclaimed Yahweh's impending judgment but did not live to see it occur also included oracles of hope for the future (e.g., Hosea, Isaiah). Perhaps Zephaniah likewise looked with hope for a future beyond the time of judgment, even if he did not live to see the events of 598–586 B.C.

HAGGAI

Haggai is usually dated ca. 520 B.C. Persia had defeated Babylon, and many Jews, liberated from exile by Cyrus's decree in 538, have returned to Judah. The latter was now a province of the Persian Empire, but governed through Zerubbabel, who may have been a grandson or great-grandson of Jehoiachin (Jeconiah or Coniah), the next-to-last king of Judah (1 Chron. 3:16–19; Hag. 1:1).

Life is difficult for the returned exiles: the economy is in trouble and food is scarce, as the prophet picturesquely observes (1:6, 9–11). Haggai, addressing himself particularly to Zerubbabel and Joshua, the high priest, declares that Yahweh has brought these conditions about because the temple (destroyed by the Babylonians in 586 B.C.) has not yet been rebuilt: "Is it a time for you yourselves to dwell in your paneled houses, while this house lies in ruins?" (1:4–11).

Inspired by Haggai's (and also Zechariah's) preaching, Zerubbabel, Joshua, and the rest of the Jewish people get to work, and soon the temple's foundation is laid. Encouraged by subsequent agricultural and economic improvements (2:15–19), Haggai proclaims that "in a little while" Yahweh will cause the treasuries of all nations (presumably including valuables plundered from the first temple) to fill the new temple with splendor (2:6-9). Yahweh is about to overthrow the power of other nations (2:21-22, echoing the Song of Miriam/Moses, Exod. 15:1, 21), and make Zerubbabel messiah or king over a new and independent nation of Judah (2:23). Since all kings of Judah have been, or were expected to be, descendants of David, Haggai's statement about Zerubbabel appears to confirm the Chronicler's genealogical data concerning him. As a result of Haggai's preaching, and that of his contemporary, Zechariah, the temple was rebuilt in 515 B.C. Nevertheless, the Persians continued to rule over the Jewish people for nearly two hundred more years, and Zerubbabel vanished from the pages of history without ever becoming messiah. Though the Book of Ezra (written ca. 350 B.C.) makes a point of reporting that various Persian kings furnished money and other impetus for rebuilding the temple (e.g., Ezra 1:1-4; 5:13—6:15), nothing in Haggai or Zechariah hints that the Persians provided any such assistance.

The Book of Haggai presents several other important developments. Haggai is the first prophet to address a provincial governor. Earlier prophets sometimes spoke Yahweh's Word to kings, but now, of course, there is no king of Judah. Haggai expects Zerubbabel to become king once the temple is completed and the new era begun. Haggai also addresses Joshua, "the high priest." That title is first mentioned here and in Zechariah. Absent kingship, the newly established high priesthood is the highest office a Jewish leader can hold, other than one to which he may be appointed by a foreign ruler. Zechariah goes so far as to proclaim Joshua, the high priest, messiah (Zech. 6:9-14). The hope for a messiah from the "house of Aaron" also appears in later Jewish sources.

Though earlier prophets, too, spoke of Yahweh's sending droughts or pestilence to warn or punish his people (e.g., Amos 4:6-10; Mic. 6:14-15), they more typically proclaimed that he would bring judgment against them in the form of defeat at the hands of foreign nations. Now that the Jewish people live under foreign—Persian—domination, Haggai visualizes Yahweh's judgment only in the guise of natural disasters (cf. Zechariah, Malachi, and Joel). The preexilic prophets emphasized the horizontal dimension of the covenant, the requirements of justice, mercy, and concern for the poor and needy within the community, while often insisting that Yahweh had no interest in sacrificial offerings (e.g., Isa. 1:10-17; Jer. 7:21-23; Amos 5:21-25). Haggai, however, is silent as to the horizontal requirements of the covenant, but preoccupied with promoting the reconstruction of the temple, the only place where, since the Deuteronomic reform, sacrifices may properly be offered (see Deuteronomy 12—19). Chapters 40—48 of Ezekiel likewise focus on a new temple in Jerusalem; there, too, it is associated with the coming of the messianic age. Preoccupation with the temple and the offering of sacrifices in it is even more pronounced, of course, in the Priestly Code (PC) and Chronicles-Ezra-Nehemiah (ca. 450–350 B.C.).

ZECHARIAH

The first eight chapters are generally attributed to Haggai's contemporary, the prophet Zechariah (ca. 520 B.C.). Chapters 9—14 probably are later additions, written between the fourth and second centuries B.C. These later chapters are sometimes designated 2 Zechariah.

The setting for chaps. 1—8 is as follows. The Persians (and Medes) had defeated Babylon in 539 B.C. and become the dominant power in the Near East. Persian policy permitted captive peoples to return to their native lands. Zechariah, speaking for Yahweh, summons Jewish exiles to return to Zion (Jerusalem), assuring them that this city and Judah (for the first time called "the holy land") will be Yahweh's dwelling place (chap. 2). Zerubbabel, a descendant, perhaps, of one of Judah's last kings, has been appointed governor of Judah, now a Persian territory.

Zechariah reports a series of symbolic visions, mainly to the effect that Yahweh intends to restore Judah and Jerusalem, and bring about the messianic age. In one vision, Joshua, the high priest, is told that Yahweh will bring his "servant the Branch" (messiah; cf. Isa. 11:1), cleanse the land of guilt, and establish peace (3:8–10). Another vision identifies Zerubbabel as the messiah who will finish building the temple (4:6–10), a hope shared by Haggai. Zechariah refers in one passage to two messiahs, one priestly (Joshua), the other Zerubbabel, possibly a descendant of David (4:1–14). Later, when Zerubbabel drops out of view, Joshua is designated the Branch who shall build the temple (6:9–13). Unlike Haggai, but like earlier prophets, Zechariah also admonishes his contemporaries to keep the horizontal requirements of the covenant (5:3; 7:8–10; 8:16–17). This first part of the book closes with more assurances of Yahweh's intent to do good to his people, especially now that the temple's foundations have been laid. Like Isaiah and Micah, Zechariah declares that the time will come when many peoples and nations will worship Yahweh in Jerusalem (2:11; 8:20–23).

Chapters 1—8 present other notable features. Satan appears here for the third and last time in the OT (3:1–2; see also 1 Chron. 21:1; Job 1:6–12; 2:1–7). He is not yet an evil being, much less a cosmic evil power, but only "the accuser," or attorney general, an official in the heavenly council or court of Yahweh. Here, evidently, Satan has marked Jerusalem for condemnation because of its various offenses; but Yahweh decides to spare Jerusalem, "as a brand plucked from the fire," and so overrules Satan. Like Jeremiah, Ezekiel, the writer(s) of Lamentations, and the Deuteronomic historian, Zechariah interprets the catastrophic events of the exile as Yahweh's judgment against the people of Judah and Jerusalem for breaking the covenant (7:7–14). Several of the images represented in the visions in these chapters are particularly vivid: four horns (representing foreign nations that have defeated Judah), colored horses and chariots (which patrol the earth for Yahweh), a golden lampstand with seven lamps, and a flying scroll, thirty feet long and fifteen wide. Some of these images are later elaborated in the Books of Daniel and Revelation.

Chapters 9—14 describe the final days when Yahweh is expected to intervene on behalf of Jerusalem and Judah. Mention of Greece (9:13) suggests that these chapters were composed no earlier than the latter part of the fourth century B.C. Several neighboring peoples are condemned (9:1–7), after which the writer declares that Yahweh himself will guard Jerusalem from further oppressors and calls the people ("daughter") of Jerusalem to rejoice because their messiah (king) comes (or will come) to establish his kingdom of peace throughout the earth (9:8–10). Chapter 14 states that Yahweh himself will fight against the nations that attack Jerusalem. Mountains will be moved; there will be continuous day; a fountain of "living" (fresh or cleansing) water will flow through Jerusalem (14:8; cf. 13:1 and Ezek. 47:1–9); and Yahweh "will become king over all the earth" (14:9). No Davidic king or messiah is mentioned in chap. 14, but there are allusions to such a king in chap. 9 and perhaps chap. 12. The wealth of surrounding nations will be collected (14:14; cf. Isa. 60:5–7; Hag. 2:6–8); and all "the families of the earth" (cf. Gen. 12:3) shall worship Yahweh in Jerusalem—or else be punished if they fail to do so (14:16–19; cf. 8:22). The intervening chapters, with cryptic passages about shepherds and the house of David, also refer to the coming redemption of Judah and perhaps Israel (10:7). Enemy nations will be defeated (10:11) and those that make war on Jerusalem will be destroyed (12:6–9). "On that day" (in the messianic age) Jerusalem will be cleansed of sin; people will no longer worship idols, and prophecy will cease (13:1–5; cf. 1 Cor. 13:8).

MALACHI

The title means "my messenger," that is, the messenger of Yahweh. The term can also be translated as "angel," meaning one who is sent by God. It probably was taken from the reference to one so designated at 3:1, though possibly the prophet himself bore this symbolic name. The setting is Jerusalem around the middle of the fifth century B.C., slightly before the time of Nehemiah. Judah still is part of the Persian Empire. The temple has been rebuilt and sacrifices are being offered, but living conditions still are difficult for the Jewish people. Crops are blighted or ravaged by locusts (3:10–11; cf. Joel 1—2). Using a "diatribe" or question-and-answer format, the prophet interprets these conditions as Yahweh's judgment against these people. Men have been marrying foreign women (2:11)—a serious problem also in the eyes of Malachi's near-contemporaries Nehemiah and Ezra—and divorcing their wives (2:13–16). The Jewish people have also violated certain basic horizontal covenant requirements emphasized by earlier prophets, and have failed to fear Yahweh and keep his commandments generally (3:5, 7; 4:4). Malachi particularly focuses on the fact that priests and people alike have been offering blemished sacrifices: "When you offer blind animals in sacrifice, is that no evil? And when you offer those that are lame or sick, is that no evil? Present that [sort of thing] to your governor; will he be pleased or show you favor?" (1:6–14). They have also been holding back their tithes (3:8–10).

To make things right, Yahweh will send his messenger (or angel) to cause the sons of Levi (still equivalent to priests) once more to present proper offerings. This messenger, the prophet warns, is coming (3:1–3). The prophet implies that once right offerings are forthcoming, Yahweh will restore the fruitfulness of fields, trees, and vines (3:4, 10–12). It is unclear whether this restoration is to mark the beginning of the messianic age. (The book makes no reference to a coming Davidic king or messiah.) In contrast to the preexilic prophets, but like several other postexilic writings, the Book of Malachi regards the offering of sacrifices as Yahweh's central requirement. Before the time of restoration, Yahweh himself will judge Jews who have broken the covenant (3:5). At the time of judgment, the righteous and wicked will be separated: the former to rejoice, but the latter to be destroyed (3:16—4:3; cf. Daniel 12, which also looks for the judgment of individuals).

The book closes with what many interpreters regard as a late addition, which promises—or warns—that Yahweh will send Elijah to preach repentance "before the great and terrible day of the Lord comes" (4:5–6; cf. similar language in Joel 2:31b). Since Elijah was carried to heaven, he might also someday be sent back to earth (2 Kings 2:11–12; cf. Ecclus. 48:9–10; Mark 9:11–12). In Malachi, Elijah is expected to reconcile fathers and their children (4:6). In the later traditions, his task is more inclusive. As the text of Malachi stands, Elijah seems to be identified as the "messenger" who is to come (3:1–2). Later Jewish and Christian traditions look for Elijah as the one whose appearance will herald the advent of the messianic age. Malachi is the last of the twelve shorter prophetic writings that make up the Book of the Twelve.

THE OLD TESTAMENT APOCRYPHA, OR DEUTERO-CANONICALS

AN OVERVIEW

The Greek Bible commonly used by Jews from ca. 200 B.C. to A.D. 100 and by Christians during the first several centuries A.D. included a number of writings that eventually were excluded from Jewish and Protestant Bibles. From these writings come all but a few of those designated in the aggregate as the Apocrypha in modern editions such as *The New English Bible with Apocrypha,* or NEB, and *The New Oxford Annotated Bible with the Apocrypha,* or NOAB (Oxford University Press). To be more precise, one should say Old Testament Apocrypha, since there is also a voluminous literature known as the New Testament Apocrypha. The latter is not included in any modern version of the Bible. The two main collections of the NT Apocrypha are those by M. R. James, *The Apocryphal New Testament* (Oxford: Clarendon Press, rev. ed. 1953), and Edgar Hennecke, *New Testament Apocrypha,* 2 vols. (Philadelphia: Westminster Press, 1963, 1965). The OT apocryphal writings that derive from the old Greek Bible (or Septuagint, as it is often called on the basis of the legend that it was translated verbatim into Greek from the Hebrew by seventy— *septuaginta* or LXX—scholars in seventy days) include the following: 1 Esdras (also known as 3 Ezra), Tobit, Judith, the Additions to Esther, the Wisdom of Solomon, Ecclesiasticus (or Ben-Sirach), Baruch, the Letter of Jeremiah, the Prayer of Azariah and the Song of the Three Young Men, Susanna, the stories of Bel and the Dragon, the Prayer of Manasseh, and 1 and 2 Maccabees. Most of these constitute separate books, but some were incorporated into other OT writings, namely, Esther and Daniel.

Second Esdras (also known as 4 Ezra) was not included in the Septuagint, but was found in the Old Latin translation of it (ca. A.D.

200), and was included by Jerome in his Latin edition of the Bible, *The Vulgate* (ca. A.D. 390). Fourth Ezra is included in the two modern scholarly editions of the OT Pseudepigrapha (R.H. Charles and James H. Charlesworth). Jerome evidently was the first to use the term Apocrypha (meaning "hidden") to designate those writings which, in his time, were known in Greek or Latin, but not in Hebrew texts. In prefaces before each, he suggested to readers that the apocryphal writings were not on a par as to antiquity or authority with the biblical writings known in Hebrew. Later editions of The Vulgate—copied by hand, of course, until the age of printing—included the apocryphal writings, but often omitted Jerome's prefaces. For more than a thousand years, The Vulgate was the standard Bible of Western Christianity. Renaissance scholarship and religious concerns of the Protestant reformers occasioned further doubts as to the weight to be accorded the apocryphal writings. For a variety of reasons, Martin Luther decided in A.D. 1534 that although they were "useful and good to read," the apocryphal books were not "held equal to the Scriptures." But Luther included most of the apocryphal books in his German Bible of that same year. He omitted 1, 2, 3, and 4 Esdras and 3 and 4 Maccabees. Luther's Bible evidently was the first to place the apocryphal books as a group after the other OT writings.* All later branches of Protestantism have followed Luther's more restricted canon. At the Council of Trent in A.D. 1546, however, the Roman Catholic Church reaffirmed the canonical status of the Apocrypha, except for 1 and 2 Esdras and the Prayer of Manasseh. The official versions of The Vulgate's OT since Trent end with 1 and 2 Maccabees, but add the Prayer of Manasseh and 1 and 2 Esdras in an appendix placed after the NT.

The Eastern Orthodox churches likewise maintained a more inclusive OT canon, with some further additions. Thus the Eastern churches at present include 3 Maccabees and Psalm 151 (which were in some versions of the Septuagint and other ancient texts, but not in The Vulgate), as well as 1 Esdras, and some also include the Prayer of Manasseh and 2 Esdras. In Russian Orthodox Bibles, 1 and 2 Esdras are designated as 2 and 3 Esdras, respectively. Since the seventeenth century, the Apocrypha of the Eastern churches has consisted of Tobit, Judith, Wisdom of Solomon, and Ecclesiasticus.

The apocryphal books do not appear at all, of course, in the old

---

*On this matter, see Luther's "Prefaces to the Apocrypha" in *Luther's Works* 35:337–54, 337 n. 1 (Philadelphia: Fortress Press, 1960).

Hebrew or modern Jewish Bibles. Catholic Bibles include most of the apocryphal books. Those designated deutero-canonical are considered fully scriptural, and generally are found in the same locations or sequences as in the Greek Old Testament (LXX). Those designated apocryphal—1 and 2 Esdras, and the Prayer of Manasseh—are not considered fully canonical and ordinarily appear in a separate section at the back of Catholic Bibles. Catholic Bibles do not include 3 and 4 Maccabees or Psalm 151 at all.

Until A.D. 1827, editions of the King James Version (KJV) of the Bible usually included the OT Apocrypha, and located it either between the OT and the NT or following the NT. Uncertainty as to where to place the Apocrypha is reflected in the fact that many modern Bibles omit it altogether, while some, for instance, the *NEB with Apocrypha*, place it between the OT and the NT, and others, for instance, the *NOAB with Apocrypha*, place it after the NT. The 1977 edition of the latter is distinctive in that it includes not only 3 but also 4 Maccabees, which was in some editions of the Septuagint and other ancient versions, but has not been included in either The Vulgate or Eastern canons. This edition also includes Psalm 151. Thus it can be seen that the Apocrypha is still a somewhat open if not fluid category, both in religious and scholarly circles.

Until a few years ago, the standard critical edition of the Apocrypha and Pseudepigrapha was that of R. H. Charles, *Apocrypha and Pseudepigrapha of the Old Testament*, 2 vols. (Oxford: Clarendon Press, 1913). One should now consult the more inclusive work edited by James H. Charlesworth (*The Old Testament Pseudepigrapha*, 2 vols. [Garden City, N. Y.: Doubleday & Co., 1983–1985], hereafter OTP). See also the less inclusive but newly edited volume by H. F. D. Sparks, *The Apocryphal Old Testament* (Oxford: Clarendon Press, 1984). The basic handbook on much of this literature is the work by G. W. E. Nickelsburg, *Jewish Literature Between the Bible and the Mishnah* (Philadelphia: Fortress Press, 1981, 1987). For a popular guide to the OT Pseudepigrapha, see D. S. Russell, *The Old Testament Pseudepigrapha: Patriarchs and Prophets in Early Judaism* (Philadelphia: Fortress Press; London: SCM Press, 1987).

OLD TESTAMENT APOCRYPHA

1 ESDRAS

This writing is also known in The Vulgate and Catholic Bibles generally as 3 Esdras, but in Eastern Orthodox Bibles as 2 Esdras. The present nomenclature derives from the fact that in the Septuagint, Ezra and Nehemiah constituted a single book (1 Esdras), whereas in The Vulgate our present Ezra was named 1 Esdras and Nehemiah was called 2 Esdras. The Greek name Esdras was and still is generally used in the title, instead of the Hebrew name, Ezra, which, however, has always appeared in the text (chaps. 8—9).

Most of the book parallels and apparently borrows from portions of 2 Chronicles, Ezra, and Nehemiah. The main piece of new material is the story of three bodyguards and the Persian king Darius (3:1—5:3) which serves to introduce Zerubbabel (also known to us from Ezra 3—5, Zechariah 4, and Haggai).

As this story is told, the three bodyguards plan a contest in order to induce King Darius to bestow wealth and honors upon one of their number. Each presents, for the king to judge, his written statement and oral argument as to "what one thing is strongest." In turn, they argue persuasively for wine, the king, women, and truth. The case for truth seems to be a later addition. In the present account, Zerubbabel gets two shots at the prize by arguing both for women (4:13–32) and truth (4:33–40). Here, truth—a Greek virtue—is linked with God, for example, in Zerubbabel's summary exclamation, "Blessed be the God of truth!" The assembled crowd shouts in reply—and in unison—the famous line, "Great is truth, and strongest of all" (4:41). Zerubbabel is then named winner and granted his desire, which is that he be authorized to go to Jerusalem and rebuild it and the temple (cf.

Neh. 2:1–8, where another Persian king authorizes Nehemiah to rebuild Jerusalem). In addition, Darius issues edicts granting special privileges to all Jews who return to Judea, expelling Idumeans (Edomites) from villages claimed by Jews, and authorizing expenditures to pay for building the new temple and provision of burnt offerings.

The rest of 1 Esdras consists largely of material drawn from portions of 2 Chronicles, Ezra, and Nehemiah. The writer is particularly interested in traditions concerning the temple, ritual observances there, its destruction by the Babylonians, and especially its restoration under the leadership of Zerubbabel, and the names of priests, Levites, and other Jewish leaders who take part in that restoration. The writer also focuses on the support purportedly given for this project by the Persian monarchs Cyrus, Darius, and Artaxerxes, the sacrifices offered at the dedication of the new temple, and Ezra's leadership in promulgating the law and in breaking up marriages between Jewish men and alien women.

First Esdras begins with an account of Josiah's superlative celebration of Passover and his death in battle (1:1–33), both based on 2 Chronicles 35. The last days of Judah are reviewed in 1:34–58, following 2 Chronicles 36 with slight variations and errors which are noted in the NOAB and NEB study editions. Chapter 2 picks up, from Ezra 1, the story of Cyrus's determination to pay for rebuilding the temple and his return of the gold and silver vessels taken by the Babylonians at the beginning of the exile (2:1–15; cf. 4:57, where Darius orders these same vessels returned.) The narrative then strangely skips forward a century to the time of Artaxerxes (2:16–30). The same unfriendly neighboring officials who, according to Ezra 4:7–23, complain to Artaxerxes about Jewish efforts to rebuild the walls of Jerusalem, also object, in 1 Esd. 2:16–24, to the Jews' rebuilding the temple. Actually, the temple already was rebuilt (in 515 B.C.). Curiously, 1 Esdras makes no mention of Nehemiah, under whose leadership the walls of Jerusalem were restored in 444 B.C.

The list of returning exiles in chap. 5 corresponds closely to lists in Ezra 2 and Nehemiah 7. All three sources distinguish several classes of temple functionaries, probably in descending order of rank: priests, Levites (including, it seems, though evidently at lower levels, the orders of singers and gatekeepers), temple servants, and Solomon's servants. The report of temple-building continues in 5:47—7:15, drawing from Ezra 3:1—4:5 and 4:24—6:22. Chapters 8 and 9, which concern Ezra's reading the law, leading a mass procession of exiles from Babylon, and breaking up racially (or nationally) mixed marriages, follow closely what is found in Ezra 7—10 and Neh. 7:73—8:12.

It may be that the author thought these earlier traditions pertinent to the situation of the Jewish people during the Maccabean period, perhaps around the time the temple was rededicated in 164 B.C., following its desecration by Antiochus Epiphanes (cf. 1 Macc. 4:36–59). Copies of earlier biblical writings were always scarce and in this period might have been especially so, since many of them may have been confiscated and destroyed along with the books of the law by Antiochus's "inspectors" (1 Macc. 1:56). It would not be surprising if the author of 1 Esdras wished to assemble a compend of these earlier traditions in order to preserve and encourage traditionalist practices. The book usually is dated in the second century B.C. and, like many other books in the Apocrypha, probably was originally composed in Greek.

2 ESDRAS (or 4 EZRA)

Though not included in the Septuagint, 2 Esdras came into Christian Scripture through the Old Latin and Jerome's Vulgate editions. Modern translations are based on Latin, Ethiopic, Syriac, Arabic, Armenian, and other early versions, which often disagree. Chapters 3—14 contain accounts of seven visions, which, according to the seventh (14:1–48), were written at Ezra's inspired dictation. These visions probably were composed in Jewish circles, ca. A.D. 100. In different ways, they affirm that God will deliver the few who are righteous, if not in this world, then in the next; condemn the many who are unrighteous; and punish the enemies of the Jewish people, particularly the Romans (who had defeated the Jews and overrun Jerusalem in A.D. 66–70).

The first three visions (3:1—9:25) are presented in the form of dialogues. Somewhat like Job and Jeremiah, Ezra (also named Salathiel, 3:1) questions God (usually referred to by a circumlocution, such as "the Most High") as to why God's people suffer while unrighteous nations prosper (3:28–36), and about the human predicament generally. The archangel Uriel (one of seven archangels, each of whose name ends in "-el") answers (as God answers Job in his speeches out of the whirlwind) that there are fixed limits to human power and knowledge. Not put off by being told that he cannot comprehend the "things above" (4:21, NEB), Ezra insists that he wants to ask about matters of daily experience, namely, why the Gentiles lord it over "Israel" and why the meaning of life has become questionable. Uriel replies that all will soon become clear, for the present age is hastening to its end (4:26; cf. 1 Cor. 13:8–12). In the new age, the righteous will have their reward. But, Ezra urges, this will do little good, for most if not all men are unrighteous, and so have no hope (4:38; 7:46–48, 68; 8:35). What good is paradise or the prospect of immortality if no one will qualify to receive these blessings (7:119–126)? Repeatedly, Ezra is told not to worry: God will bless the righteous, few though they be, with immortality in the world to come—which was made for the sake of the few (8:1). As to the rest who abused their freedom by despising the Most High and forsaking his law and his ways, "So let the multitude perish" (8:55–61; 9:22).

The fourth, fifth, and sixth visions, like other apocalyptic texts, purport to be revelations to an ancient seer—here Ezra—which were written and sealed long ago for later reference, concerning the subsequent course of history, most notably the "last days" of the present age and the onset of the coming age, which now—from the standpoint of those who were to read the unsealed visions—is soon to appear (see, e.g., 12:37–38; 14:8–48). The fourth vision, of a woman in mourning (9:38—10:59), refers to the plight of Zion (Jerusalem) after the temple is destroyed, probably in A.D. 70 (10:21–23). It affirms that Jerusalem will be rebuilt in splendor (10:55). The fifth vision (11:1—12:51) depicts an eagle with three heads and twelve wings that controls and oppresses the earth. This eagle evidently stands for the Roman Empire. Its dominion will end (11:44–46), and the lion (i.e., the messiah) will deliver God's people (12:34). The sixth vision or dream, of a man from the sea, shows that God will defeat his enemies but protect his people (chap. 13). Here also we see an early version of the popular legend about the ten tribes dwelling in "another land" until the "last times" (13:39–50).

Several other distinctive features appear in chaps. 3—14. Here for the first time in biblical tradition, we find the idea that human depravity ("the evil heart") has been transmitted to Adam's descendants (3:20–27; 7:118). As in 1 Esdras, truth is an important value; here it is expected to prevail in the coming age (6:28; 7:34; cf. 1 Esd. 4:33–41). The two primeval sea monsters, Behemoth and Leviathan, will serve as food—evidently in the coming age—for those whom God will choose (6:49–52). Several visions refer to the coming time of judgment (e.g., 7:32–44, 61–74) and depict the fate of the spirits of those who die in the meantime. The unrighteous will dwell in seven "ways of torment" (7:79–87), the righteous in seven orders of blissful habitation (7:88–99; cf. 4:35). As in Ezekiel 47, the coming age is pictured as paradise, with perpetual and abundant fruit (7:123; cf. Rev. 22:2). The visions tell that the world has grown old, explaining that this is why people are smaller than in earlier times (5:51–56). Nine and a half out of twelve parts of the old age have already passed, and as the world becomes weaker through old age, the evils of life in it multiply all the more (14:10–17). Ezra himself is one of those "taken up" into heaven (8:19; 14:9; cf. 6:26), but not until, under divine inspiration, he dictated the twenty-four books of the OT in order to warn those born after his ascension but before "the times are ended" (14:9), along with seventy other books reserved for the edification of the wise (14:19–48; cf. 12:37–38). It is curious that the only claim for plenary inspiration of the OT (and other writings) is in 2 Esdras, which itself enjoys only the most tenuous canonical status. The original book of 2 Esdras seems to have ended here, with chap. 14.

The last strata in 2 Esdras consist of Christian additions, mainly in chaps. 1—2, commonly dated ca. A.D. 150, and chaps. 15—16, which may have been written as late as ca. A.D. 250. Both sets of additions promise their readers that the close of the age or kingdom of God will soon come (2:13, 34–35; 16:52). The time of tribulation that will herald the advent of the new age is also at hand (16:37–39, 74). The later addition appears to reflect Christian experience of active persecution by Roman authorities, possibly in the time of the emperor Decius (see 15:52). The writer's enthusiasm for the coming destruction of the enemies of the chosen people probably reflects hatred engendered by such persecution (see 15:34–45, 56–63). As in the books of Daniel and Revelation, "Babylon" is a code name for the oppressors of God's people—here, as in Revelation, the Roman Empire.

Chapters 1—2 reflect relatively peaceful times. Special features include the thesis that if "Judah" will not obey him, God will bestow his favor on "other nations"—implicitly, Gentile Christians (1:24–40). The latter will enjoy the "everlasting habitations"—those prepared for the former (2:11; cf. 7:88–99, and Luke 16:9)—which include the tree of life and the twelve trees loaded with all kinds of fruit (2:12, 18, 38) anticipated in earlier prophetic and NT traditions. In the meantime, God's people are to live according to the provisions of the law governing love and justice in human society: "Guard the rights of the widow, secure justice for the fatherless, give to the needy, . . . clothe the naked, care for the injured and weak . . . ."

(2:20–22; cf.Matt. 25:31–46; Luke 10:29–37). Proper burial takes on new meaning, in view of the hope for the resurrection of the dead (2:23).

Nothing in the visions or the later Christian additions suggests that either Jews or Christians are to concern themselves with worship at the Jerusalem temple or the offering of sacrifices there, in contrast to emphasis on these activities in Ezra and 1 Esdras. (The Romans had destroyed the temple in A.D. 70; it was never rebuilt, and both Jews and Christians had to accommodate their traditions and practices to its absence.) Instead, both the visions and the additions look for God's intervention on behalf of his people, a deliverance associated in some passages with the coming of God's Son (2:43–47; 7:28).

TOBIT

This charming narrative provides many insights as to Jewish practices and beliefs ca. 400–170 B.C., the period during which, at some point, it evidently was written. We see the ideal (honored, to be sure, only by Tobit) that Israelites should keep the feasts in Jerusalem (1:4–8; cf. Deut. 12:1–14); the distinction between priests (sons of Aaron) and Levites (1:6–7) that emerged ca. 400 B.C.; the virtue of abstinence from gentile (non-kosher) food (1:10–12; cf. Dan. 1:8, Jth. 12:2; Add. to Esther 14:17); belief in the seven holy angels or archangels of God (12:15), guardian angels (5:21; 12:12–13), and demons, which reflects Persian (Zoroastrian) influence; the importance of a good burial (1:17; 6:14; 14:11, 13; cf. 2 Esd. 2:23; Mark 15:43–46); the practice of placing bread on the graves of the righteous, but not on those of sinners (4:17; cf. Ecclus. 30:18); an anxious father's advice to his only son as the latter goes forth into the world—much of it in the form of wisdom sayings (4:3–19); mention of a man-eating fish (6:2); use of fish parts in demon exorcism and healing; conflicting ideas as to whether angels can (6:5) or cannot (12:19) eat fish; an otherwise rarely reported insistence on intratribal marriage (4:12–13; 6:9–12; cf. Num. 36:6–12); the idea of divinely foreordained marriage (6:17); a glimpse of the marriage service (7:11–15); the touching words of a bride's parents to the newlyweds (10:11); some fine examples of personal prayer (3:2–15; 8:5–8); the entertaining quarrels of the old married couple, Tobit and Anna (2:11–14; 10:1–7); and several more wisdom sayings, this time attributed to the angel Raphael (12:6–10). "Brother" and "sister" are frequently used as terms of endearment, rather than indicators of biological kinship (e.g., 5:20; 7:4, 16; 8:4, 7).

There are three plots: the story of Tobit, a singularly righteous Israelite afflicted, like Job, for no apparent reason, here with blindness while practicing ritual purity; that of Sarah, whose seven husbands have been killed, one after the other, by a jealous demon, and now has little prospect of finding an eligible (and willing) spouse (3:15); and Tobit's recollection that he has lent some money to a certain Gabael at Rages, and his decision to send his son, Tobias, to collect it. The plots are skillfully interwoven. All on the same day, Tobit and Sarah who, like Job, have been falsely accused by victim-blaming associates, pray that they may die and be delivered from their troubles. The prayers of both are heard in the heavenly council, and the angel Raphael is sent to cure their ills (chap. 3); and, still the same day, Tobit remembers the money (4:1). Tobias's journey, during which he is accompanied by the angel Raphael (disguised as "brother Azarias") and "the dog" (5:16; 11:4), leads to the resolution of all their problems.

Along the way, the angel instructs Tobias to catch a fish that has tried to swallow him and set aside its inner parts for later use in smoking out the demon and healing his father's eyes. As they approach Ecbatana, Azarias advises Tobias to think about marrying his cousin Sarah, who is not only eligible and heiress to a large fortune, but also beautiful and sensible (6:1–12). Brother Azarias briefs Tobias as to how to handle the demon—a matter Tobias has been quite concerned about (6:13–17). After they arrive, Azarias suggests the marriage to Sarah's father, Raguel, who is well disposed, and, as they sit down to dinner, tells Tobias to "eat, drink and be merry" (7:9; cf. Eccles. 2:24). He also tells him about the previous seven unfortunate husbands (without mentioning the demon). Undaunted, Tobias insists on marriage forthwith. The ceremony is quickly performed, Tobias and Sarah go up to bed, and Raguel goes outside to dig another grave. But the demon is overcome by the smoke and flees to Egypt, where the angel binds him. *Now* Sarah's parents put on a two-week wedding feast (chap. 8). Somewhat incidentally and anticlimactically, Azarias goes to Rages and collects the money from Gabael (chap. 9). Back in Nineveh, Tobit worries about the money, Anna about her son, and the two take the occasion to have a good domestic argument: "Am I not distressed, my child," says Anna, "that I let you go, you who are the light of my eyes?" But Tobit tells her, "Be still and stop worrying; he is well." And she answers him, "Be still and stop deceiving me; my child has perished" (10:5–7). Then the young couple returns, Tobias heals his father's eyes, and all ends happily (chaps. 11—12). Before ascending back to heaven, Raphael identifies himself as one of the seven holy angels, offers Tobit and Tobias some advice, especially recommending that they praise God and give alms, and instructs Tobit to write down in a book "everything that has happened" (12:11–20), thus, implicitly, accounting for the composition of the book.

Chapters 13 and 14 may be later additions. Chapter 13 consists of a psalm. Many biblical and apocryphal books contain one or more psalms. This one praises God as Father, King of the ages, King of heaven, and looks for the messianic age when Jerusalem will become a city of gold, emeralds, and other precious stones. Chapter 14 reports Tobit's further acts of virtue (notably, giving alms), and his last words (in which he looks for the restoration of Jerusalem and the time when all the Gentiles will turn to God), his death at the ripe age of 158 (cf. Gen. 6:3; Job 42:16), and his "magnificent funeral." The book closes with the further information that Tobias also gives his mother- and father-in-law magnificent funerals, inherits their property (as well as Tobit's), and dies at the age of 127, after hearing the good news of Nineveh's destruction at the hands of Nebuchadnezzar and Ahasuerus (cf. the Books of Jonah and Nahum).

JUDITH

The story probably was written during the first third of the second century B.C. in order to encourage the writer's fellow Jews to keep tradition and resist their enemies despite the seemingly overwhelming power of other peoples, particularly, perhaps, the Syrians. Unlike the Book of Daniel, which encouraged its readers to await supernatural deliverance, the writer of Judith implies that contemporary Jewish readers should emulate her example by trusting God and taking arms against their oppressors. This, at all events, is what many Jews did in the time of Antiochus IV and the early Maccabean period. (See 1 and 2 Maccabees.)

Bethulia—a place otherwise unknown—may stand for Jerusalem. As the story is told, it is the last bastion: if it falls, all Judah will be captured, and, worst of all, the Jerusalem temple ("the sanctuary") will be captured and desecrated by the idolatrous and malicious Gentiles (4:2, 12–13; 8:21–24; 9:8). The Syrian overlord, Antiochus IV, did, in fact, plunder and desecrate the temple in 167 B.C. (1 Macc. 1:21–24, 54; cf. Dan. 8:9–13). The historical setting described in the story is impossible: the author portrays Nebuchadnezzar as king of Assyria after the exile. This confusion may have been intended to alert readers to look for the real meaning of the book: namely, a summons to resist contemporary foes. The Syrians, of course, would have taken a dim view of any resistance literature explicitly naming them. The arrogance of "Nebuchadnezzar" and his adherents, together with the demand that conquered people give up their religion (3:8; 6:2–4) corresponds closely to the situation of the Jewish people at the time of Antiochus IV.

As the story goes, Holofernes has been dispatched by Nebuchadnezzar to punish those nations, including "Israel," that had refused to help him in his war against Arphaxad, the Mede. It is understood that these nations will be required to give up their religion and worship Nebuchadnezzar as god (3:8; cf. 1 Macc. 1:14–50; Dan. 3:3–15). In this setting, Judith summons the elders of Bethulia to her house, speaks of God's transcendent power and purpose, exhorts them to remain true to him, prays for his aid in carrying out her plan (chaps. 8—9), and puts this plan into operation, thereby bringing about the deliverance so desperately needed (chaps. 10—15).

After adorning herself with elegant finery, the better "to entice the eyes of all men who might see her," Judith crosses into no man's land and explains to an Assyrian patrol there that she wants to tell Holofernes how he can defeat the Hebrews. All the soldiers eagerly volunteer to escort this marvelously beautiful woman to their general, but only a hundred are chosen for this pleasant duty (10:3–19). She proceeds to tell Holofernes with various double-entendres and ingenious prevarications that as soon as the people of Bethulia eat and drink the consecrated offerings which, she says, they are on the verge of doing lest they starve, God himself will destroy them by way of punishment for so doing (11:5–19). Holofernes is impressed with Judith's wisdom, but especially with her beauty. He schemes to get her alone, that he might "embrace" her (12:10–12); but when the time comes, he breaks his own previous record for wine consumption, passes out, and Judith lops off his head—a favorite scene in later Western art—placing it in her now-empty kosher food bag. Back in Bethulia, she instructs her brethren what to do next (14:1–4). Just as she predicted, after the Israelites sally forth in the morning, the Assyrians panic on finding their general headless, the Israelites defeat them with "great slaughter," and take possession of nearby towns and villages and a vast quantity of booty (14:11—15:7).

Judith's words summarize the main thrust of the book: "Our God is still with us, to show his power in Israel, and his strength against our enemies" (13:11; see also 16:17). Judith epitomizes the bravery of

Jael against Sisera and David against Goliath, the alluring beauty of Abraham's Sarah, Esther, and Susanna, and the shrewd strategies of Tamar (Gen. 38) and Gideon. Like the Book of Tobit, Judith concludes with a psalm and final biographical notes (chap. 16).

Several points of religious and cultural interest may be noted. Like Daniel and Esther (of the Additions), Judith keeps kosher (10:5). Like Tobit and Sarah in the Book of Tobit, and like Esther and Mordecai in the Additions to Esther, she prays at length to God for assistance (9:2–14). Like Deborah, she rallies her contemporaries to go and fight bravely against their oppressors (8:11–27; cf. Judg. 4:6–9, 15). Like Miriam and Deborah, she composes a song or psalm of victory to commemorate the events (16:2–17). The psalm looks forward to the eternal torment (by fire and worms) of all nations that oppose God's people (16:17; cf. Isa. 66:24; Ecclus. 7:17; Mark 9:43–48). Before she dies, she grants her maidslave freedom—an unprecedented act of liberation—and distributes her property to both her husband's and her own nearest relatives—again, an unprecedented procedure (16:23–25; cf. Num. 27:8–11; Job 42:15). We also learn from the story that widows may receive substantial inheritances (or bequests) from their husbands (8:7). In general, Judith represents a model of Jewish piety, virtue, and bravery: qualities evidently not reserved to men in Judaism of the second century B.C. (see also 4 Maccabees 15).

ADDITIONS TO ESTHER

The Additions are those parts of the Greek version of Esther that were not known in Hebrew at the time Jewish Scripture was defined and delimited at Jamnia, ca. A.D. 90. They were probably added around the time Esther was translated into Greek, ca. 100 B.C. According to 11:1, the translation—probably meaning the whole Book of Esther—was the work of a certain Lysimachus of Jerusalem. Six sets of additions, not all necessarily written at the same time, are scattered through the book at various points. Their author(s) evidently wished to clarify certain matters left in doubt in the original, and, particularly, to introduce religious elements notably absent from it. For example, in the original book, God is never mentioned, and no one prays or observes any other religious practices.

Lest anyone wonder, the Additions now explain why Mordecai (Mardochaeus, NEB) refused to bow to Haman—thereby provoking the latter's animosity against all Jews—so that he might not "set the glory of man above the glory of God" (13:12–14). Esther tells God that she finds her marriage to the gentile king Artaxerxes (Ahasuerus) abhorrent (14:15); moreover, lest she be thought proud of herself as queen, she explains that she wears her crown only on public, not leisure, occasions (14:16). These explanations are set in the form of Mordecai's and Esther's prayers to God—who already knows all things (13:12; 14:15–16); thus their actual function is to edify the reader (cf. John 11:41–42, where Jesus prays in order to be heard by the people standing around him). Lest contemporary Jewish scruples be offended, the Additions note that Esther avoids gentile food; like Daniel and Judith, she keeps kosher.

The Additions try again to explain the murky connections between lots, Purim, and the story (10:10–13). Here the idea is that God has "made" one "lot" for the Jews (Israel), and another for all other nations (Gentiles), some or all of whom had come to destroy Israel, and that in the course of events, God decided for and saved Israel and defeated the Gentiles (10:8–12; cf. Luke 1:68, 71). Purim, implicitly, celebrates this "day of decision." The whole Book of Esther, including the Additions, is now characterized as the Letter of Purim (11:1).

The Additions frequently refer to God, who is ultimately credited with saving his people (15:8; 10:9). Even the Persian king, Artaxerxes, testifies to God's justice, omniscience, and sovereignty (16:4, 16, 21). The Jews' subjugation to their enemies is explained as God's punishment for their worship of other gods (14:6–7)—a theory of history congruent with earlier prophetic and Deuteronomic views. Mordecai's dream (11:5–11) is also of religious interest. Earthquake, tumult on earth, the gathering of two great dragons and all the nations for battle, darkness, gloom, and the like, are standard features of Jewish and early Christian representations of the time of tribulation expected before the establishment of God's kingdom on earth (see, e.g., Isa. 27:1; Ezekiel 38—39; Dan. 12:1; Zechariah 14; Mark 13; Revelation 12; 13; 20). The interpretation of some of these features in 10:5—9 is probably a later demythologizing attempt to explain allegorically that these expectations have been fulfilled (see esp. 10:5).

The tendency of tradition to exaggerate as it grows may be seen in the characterization of Haman as an accomplice of the two conspiratorial eunuchs (12:6) and as a Macedonian bent on treason (16:10–14). The Additions supply several melodramatic touches when Esther goes before the king; for example, though "radiant with perfect beauty," her "heart was frozen" as she approaches the royal presence; the king was "most terrifying," and "glanced at her in towering anger" (NEB), with the result that she falls fainting not only once but twice (15:1–16; cf. Esther 5:1–2). Few interpreters propose that the Additions should be taken as literal history. Nevertheless, the Additions, like other writings from the same period, do provide a treasury of historical information as to the beliefs, concerns, and practices of Judaism in the second and first centuries B.C.

WISDOM OF SOLOMON
(or WISDOM)

The author of Wisdom implicitly identifies himself with Solomon in chaps. 7—9 (cf. Eccles. 1:12—2:12). Unmistakably Greek terms (e.g., Hades) and ideas (e.g., 8:7, 19–20; 12:1), however, suggest that the book was not composed before the fourth century B.C. Usually Wisdom is dated in the first century B.C.

Like traditional wisdom (e.g., Proverbs) this book holds that righteous individuals are rewarded and wicked ones punished, but it differs from the orthodox wisdom theology by proposing that such rewards and punishments will be dispensed after death rather than in this life. As in Proverbs 8, Wisdom itself is represented as a female being closely associated with God from the beginning of the world (9:9). Here, Wisdom, which is identified with God's spirit or breath, is said to fill the whole earth, holding all things together (1:5–7; 7:22—8:1; cf. John 1:1–5; Col. 1:15–17). Several other passages also evidently influenced NT ideas and expressions: for example, 3:7 (cf. Matt. 13:43); 3:8 (cf. Rev. 2:26–27; 20:4); 3:14 (cf. Matt. 19:12); 5:16 (cf. Rev. 2:10); 5:16–19 (cf. Eph. 6:11–17); 6:3 (cf. Rom. 13:1–2); 14:22–31 (cf. Rom. 1:18–32). Like many NT writings, Wisdom looks for the time of Judgment, when the righteous will be rewarded and the unrighteous punished (chaps. 3—5). These several affinities may explain why Wisdom is listed with NT writings in the Muratorian fragment, an early Christian document written ca. A.D. 200.

The book contains several kinds of material. Like other wisdom writings, it praises wisdom, commending it particularly to the kings of the earth (1:1–15; 6:1–25). The writer reflects thematically upon the respective destinies of the wicked and the righteous (1:16—5:23) perceptively portraying the desperate and exploitive attitudes and ethics of the ungodly (2:1–11). In chaps. 7—9, "Solomon" tells about himself and the wonders of wisdom, and prays for its continuing gifts. This leads into a review of stories about early humankind and Israel, in which wisdom is said to have delivered the ancients who heeded her (chaps. 10—11). This section blends into the concluding rumination—probably by another writer—on God's dealings with Israel and Egypt long ago (chaps. 11—19). This last also includes a brief allusion to God's attempt to bring the Canaanites to repentance, even though, in his omniscience, he knew beforehand that this "accursed race" would never change (12:3–11); and a longer discourse on the foolishness of making and worshiping idols (13:1—15:17), a theme featured in other more or less contemporary writings, such as Bel and the Dragon, and the Letter of Jeremiah. In this connection, the author indicates his general antipathy toward art, especially painted sculpture (15:4–6; cf. Exod. 20:4 and Deut. 5:8, which can be read to prohibit not only worshiping, but even making artistic representations of anything).

Like 2 Esdras, Wisdom promises immortality to the souls of the righteous (3:4; 5:15), but is more optimistic as to the number that might qualify for this blessing. At times, Wisdom seems to view all Israelites as "sons" of God (12:21; 16:10), or even as "a holy people and a blameless race" (10:15; cf. Ezra 9:2). Wisdom affirms God's providence, and, like Tobit, addresses God as Father (14:3; Tob. 13:4; cf. 2 Esd. 1:29). For the first time in biblical tradition, death's entry into the world is blamed upon "the devil" (2:24; cf. Genesis 3, which refers only to the serpent, one of the creatures God had made, and understands human mortality as part of *God's* punishment for the first couple's disobedience). Nevertheless, cosmic dualism is quite limited, for Wisdom praises God as the creator and lover of all that exists (1:4; 11:24).

The final chapters present a highly idealized and imaginative interpretation of Israel's early history (e.g., 16:20–21, which says that the manna given in the wilderness was made to suit the individual tastes of every Israelite; cf. Num. 11:4–6, where, as elsewhere in earlier tradition, the Israelites repeatedly complain that manna was scarcely fit to eat). An imaginary prototype of medieval and Chinese dragons appears in a list of newly created beasts that Yahweh might have sent—but mercifully did not do so—to punish the Israelites for their apostasy in the wilderness (11:18–19; cf. Job 41). These several chapters of revisionist history evidently were meant to encourage fellow Jews to believe that God would still act in history on behalf of his people when they needed his help (see esp. 16:7–8; 19:22).

ECCLESIASTICUS
(or THE WISDOM OF
JESUS, SON OF SIRACH)

Ecclesiasticus (not to be confused with Ecclesiastes) or Sirach (as it is often called) is the longest of the wisdom writings. The author reveals not only his name, Joshua (Heb.) or Jesus (Gk.), 50:27, but also various personal experiences and insights (e.g. 34:11–12; 39:32–34; 51:13–22). One infers that he was a man with wide interests, a gentle spirit, and a firm faith. Probably a teacher and philosopher, he comments that devising proverbs "requires painful thinking" (13:26). He values priests and sacrificial offerings (7:29–31; 45:6–26), but warns against supposing that God can be bribed (7:9; 35:12), and generally urges a high standard of justice, kindness, and consideration for others. Wisdom is closely associated with the law or commandments, which are understood mainly in terms of ethics or practical reason. Sirach probably was written ca. 180 B.C. and translated into Greek ca. 130 B.C.

The prologue, written by the anonymous grandson of Jesus who translated it from Hebrew, commends the book to those who love learning as a guide to progress in living according to the law. Chapters 1—43 consist largely of proverbs (short observations and admonitions), which often are grouped by topics. A briefer section (44:1—50:21) praises certain famous men of yore, showing how they were favored by God for their righteousness, beginning with Enoch and ending with Simon the high priest (ca. 200 B.C.). The book concludes with a psalm of thanksgiving (51:1–12) and exhortations to heed the instruction presented.

Many traditional wisdom themes are repeated here. Wisdom is praised and said to begin with the "fear of the Lord" and to come from him (chap. 1). Those who love and heed wisdom are righteous; those who do not are foolish and wicked. The former may look for reward in the form of prosperity, long life, a famous name, and posterity; but the latter will be punished in this life. (The author offers no hope for resurrection or immortality.) The reader, often addressed as "my son," is warned against the enticements of loose women and the perils of adultery (9:3–9). A bad wife is a great catastrophe; a good one, a great blessing (25:16—26:4, 13–18). Fathers are to use the rod rather than spoil their sons (30:1–13). Excessive drinking leads to trouble (31:25–31). The author makes many shrewd observations and comparisons regarding the human condition (e.g., 20:18, 29; 21:2, 14;

40:17–27). Numerous sayings offer advice, particularly for those in authority and those who aspire to success in various kinds of enterprise (e.g., 10:1–3; 11:7–9; 20:27–28; 37:7–35). Many also refer to matters of etiquette (e.g., 31:12–18; 32:1–13). And several are prudential (e.g., 8:10–19; 13:1–13).

The author is fond of balanced statements, which often show considerable sophistication and delicate irony (e.g., 5:1; 6:13, 23, 31; 11:2; 33:14–15; 41:1–2). Repeatedly, he emphasizes the importance of giving alms and otherwise helping the poor and needy (e.g., 4:1–10; 29:9–13). Almsgiving is also commended in Tobit (Tob. 4:7–11; 12:8–9) and by a later Jesus (Luke 12:33; 16:1–9). But Sirach advises against helping sinners (12:1–7). Numerous other passages are later echoed in sayings attributed to Jesus in the first three gospels (e.g., 7:14b, 35; 9:5a; 11:19; 19:17; 27:6; 28:3–4). Sirach apparently opposes placing food on graves (30:18), a practice endorsed by Tobit with respect to the graves of the righteous (Tob. 4:17; cf. Letter of Jer. v. 27). Sirach holds a low view of women (22:3; 25:24; 42:14) but recommends marriage (36:22–26).

Many topics are considered: friendship (6:7–17); treating oneself well (14:3–19); freedom of the will and responsibility (15:11–20); lending and borrowing (29:1–20); matters of health and table manners relating to eating and drinking (31:12—32:13); dealing with servants (33:24–31); mourning (38:16–23); and the value of physicians, scribes, and craftsmen (38:1–25, 24–34). Throughout, God is praised as creator and sovereign of all that is, who cares for his creation, and governs it well (10:4; 39:16–35; 42:15—43:33).

The long section in praise of famous men highlights the great deeds of biblical heroes. Though the writer makes no mention of resurrection or immortality, he is confident that their fame and names "will live for ever" (44:1–15). In several instances, the earlier tradition is expanded by legends previously unrecorded, such as the ascension of Enoch (44:16; cf. Gen. 5:24); the youthful David's playing with lions and bears (47:3); Solomon's filling the earth with parables and riddles (49:17). Most of the figures are somewhat idealized: Noah was perfect (44:17); Abraham was unique "in glory" (44:19); Moses, who was equal in glory to the angels (45:2), was chosen by God "out of all mankind" (45:4); and Aaron was chosen "out of all the living" (45:16). Together, these recitations served as reminders to contemporary Jews (ca. 200 B.C.) that God sustained his people in the past by raising up strong leaders and making covenants with them that would endure to all times. By implication, Sirach's contemporaries could look to God to raise up such leaders and to continue to honor his covenant promises in their time and in the future. Such hopes would have been very important in the era of Antiochus IV and the Maccabean period.

BARUCH

The book is implicitly ascribed to the Baruch who was Jeremiah's secretary (see Jeremiah 36; 45). It is set, ostensibly, among certain Jewish exiles in Babylon ca. 580 B.C. Jerusalem has been burned (1:2); the temple devastated (2:26); many of the people of Jerusalem and other cities of Judah have perished miserably (2:25), and the rest are now scattered in exile (3:8). Several features point to more recent composition, however, such as references to demons and Hades and various errors as to names and chronology. Interpreters generally suggest that the book was written in the second or early first century, B.C. Stylistic and substantive considerations suggest that there may have been more than one author. The book consists of four sections, each with special characteristics and concerns. The first two are in prose; the last two, which are in poetic form, seem to have been modeled on earlier psalms, proverbs, and prophetic forms and themes.

The first section, 1:1–4, introduces "this book" as one written by Baruch ca. 582 B.C. in Babylon and read to the Jewish exiles there (1:1–3), and then sent to the high priest and other priests and people in Jerusalem, so that they might make their "confession" by reading it in the temple on special holy days (1:14). Thus the first section introduces the second (1:15—3:8), a kind of general confession, but seems unrelated to the third or fourth sections. Both the first and second sections typically refer to God as the Lord or the Lord God. The first section also says that the exiles collected money, "each giving what he could," to be sent to the priests and those with them in Jerusalem, to buy sacrificial offerings at the temple. Curiously, the writer seems to assume that the temple is still standing, and that the customary ritual functions continue in it, despite its destruction in 586 B.C. (see 2 Kings 25:9). Confusion on this point would be understandable if the author was writing several generations or centuries later. He evidently meant to imply that all diaspora Jews who were unable to attend the prescribed festivals in Jerusalem themselves could, by sending money, have sacrifices and prayers offered there on their behalf (cf. Deut. 14:22–26). We may see here a precedent for Paul's collecting money from the gentile churches on behalf of "the saints" in Jerusalem (e.g., 1 Cor. 16:1–4), and for the later Catholic practice of making contributions for the saying of masses. In Baruch, prayers are requested not only for the contributors, but for the Babylonian kings Nebuchadnezzar and Belshazzar (1:10; cf. Jer. 29:7, where the prophet instructs the exiles in Babylon to seek the welfare of that city and pray to Yahweh on its behalf; and Matt. 5:44 = Luke 6:28, where Jesus tells his hearers to love and pray for their enemies).

The second section, 1:15—3:8, is a prayer of confession to be offered to God, along with sacrifices and other prayers, on special days (1:14). The first part, 1:15 through 2:5 (or perhaps, 2:12), fits the situation of those left in Jerusalem; the latter part of the section is from the standpoint of the exiles (see, e.g., 2:13–14). Both sections draw on language and themes found in earlier biblical texts, especially Deuteronomy, Jeremiah, and Daniel. The confession initially acknowledges that the calamities experienced are God's punishment for the victims' sins and disobedience (1:17–21); but at the end, the confession suggests that the punishment is for the sins of the fathers, after all (3:4–8; cf. Lam. 5:7). The confession concludes with a promise (attributed to Moses), that if Israel changes its ways, God will bring them back from exile and make an everlasting covenant with them (2:28–35; cf. Jer. 32:38–40). We see here, and also in 2:2, the understanding that the Deuteronomic law, which includes warnings as to the consequences of disobedience, could be understood to prophesy coming events (cf. Matt. 11:13, ". . . the prophets and the law prophesied until John").

The third section (3:9—4:4) is addressed to "Israel," and explains that the reason its people dwell in the land of their enemies is that they have forsaken wisdom. Wisdom either has not been granted to other nations, or has been foolishly ignored by them. Thus those who have lived for pleasure and glory, hunting wild animals and birds for sport, or hoarding silver and gold, all have perished for lack of wisdom, along with the famous giants of old (3:16–17, 24–28, NEB). But God, who knows all things, and by wisdom established the earth for all time, filling it with four-footed creatures, sending forth light, calling to the stars, has given wisdom to Israel (3:32–36). Thus there is hope for Israel, since through the Law, Israel knows what is pleasing to God (4:4). Wisdom here is equated with the Law or Torah (4:1; cf. the equation of reason and law in 4 Maccabees).

The fourth section (4:5—5:5) is likewise addressed to Israel (typically called "my children" or "my sons and daughters") and Jerusalem (in 4:30—5:5). The writer summons them to "take courage," for God will soon (4:24–25) bring them back to Jerusalem and act in judgment against those cities that have afflicted them. The writer's enthusiasm for the devastation of these foreign cities contrasts with the first section's positive attitude toward the Babylonian kings (1:11–12). It is unclear whether the speaker in this fourth section (who addresses hearers/readers as "my people" or "my children") is meant to be Baruch (who is mentioned only in the first section), Wisdom (speaking as in Proverbs 8), or some prophet, pronouncing oracles on behalf of God. The speaker frequently refers to God, typically as "the Everlasting," indicating that the speaker distinguishes between himself and God. Wisdom is not mentioned in this section; but possibly the author or editor understood Wisdom, which is named at the end of the third section (3:37—4:4) to be the speaker in 4:5—5:9 as well. The message of hope in the fourth section contains numerous echoes of Second and Third Isaiah (Isaiah 40—66), from which several verses may derive. The substance of this message is that the exiles will be gathered once more to Jerusalem, "from east and west" (4:36–37; cf. Matt. 8:11). Other features of prophetic and apocalyptic eschatology are notably absent, such as the appearance of a messiah, a new covenant, the resurrection of the dead, or the judgment of the righteous and unrighteous.

LETTER OF JEREMIAH

This book is presented as a letter by Jeremiah to those about to be taken into exile by the Babylonians (v. 1). A letter from Jeremiah to the Jewish exiles in Babylon is preserved in Jeremiah 29. But the Letter treated here probably comes from a later author who wrote between 331 and 100 B.C. In some ancient Bibles, the Letter is treated as a separate book, and placed between Lamentations and Ezekiel; in others, it is part of Baruch, and so some English translations designate it as chapter six of that book.

"Jeremiah" wishes to warn the prospective exiles lest in Babylon they be tempted to worship images or idols as if such really were gods. Thematically, the writer asserts that idols cannot save themselves (vv. 12, 15, 49, 57) or anyone else (vv. 36–39) from the vicissitudes of life, argues that they ought not be considered as gods (vv. 40, 44, 52, 56), and urges readers not to fear them (vv. 16, 23, 65, 69). This is perhaps the most extensive or sustained polemic against the worship of idols in the Bible. (See also Ps. 115:4–8; Isa. 40:18–20; 41:7; 44:9–20; 46:1–2, 5–7; Jer. 10:2–16; Wisdom of Solomon

Prayer of
Azariah and
the Song
of the Three
Young Men
(Additions
to Daniel)

13—15; and Bel and the Dragon.) The impotence of idols is vividly and sardonically stressed: they cannot save themselves from rust and corrosion (v. 12) or from war and robbers (v. 15); their eyes are coated with dust kicked up by the feet of visitors to their shrines (v. 17); bats, birds, and cats perch ignominiously on their bodies and heads (v. 22); they are no more than scarecrows in a cucumber patch (v. 70).

Several distinctive features may be noted. The Letter interprets the exile as God's judgment against the exiles for their own sins (cf. Lam. 5:7 and Bar. 3:5, 8, which blame their "fathers"). The writer warns that the exiles may remain in Babylon up to seven generations (v.3; cf. Jer. 29:10, which anticipated that the exile would last for seventy years). Reference in v. 7 to God's angel watching over the exiles is reminiscent of the guardian angel Raphael in Tobit; angels are some-times called "watchers" in various writings in the Pseudepigrapha. The writer has no respect for priests who officiate at the idols' temples: they steal silver and gold from the idols, spend it on themselves or give it to brothel harlots (v. 10), sell the sacrifices offered to the idols and use the proceeds for their own benefit (v. 28), take the gods' clothing for their wives and children (v. 32), and in case of fire, save themselves, but let the idols burn (v. 55). Like Sirach (and earlier legal and prophetic writings), the author of the Letter shows concern for the poor, the helpless, the blind, the distressed, widows, and orphans—noting that neither the idols nor their priests do anything to help them (vv. 28, 37–38).

THE PRAYER OF AZARIAH AND
THE SONG OF THE THREE YOUNG MEN
(ADDITIONS TO DANIEL)

Here we have the first of three sets of additions to the Book of Daniel found in the Septuagint and other early versions. This first set consists of three psalms or hymns joined together with a minimum of connecting narrative. Purportedly, they were recited by one or all of Daniel's three friends, Shadrach, Meshach, and Abednego, after King Nebuchadnezzar had them bound and cast into a "burning fiery furnace" because they had refused to bow down and worship the golden image erected by the king (see Dan. 3:1–18). In the Additions, the friends have Hebrew names (Azariah, Hananiah, and Mishael), possi-bly to underscore their traditionalist character. Except for vv. 66 and 68 (which may have been appended to tie them into this setting), the

125

psalms themselves do not refer to the fiery furnace. Verses 23–27 pick up the story from v. 1, presenting a vivid prose account of the events implicit in Dan. 3:19–27. Only here do we learn that the angel of the Lord "came down" and "drove the fiery flame" away. In the apocryphal or augmented versions, the Prayer and Song are inserted after Dan. 3:23. This first set of additions is dated ca. 170–150 B.C.

The Prayer of Azariah (vv. 2–22) is a psalm of communal lament (cf. Psalms 83; 85). Its acceptance of national calamity as God's judgment recalls Lamentations 1. Several passages are suggestive of the era following Antiochus Epiphanes's desecration of the temple (ca. 167 B.C.): the Jewish people have been given over to lawless enemies and to an unjust king—the most wicked in the world; there is no Jewish prince, prophet, or leader, no offering of sacrifices, and no place to offer them (vv. 9–10, 15). Since sacrifices cannot be given, God is asked to accept a contrite heart and a humble spirit instead (v. 16; cf. Ps. 51:16–17). The psalmist calls on God to remember his promises to Abraham, Isaac, and Israel ("thy holy one"—a rare characterization of Jacob!), and to put down the oppressors of their descendants, so that they will know that he is the only God, sovereign over all nations (vv. 11–14, 20–22). Here we see an expression of explicit monotheistic faith (cf. v. 68).

The Song of the Three Young Men comprises two psalms of thanksgiving, at vv. 29–34 and 35–65, each with distinctive repeated congregational responses. Both psalms are preserved in Christian liturgy as the *Benedictus es, Domine* and *Benedicite omnia opera Domini*, respectively. In the former, God is blessed and glorified in all places: in the temple (now evidently reconsecrated), seated upon the cherubim (cf. Ezekiel 1; 10) contemplating the seas; upon the throne of his kingdom (presumably the land); and in the firmament of heaven. In the latter, celestial and atmospheric powers, along with earth and sea, mountains, springs and rivers, everything that grows, whales and all other sea creatures, all birds, all beasts, together with Israel, priests, and the souls of the righteous (including, perhaps, those who have died), are called upon to praise the Lord. (Cf. Psalms 148; 150:6; also Job 38—40, which likewise affirms Yahweh's creation of, compassion for, and dominion over all creation and all living beings.) The celebration of creation appears later in such magnificent compositions as Saint Francis's "Canticle of the Sun," the hymn "Old One Hundred," Haydn's "Creation," and Beethoven's "Ode to Joy." Verse 66 again refers to the three young men, calling on them, too, to "bless the Lord"—here because he has delivered them from the fiery furnace—while the last two verses, echoing earlier psalms, call on all who worship the Lord to bless and praise him. The tone of rejoicing in the Song of the Three Young Men may reflect important victories by the Maccabeans in their war of liberation against the Syrians (see, e.g., 1 Macc. 7:39–48).

SUSANNA
(ADDITIONS TO DANIEL)

Like several other writings from later times, Susanna is set during the Babylonian exile (586–539 B.C.). Greek terms (such as the wordplays in vv. 54–55 and 58–59) and other features, however, suggest that it probably was written between the third and first centuries B.C. Its narrative qualities rank among the best of biblical writings, and it is one of the earliest known detective stories in world literature. (Daniel, as zealous attorney for the defense, not only saves his client but solves the case and catches the true culprits in the courtroom.)

Its theological and moral thrust, summarized in vv. 60–62, accords with the traditional wisdom viewpoint: the righteous (also beautiful) Susanna is vindicated, and the wicked elders are punished. The book emphasizes law and, implicitly, due process. Susanna has been instructed in the law of Moses (v. 3). She refuses to violate the Seventh Commandment even to save her own life (vv. 22–23; cf. Deut. 22:22). The elders, who are also judges (vv. 5–6), not only covet their neighbor's wife, but maliciously bear false witness against her, and want her killed to cover up their own wicked scheme (see Exod. 20:13–14, 16–17). These shameless elders even order Susanna unveiled during trial so "that they might feast upon her beauty" (v. 32).

Susanna's piety is shown in her refusal to sin, her trust in God, and her prayer for his help. The Lord hears her prayer (cf. Tob. 3:16–17) and arouses Daniel to the rescue. This inspired youth declares her innocent and proceeds to so prove, urging attention to "the facts," ordering witnesses sequestered and cross-examining them separately. They offer conflicting testimony, thereby revealing that each has lied, and so, in accordance with the law as to false witnesses (Deut. 19:16–21), they suffer the punishment that would have been inflicted upon the falsely accused (vv. 61–62).

A few incidental points of interest may be noted. The story illustrates the OT law requiring at least two witnesses to sustain a criminal allegation (Deut. 19:15); but, curiously, no one in either trial scene takes an oath to tell the truth (cf. Exod. 20:7; Lev. 19:12). Daniel is the only biblical figure who appears as an attorney, that is, an advocate for someone else at trial (but see Gen. 18:22–33). In the course of interrogation, he badgers the witnesses, accusing the first of making unjust judgments, and the second of having Canaanite (rather than Judahite) ancestors. The writer also has Daniel aim an ethnic slur at "Israel": the wicked judges might be able to intimidate Israelite women into compliance with their lustful schemes, but not a daughter of Judah (vv. 52–57)!

The central point or "moral" of the story is underscored in v. 60: God "saves those who hope in him." The writer evidently intended the story to encourage Jews to remain faithful to the law and tradition despite temptations and pressures towards acculturation to the ways of their gentile neighbors. The same concern appears in the rest of Daniel, in such stories as Tobit and Esther, and in the many other relatively late writings, such as the Wisdom of Solomon, the Letter of Jeremiah, and the Books of the Maccabees.

BEL AND THE DRAGON
(ADDITIONS TO DANIEL)

These two stories of rather uneven literary quality present Daniel as an exemplary disbeliever (in all gods except God) and iconoclast who literally smashes or destroys false gods. As in Daniel and the other Additions, the setting is Babylon, but now, supposedly, in the days of Cyrus, the sixth century B.C. Persian emperor hailed by Second Isaiah as God's messiah (Isa. 45:1). Here, as elsewhere in Daniel and some other relatively late OT and apocryphal writings such as Esther, Baruch, and the Letter of Jeremiah, as well as Revelation, in the NT, "Babylon" is a code term, standing for latter-day enemies or oppressors of God's people. These Additions, like the others, probably were written in the second or first century B.C. In the Greek versions of Daniel, these two stories are added at the end, either before or after Susanna.

According to the first story, Bel is a Babylonian god represented by a large statue (cf. Isaiah 46), which regularly is served huge quantities of food and drink by seventy priests. Because these offerings are consumed each day, it seems that the image really is a living god (v. 6). But Daniel knows that there is only one living God, the creator and sovereign of all that is (v. 5). Consequently, he realizes that Bel is bogus. In the king's presence, Daniel secretly sprinkles a layer of ashes on the floor of Bel's temple—a stratagem worthy of heroes in modern detective novels. The next morning, in a moment of high melodrama (cf. Esther 7; Add. to Esther 15), Daniel draws the king's attention to fresh footprints: "Look at the floor and notice whose footsteps these are." The king then has the priests and their families, who have been perpetrating this fraud, put to death. Here, as in Let. of Jer. 6:28, priests who worship idols are seen not only as idolaters, but as self-serving swindlers preying upon the piety of a gullible populace. In its way, the story of Bel stands with Susanna among the world's earliest detective stories. It might also be seen as a precursor to the famous scene in *The Wizard of Oz* in which Dorothy unmasks the man behind the machinery.

The story of the Dragon (or Snake, NEB) follows. "You cannot deny that *this* is a living god," the king tells Daniel (v. 24), pointing to a large snake or lizard, presumably moving about its cage at another shrine. It obviously is alive. But since the Lord is the only living God (v. 25), Daniel knows that this can be no god. He feeds the poor creature poisonous pancakes and it promptly dies, to the great consternation of its worshipers who force the king to hand Daniel over to them for retribution. They throw Daniel into the lions' den—his second time there, it seems (cf. Dan. 6:16–24). The lions' rations (two human bodies and two sheep a day) are suspended in order to encourage them to eat Daniel. At this point, the plot gets muddled. The prophet Habakkuk has been innocently carrying dinner to some local farm workers in Judea (cf. 1 Sam. 17:17–18). Suddenly "the angel of the Lord" orders him to take the dinner to Daniel in the lions' den in Babylon. When Habakkuk protests (understandably) that he has never been in Babylon and knows nothing about the den, the angel abruptly seizes him by the hair, and carries him—while he carefully balances the dinner bowl—to within a few feet above the den, apparently just out of the zone of danger. Daniel gets the dinner, and the angel returns the prophet safely home. Why the lions refrain from eating Daniel is not explained. Possibly the story mixes the lions' den plot with another version in which Daniel faces starvation. At all events, when the king discovers Daniel alive six days later, he declares that Daniel's God is great, releases Daniel from the den, and throws Daniel's enemies to the lions, who devour them on the spot. Again we see an instance, albeit fictive, of "death to the idolaters" (cf. Exod. 32:25–29; 1 Kings 18:40).

As in canonical Daniel, the Letter of Jeremiah, Wisdom of Solomon

13—15, and Isaiah 40; 44; and 46, the basic theme in these Additions is that God alone is to be worshiped as such, never idols and false gods. The latter may have posed a serious temptation to Jews living in the midst of pagan neighbors and under domination of foreigners who were devoted to their gods. In positive terms, the two stories illustrate obedience to the first two commandments (see Exod. 20:3, 5) and persistent faith in God, despite social or political pressures.

THE PRAYER OF MANASSEH

This shortest book in the Apocrypha, indeed, in the OT, is also distinguished by its quality of personal piety. It resembles certain psalms of individual lament (e.g., Psalms 69—71), but makes no mention of enemies or desire for vengeance. Instead, the writer consistently acknowledges his own sin (cf. 2 Esd. 7:116–126). Unlike 2 Esdras, "Manasseh" looks with hope to God for the gift of repentance and forgiveness for all who have sinned. Unlike Jonah, he knows himself as a sinner and therefore rejoices that God is "of great compassion, long-suffering, and very merciful, and repentest over the evils of men" (v. 7a; cf. Jonah 4:1–3). While the prophets called for repentance by the whole people of Israel or Judah, this writer assures readers that God has appointed repentance for individual sinners, and identifies himself as one of these (vv. 7c–8). He uses a striking metaphor for repentance: "Now I bend the knee of my heart . . ." (v. 11). Several apparent parallels are found to NT passages: v.6 and Rom. 11:33; v. 8 and Luke 5:32; v. 9 and Luke 18:13; and v. 15c and Matt. 6:13, added ending. The Prayer may well have been familiar at least to Greek-speaking Jews and Christians in the first century A.D.

According to the Deuteronomic editor of 2 Kings 21, Manasseh was the worst of Judah's kings: in particular, he worshiped the gods or "abominations" of other nations and peoples, and—like earlier and later moguls and dictators—"shed very much innocent blood" (cf. 1 Macc. 1:37). Later, the Chronicler undertook to rehabilitate Manasseh, probably in order to understand and explain how so wicked a king could have reigned fifty-five years—longer than any other king of either Judah or Israel. According to the Chronicler, Manasseh prayed to God, who received his entreaty, and then changed his ways (2 Chron. 33:12–19). The present book purports to tell what Manasseh said in that prayer. Only vv. 9–10 correspond with what is known of Manasseh, however, notably, that he had practiced idolatry on a grand scale.

Like many other texts, this Prayer acclaims God as maker of heaven and earth (e.g., Psalm 148; Isaiah 45; Song of the Three Young Men; the Apostles' Creed). In accord with the first creation story (Gen. 1:2, 9–10) and Job 38:8–11, the writer does not say that God created the sea; rather he "shackled" or confined it (v. 3; cf. Jonah 1:9, where that prophet acknowledges—unhappily, it seems—that Yahweh "made the sea and the dry land").

Later biblical tradition often sanctifies earlier figures whose character, as originally described, was less than impeccable, such as David (2 Kings 22:2) and Jacob (Prayer of Azariah v. 12). Here the writer states that neither Abraham, Isaac, nor Jacob sinned against God. The present writer implicitly views Manasseh quite favorably.

This outstanding example of Jewish devotional writing is commonly dated in the second to first century B.C. Notwithstanding its religious quality, which he highly valued, Luther—followed by all other Protestants—concluded that the Prayer belonged in the Apocrypha. Later in the sixteenth century, the Council of Trent decided to exclude the Prayer of Manasseh, together with 1 and 2 Esdras, from Catholic Scriptures. Some Eastern Orthodox churches, however, still include the Prayer, with most of the rest of what Jews and Protestants call the Apocrypha, in their Bibles. Charlesworth includes the Prayer of Manasseh, along with full commentary, in his new edition of the Pseudepigrapha (OTP).

1 MACCABEES

Here we have a detailed history of the Jewish people during the brief but tumultuous period ca. 175–135 B.C. Most of the book probably was written within a few decades of the events. Generally it is considered an accurate account, though obviously told from a partisan Jewish standpoint and concerned with emphasizing the heroic and splendid accomplishments of "the family": Mattathias, his three sons (Judas, Jonathan, and Simon), and Simon's son John Hyrcanus. Judas was nicknamed the Maccabee or Maccabeus, probably meaning "the hammer," in recognition of his military prowess. The members of Mattathias's family are known both as Hasmoneans and Maccabeans. The era in Jewish history from ca. 167–63 B.C. is commonly designated the Hasmonean or Maccabean period because of the leadership roles of various family members during these years.

A cursory introduction reports the triumphs of the Greek conqueror, Alexander the Great, his death (ca. 323 B.C.), his generals' succession to power, and the appearance of Antiochus Epiphanes (or Antiochus IV), who gained control over the Syrian portion of Alexander's former empire in 175 B.C. Even before Epiphanes's time, certain "renegade" Jews began to follow gentile, that is, non-Jewish practices (1:11–15). For reasons that are not entirely certain, Antiochus determines to put an end to Jewish religion, condemns to death any Jews who persist in their religious practices, desecrates the temple, and orders Jews to sacrifice to pagan gods (1:20—2:18). Mattathias, a traditionalist Jew of priestly lineage, refuses to offer such sacrifice, kills a Jew who has done so, along with the Syrian officer who has been enforcing the order, and thereby (ca. 167 B.C.) initiates a movement for religious freedom that soon has major military and political consequences.

Emphasis on Sabbath observance apparently increased during the course of the four centuries since Jews last had occasion to fight for their nation. Thus when attacked on the Sabbath, the first group of traditionalists chooses to die rather than break the law by "working," that is, fighting back. Jewish leaders quickly recognize that such a policy can only lead to further disaster, and so determine that in the future, Jews will fight if attacked on the Sabbath (2:29–41). Mattathias and the Hasideans, ardent traditionalists, enforce orthodoxy upon those less zealous for the law, massacring backsliding "sinners," and forcibly circumcising Jewish youths whose parents have neglected to attend to that requirement (2:42–48; cf. 3 Macc. 7:10–15).

Subsequently, under Judas's direction and invoking the help of Heaven (a circumlocution for the name of God), Jewish forces begin to win a series of battles, usually against much larger armies. By 164 B.C., Jerusalem is regained, the temple restored, a new altar built, and sacrificial worship resumed (4:36–59). This restoration is commemorated in the later Jewish festival of Hanukkah or lights. Chapter 5 reports numerous additional victories by the Jews (sometimes called Israelites) over their gentile enemies, under Judas's formidable leadership.

In the following years, the Jews find themselves now on one side, now another, of the numerous contenders for control of the Syrian or Seleucid kingdom. As he lies dying, Epiphanes names his friend Philip as regent (6:14–15). Lysias, who has been Epiphanes's chief of staff, now puts forward the latter's son (also named Eupator), as King Antiochus V. Lysias leads a great army (including thirty-two elephants, each with its Indian driver) against Judas, but hearing that Philip is trying to seize the throne, Lysias comes to terms with the Jews and hastens back home to fight Philip. Soon (chap. 7), Epiphanes's nephew, Demetrius (or Demetrius I),makes himself king and has both Antiochus V and Lysias put to death. Alcimus, "an ungodly Jew" who aspires to be high priest, ingratiates himself with King Demetrius and accuses Judas of sedition. Demetrius sends an army under General Nicanor against Judas. Nicanor's army is defeated, and his head is cut off and displayed in Jerusalem (cf. Judith 13—14).

Hoping to gain support against Demetrius, Judas makes alliance with the Romans (chap. 8), but then dies fighting a huge Syrian army under Bacchides, another of Demetrius's generals. Judas's brother Jonathan becomes leader of the traditionalist Jewish forces, which succeed in compelling Bacchides to withdraw (chap. 9). Alexander Epiphanes (or Balas) now comes forward as king. Both he and Demetrius bid for the Jews' support (chap. 10). The latter side with Alexander, who offers Jonathan the high priesthood. After Demetrius dies in battle, Alexander honors Jonathan, making him provincial governor under the Syrians (10:59–66). Demetrius's son Demetrius II then arrives with an army commanded by Appolonius, which Jonathan's men put to rout, much to the delight of King Alexander.

Next, Ptolemy, king of Egypt, invades the land. In the course of further intrigue, battle, and insurrection, Alexander is killed and Ptolemy dies. Demetrius II becomes king of Syria, and Jonathan pledges allegiance to him; in return, Demetrius awards Jonathan the office of high priesthood and releases the Jews from the requirement of paying taxes. At this point, Trypho, an adherent of the late Alexander, pushes Alexander's son forward as King Antiochus VI, and Jonathan eventually agrees to accept the latter's sovereignty. Miraculously, Jonathan defeats a large army sent by Demetrius II (11:63–74) and attempts to renew relations with Rome and Sparta. But then, through a devious stratagem, Jonathan is captured (and later killed) by Trypho, who now wants to be king himself (chap. 12).

The third Maccabean brother, Simon, is chosen leader of the Jews, and negotiates a treaty with Demetrius II. The treaty results in virtual Jewish independence (ca. 142 B.C.) and the beginning of an ideal, if brief, era under Simon's leadership as high priest and ethnarch (chaps. 13—14). Next, Antiochus VII (son of Demetrius I) bids for the Seleucid throne, but when his initially promising relations with the Jews break down, he sends his commander Cendebeus (Kendebaeus, NEB) to attack them. Simon, now old, appoints his sons Judas and John (or John Hyrcanus) to lead the nation, and they rout the forces of Cendebeus (16:1–10). A certain Ptolemy, evidently hoping to regain the office of high priesthood for his own family, assassinates Simon and two of his sons, but John Hyrcanus survives the plot, kills the assassins, and becomes high priest, ca. 134 B.C..

The first Hasmonean to claim the title of king of the Jews probably was John's successor and son, Aristobulus I (ca. 104–103 B.C.). Thereafter, a quasi-independent Jewish kingdom under Hasmonean rule survived until 63 B.C., when the Romans annexed what they were to call Palestine and made it a province of their own mighty empire.

The period described in 1 Maccabees may well have been the context for other writings that also report persecution of the Jews, their brave resistance, and hopes for the future, such as Esther, Daniel, and Judith. The Jews had not yet reestablished a kingdom, but they had regained their religious freedom. Other traditions and lore purporting to describe events in the early Maccabean period are to be found in 2 and 4 Maccabees.

2 MACCABEES

This writer's main purpose is to encourage his readers (or hearers, 15:39) scrupulously to maintain their Jewish traditions and practices despite both constant temptations to assimilate to the ways of gentile, particularly Greek, culture and the danger of religious persecution. In a somewhat self-conscious preface (cf. prologue to Ecclesiasticus), he states that he is summarizing a detailed five-volume history by an earlier writer, Jason of Cyrene (2:19–32). Jason may have written in the last quarter of the second century B.C., while the anonymous final author of 2 Maccabees possibly composed his summary fifty to seventy-five years later. We may assume that Jason was primarily responsible for the stories and most of the details, while the present author provided most of the commentary and interpretation.

The book begins with what purport to be two letters intended to encourage Jews living in Egypt to observe the festival of Hanukkah, which celebrates the rededication of the temple by Judas Maccabeus in 164 B.C. (1:1—2:18; cf. 1 Macc. 4:36–61). The writer later returns to the temple purification scene, noting that Judas and his followers voted that all Jews should observe this festival each year (10:1–8). Subsequently, they also vote to require celebration of Nicanor's Day, commemorating the defeat of that hated enemy (15:36). (Neither observance, of course, was contained or authorized in the Torah or Mosaic law.) Pious legends about Nehemiah and Jeremiah stress continuity with ancient rituals and artifacts (1:30—2:8), and the writer claims to possess all the old books and records, in order to authenticate his ties to earlier tradition (2:13–15).

The main narrative (3:1—15:37) covers the relatively brief period from the time of the high priest Onias III to Judas's defeat of Nicanor (ca. 180–160 B.C.) and tells the story of traditionalist Judaism's struggle for survival and religious freedom against Syrian oppression. Judas is still alive and is the main leader of the Jews ("Israel") at the close of the book (cf. 1 Macc. 9:14–22).

Some information adds to that given in 1 Maccabees, such as descriptions of the corruption of the high priests Jason and Menelaus and the apostate zeal of these and other priests for Hellenistic (Greek) culture, for example, their enthusiasm for the gymnasium, the Greek hat, the wrestling arena, and the discus—to the neglect of their proper priestly duties (4:7–34). But generally 2 Maccabees is not viewed as reliable history. The author passes along several legendary stories illustrative of the importance of fidelity to Jewish religion and of God's power to deliver his people, such as the stories of Heliodorus's attempt to plunder the temple bank (chap. 3), the martyrdom of Eleazar (6:18–31) and of the seven brothers and their mother (chap. 7) for refusing to eat pork, and Razis's death at his own hand for the sake of Judaism (14:37–46). Apparitions—typically featuring gold-clad horsemen and golden weapons—regularly inspire faithful Jews and terrify their enemies (e.g. 3:24–30; 5:1–4; 11:18). The author's perspective is suggested at 11:13: "The Hebrews were invincible because the mighty God fought on their side." As in Judith, the focal interest is preservation of the "holy place," the temple (15:17–18). Throughout, the author presents incidents demonstrating that God punishes oppressors of the Jews, but defends the latter—at least those who remain true to the law (e.g., 8:38; 10:38). Numerous episodes concern the Jews' slaughtering gentile enemies pursuant to the will of God (e.g., 12:1–28). The writer interjects numerous interpretive comments, somewhat along the lines of the Deuteronomic and wisdom theologies, to the effect that God brings disaster on Jews who commit idolatry, and that individuals suffer because they have sinned (e.g., 6:12–16; 7:18, 32; 8:36; 12:40–42).

The book contains a number of other points of religious interest. Here we see several instances of belief in the future resurrection of martyrs, and, perhaps, of other righteous Jews (e.g., 7:9, 14; 14:46; cf. Dan. 12:2–3). The living may make atonement for the dead by prayer and offerings, looking to their resurrection (12:43–45); and certain righteous dead are visualized as praying for the benefit of Jews who are alive (15:12–14). Throughout most of the period described here, Jews refrain from fighting on the Sabbath, sometimes to their detriment (e.g., 5:25–26; 6:11; 8:26), but eventually Judas is granted the vision of a golden sword, apparently understood to authorize doing battle on Sabbath days (chap. 15). As in Tobit, burial, including a magnificent funeral, is a matter of great importance (4:49; cf. 5:10; 13:7). The temple's function as a bank of deposit is noted (3:10–21; cf. 4 Macc. 4:3–10). Second Maccabees contains the first references to "Judaism" (2:21; 14:38)—which accords with the book's emphasis on keeping Jewish tradition—and refers in passing to belief in God's creation of the world out of nothing (7:28; cf. Gen. 1:1–2). Two distinctive religious developments appear frequently. One is the common use of the term "holy" for entities other than God: the holy city (3:1); the holy place or temple (e.g., 5:15, 17); holy vessels (5:16); the holy Sabbath day (5:25; 6:11); the holy book (8:23); and the holy people (15:24). The other is the use of new and special titles or circumlocutions for the name of God. He is not only the Most High (3:31), but also the Sovereign of spirits (3:24), the Savior of one's life (3:35), Creator of all things or of the world (7:23; 13:14), the Defender of the Jews or their nation (8:36; 14:34), the Great Sovereign of the world (12:15), the King of kings (13:4), and the Sovereign in heaven (15:4). The most frequently used title is simply the Almighty.

3 MACCABEES

Unlike the other books of the Maccabees, the present writing contains no references to the Maccabean period. Instead, it purports to tell about the harrowing experiences of traditionalist Jews in Egypt during the reign of that nation's "audacious" (and intermittently befuddled) ruler, Ptolemy Philopater. Though a king by that name did rule Egypt, ca. 220–203 B.C., it is more likely that 3 Maccabees reflects the experience of Jews, possibly in Egypt, during the course of the next two or three centuries. The precipitating incident in the plot is Ptolemy's thwarted attempt to enter the "Holy of holies," that is, the inner temple at Jerusalem. According to 2 Maccabees, one Heliodorus entered the temple to plunder bank deposits ca. 175 B.C.—a story similar in several respects to that in 3 Maccabees about Ptolemy (2 Macc. 3:8–40; cf. 3 Macc. 1:8—2:23). Antiochus Epiphanes entered the Holy of holies ca. 170 B.C. in order to take its treasures; the Roman general Pompey entered it in 63 B.C.; and the mad Roman emperor Caligula proposed to erect a statue of himself there ca. A.D. 40. Which of these episodes may be reflected here is uncertain. Several interpreters think that 3 Maccabees was written in the first century A.D. Though present in some important ancient biblical manuscripts, 3 Maccabees was omitted in Jerome's Vulgate and does not appear in Western Bibles other than the NOAB. It is included in the Scriptures of the Eastern Orthodox churches. For an alternate translation and additional commentary, see OTP 2/509–29.

The story line is relatively simple, in contrast to the complexities of 1 or 2 Maccabees. Here, Ptolemy, while touring shrines around his realm, develops a compulsion to enter the Holy of holies—which was supposedly barred not only to Gentiles, but to everyone other than the high priest (1:11–15). In response to the anguished cries of the faithful and the prayer of Simon, the high priest, God intervenes, shaking and temporarily paralyzing the audacious and profane Ptolemy (1:16—2:24). Later, back in Egypt, and egged on by his drinking companions, this impious king resolves to take revenge by harassing Jews both in Alexandria and in the countryside. Still smarting because he has been prevented from entering the inner temple, and further enraged at what he perceives as the Jews' subsequent ingratitude (i.e., their refusal to renounce Judaism in exchange for initiation into the mystery cults), Ptolemy orders his soldiers to arrest all the Jews in Egypt, so that he may inflict "sure and shameful death" upon them (chap. 3). Amid the joyous shouts of the bloodthirsty Gentiles, the Jews are rounded up and herded into a large racetrack or amphitheater known as the hippodrome, to be tortured and destroyed (chap. 4). The king orders Hermon to drug the five hundred elephants of which he is in charge so that they will be all the more ferocious when they charge the bound and hapless Jews the next day. The Jews cry to their God and Father in heaven, who then sends the king into such a deep sleep that the hour appointed for their destruction passes, and they are spared, for the time being. The eager crowd of would-be spectators eventually arouses the king, but instead of getting on with the bloodshed, he resumes drinking and calls on all his guests to join in. The Jews' execution is then rescheduled for the next day.

Next morning, however, again answering the Jews' entreaties, God confuses Ptolemy's mind, so that he forgets his evil design, and instead, threatens Hermon and his other officials for plotting against the Jews, whom he praises for their "full and firm loyalty." Later, however, Ptolemy reconvenes the party and demands to know why Hermon has not yet sent the elephants to trample the Jews. He then reschedules their destruction for the following day. But, when his officers complain that he is treating them like idiots by his frequent changes of orders, Ptolemy swears that he will get on with the massacre immediately. The thundering herd of elephants, again maddened by substance ingestion (5:45–48; cf. 5:1–3 and 1 Macc. 6:34), now charges towards the hippodrome, while "countless masses" of depraved Gentiles surge in, eager to witness the impending gory spectacle (chap. 5). An old priest named Eleazer (cf. 2 Macc. 6:18–31) now calls at length (6:2–15) on God to remember the descendants of Abraham and "the sainted Jacob" (6:3; cf. Prayer of Azariah v. 12), as he had done in the days of Pharaoh, Sennacherib, Daniel and his three friends, and Jonah. (Jonah here is regarded as a model of piety; cf. his characterization in the Book of Jonah.) When all the Jews raise a great cry to heaven, the sound terrifies the Egyptian army (which has been following the elephants into the hippodrome), and when two fearful angels suddenly appear, the great beasts turn round, trampling many of the Egyptian troops to death. The king now repents of his wicked scheme, blames it all on his officials, orders the Jews released from their bonds, and gives provisions for a seven-day festival so that the Jews might celebrate their deliverance. The king also holds a great banquet in celebration of the occasion, and grants the Jews' petition that they be allowed to return to their homes (chap. 6).

Chapter 7 reports the king's letter to all his officials, in which he professes his faith in God, and blames the plot against the Jews on certain malicious "friends" or officials in his court (7:1–9; cf. Add. to Esther 16:1–14). Before departing, the Jews request and receive permission to massacre fellow Jews who have transgressed the law, which they proceed to do joyfully, praising God. Finally, the good traditionalist Jews return home safely, there to enjoy great prestige and recover all their property.

Like the writer of 2 Maccabees, the present author characterizes the temple as the holy place (1:23; 2:14), and faithful Jews or Israel as holy people (2:6; cf. Ezra 9:2). He introduces even more new or uncommon titles for God than are found in 2 Maccabees. Some of the more unusual are as follows: Ruler over the whole Creation (2:7), the First Father of all (2:21), Ruler of all Power (5:7; 7:9), Almighty God Most High and King of Great Power (6:2), Eternal One (6:12), Honored One (6:13), the Eternal Savior of Israel (7:18), and the Deliverer of Israel (7:23). God's providence is implicit in several such titles, in certain explicit expressions (e.g., at 4:19–21; 5:30), and in the story as a whole. The book's implicit message seems to be that God will deliver faithful Jews who call on him, even when there is no hope in sight. Deliverance is conceived of as providential rescue of the living from torment and death, rather than as the resurrection of the

righteous (cf. 2 Maccabees) or the reward of eternal life (cf. 4 Maccabees).

4 MACCABEES

Fourth Maccabees has not been accorded full canonical status in any
known Jewish or Christian Bibles, but is found in the appendix section
of Greek Orthodox Scriptures. Many early Christian bishops and
theologians found the book inspiring, if not authoritative, and frequently cited it with approval. It consists largely of an elaboration
upon the stories of the martyrdom of Eleazer and of the anonymous
seven brothers and their anonymous mother that appeared earlier in 2
Maccabees 6:18—7:42. Here these stories are retold and embellished
in order to illustrate the present author's concern, which is to present
Judaism as a reputable philosophy, and demonstrate that Jews who,
through reason, control their emotions and thereby remain faithful to
the law, will be rewarded—at least if they die as martyrs—with
immortality or eternal life. Like 3 Maccabees, 4 Maccabees is included in the standard editions of the Pseudepigrapha. See OTP
2/531—64 for another modern translation and detailed commentary and
notes.

The author's characterization of Judaism as a philosophy recalls
Philo's and Josephus's attempts to so represent it, in order to find an
acceptable place for it in the world of Greek culture. The present
author reflects acquaintance with Platonic and Stoic concepts, but is
concerned to stress the necessity of keeping strict Jewish tradition at
all cost by refusing to eat pork and food previously sacrificed to idols
(cf. 1 Cor. 8:1–13; 10:14—11:1). Repeatedly, he relates reason to
Jewish law, at times equating the two. Both reason and law function
to control or restrain the emotions, which include, particularly, pleasure and pain, and affect both body and soul (1:20) and also brotherly
and maternal love (14:1, 20; 15:20). Virtue, self-control, and knowledge also figure frequently in the writer's argument. His basic position
is that Jews, who know that eternal life awaits those who keep the law
zealously, act with reason when they preserve their virtue by fidelity
to the law, notwithstanding the prospect of torture and death for
so doing. (See esp. the homilies in chaps. 1—2; 13; 16; and 18.)
Clearly, the writer's intention is to summon fellow Jews to keep the
law and tradition despite persecution (see, e.g., 17:8–10; 18:1–2).
The emphasis on persecution suggests that the writer lived at a time
when Jews were seriously threatened for practicing their religion. The

rather persuasive arguments advanced by "the tyrant Antiochus" (5:5–13; 8:5–14) may contain echoes of real controversies in the author's time. The book, probably written in Greek, seems dependent on 2 Maccabees, and dates from some time between the late second century B.C. and A.D. 120. Jews were subjected to persecution or other forms of hostility several times during those years under Seleucid and Roman authorities.

The embellished accounts of the martyrs purportedly illustrate the supremacy of reason over the emotions. Reason, however, is understood broadly as "devout reason" (16:1, 4). Thus the martyrs undergo torture and death not so much for the sake of reason as such, as for their religion, or that of their fathers (6:22; 9:7, 29; cf. 11:21), or just plain "religion" (9:24; 13:27; 16:13); the law, or their ancestral law (6:27, 30; 16:16); virtue (11:2; cf. 9:18); or God (16:19). They thereby serve and vindicate "the way of the Hebrew people" and their nation (17:9–10).

Unlike 2 Maccabees, which looks for the *resurrection* of the martyrs (if not of all the righteous who have died), 4 Maccabees gives assurances that those martyred for keeping the law will enjoy *immortality* or *everlasting life* with God in the presence of Abraham, Isaac, Jacob, and other patriarchs who, though they have died, "live in God" (e.g., 5:37; 7:19; 13:17; 16:25; cf. Mark 12:26–27). The martyrs, the author tells us, now stand before the divine throne (17:18; cf. Rev. 20:4–6). Fourth Maccabees 10:15 suggests that all pious Jews will experience everlasting life when they die. Jews who transgress the commandments of God, however, face the prospect of eternal torment by fire (13:15; cf. Isa. 66:24; Rev. 14:9–11). The wicked oppressors of the Jews also will suffer eternal torment by fire and otherwise (9:9; 12:12; cf. Jth. 16:17; Rev. 20:10). Some other possible echoes of 2 and 4 Maccabees appear in the Book of Revelation.

Several passages suggest that God might accept the martyrs' deaths in exchange for those of the rest of the Jewish people (6:28–29; 17:21–22; 18:4). The underlying rationale is similar to that of the Deuteronomic theology of history: when God's people break the commandments, he will punish them for doing so. Here the idea seems to be that God might accept the deaths of some, rather than punish all. The writer explains that God ("the Divine Justice") moved Antiochus to oppress the Jews because—under the influence of the wicked high priest Jason—they had changed their ways in favor of Hellenism, even to the extent of abandoning the temple service (4:17–21; cf. 2 Macc. 4:7–20). Prior to that time, they enjoyed peace and prosperity because they observed the law (3:20). Thus, unlike the author of Revelation, the writer does not invoke cosmic dualism in order to explain the disasters that befall the martyrs and other righteous persons. There is no mention of Satan in this connection. Instead, the writer understands that Antiochus has received his kingdom from God (12:11). Consistent with this affirmation of God's universal sovereignty, the author refers to him three times as Providence (9:24; 13:19; 17:22). This God is not only Creator of all things (11:5), but also Ruler over all history. One passage probably does refer to a demonic figure, "the destroyer, the deceitful serpent," in the limited role of one who goes about defiling the virginity of young women (18:8; cf. that of the demon Asmodeus in Tob. 3:7–8).

The mother of the seven brothers receives special attention in 4 Maccabees. The writer mentions, in passing, that "mothers are the weaker sex" (15:5), but then goes on to praise this mother in striking terms. She is "mother of the nation, vindicator of the law, and champion of religion" (15:29). Moreover, she is "more noble than males in steadfastness, and more manly than men in endurance!" (15:30), a "soldier of God in the cause of religion" and an "elder" (16:14). Clearly she is exemplar par excellence of the kind of "reason" the author commends to all his Jewish readers.

PSALM 151

The current edition of the *New Oxford Annotated Bible with Apocrypha* (NOAB) includes two versions of Psalm 151. The longer is translated from the Hebrew version in the Dead Sea Scrolls (DSS), the shorter is from the Septuagint (LXX). No other modern Western Bible contains this psalm (or 3 and 4 Maccabees), but it was present in several important Septuagint manuscripts, and the LXX version of Psalm 151 (along with 3 Maccabees) is recognized as fully canonical in Bibles of the Eastern Orthodox churches, where it appears at the end of the Book of Psalms. The DSS version, which is in Hebrew, seems to have been part of the Scriptures of the Qumran sect. A Syriac version of Psalm 151 was also found among the Dead Sea Scrolls. The psalm probably was first composed sometime between ca. 200 B.C. and A.D. 70.

Both the DSS and LXX versions of this short psalm take the form of an autobiographical statement by David, which might be paraphrased as follows: I was smaller and younger than my brothers; I tended my father's flock; my hands and fingers fashioned a lyre to play for the glory of God, who sent his messenger or prophet to take me from following the flock and anoint me; even though my brothers were tall and handsome, the Lord did not choose them.

Verses 3, 4, and 7b of the DSS version are without parallels in the LXX version. The last two verses of the LXX version, which refer to David's encounter with "the Philistine" (presumably Goliath), may have paralleled a description of the encounter found at the beginning of another psalm that follows immediately afterwards in the DSS, identified in OTP as Psalm 151B. Psalm 151 contains several echoes of passages and events in 1 Samuel 16 and 17. Some of the psalms ascribed to David in the Book of Psalms are set in particular situations in the course of his career (e.g., Psalms 56; 59; 60; 63; captions included in NOAB but omitted in NEB), but these are in the form of prayers to God for deliverance from personal or national enemies generally, rather than autobiographical reminiscences. Four additional psalms found among the Dead Sea Scrolls in Syriac and Hebrew versions are included in the OTP as Psalms 152; 153; 154; and 155.

THE NEW TESTAMENT,
OR CANONICAL
EARLY CHRISTIAN WRITINGS

AN OVERVIEW

The Bible of the early Christian churches was the same as that of their Jewish contemporaries, namely, the collection of writings known among later Christians as the Old Testament (OT). Both Jews and Christians during the first century A.D. mainly used the Greek translation of the OT, the Septuagint (and other Greek versions), which included most of the writings contained in what later was called the OT Apocrypha. There was as yet no New Testament, and no one yet referred to the Old Testament. The earliest references to an Old and a New Testament appeared ca. A.D. 200, but it was not until near the end of the fourth century that Christians generally agreed on which writings were to be included in this supplement to their earlier Scriptures.

The term New Testament is a misleading translation of Hebrew and Greek expressions meaning a "new covenant." Jeremiah had looked for the time when God would make a new covenant with Israel and Judah, one written on people's hearts (Jer. 31:31–34; cf. 32:38–40; Hos. 2:18–20; Ezek. 11:19–20). The Book of Hebrews draws directly on the Jeremiah passage in characterizing the new covenant Christians have with God (Heb. 8:8–12; 10:16–17; cf. 1 Cor. 11:25), arguing that Christ mediates better promises and a better covenant (Heb. 8:7, 13; 9:15; 12:24). In the course of time, the term was extended to refer to Christian writings that, in general terms, described this new covenant, and in time came to be regarded as Scripture.

By ca. A.D. 140, if not earlier, many Christians came to regard Paul's letters as authoritative writings, if not Scripture, and as a supplement to the OT (see 2 Pet. 3:15–16). Marcion was the first Christian known to have proposed the creation of an entire new set of

Scriptures for Christianity, ca. A.D. 140. He observed that the God described in Jewish Scriptures delighted in bloody sacrifices and revenge, and concluded that this God must be evil by nature, since he had created such an evil world as the one in which humans were condemned to live. He rejected both the God of Judaism and its Scripture. Instead, he urged Christians to worship Jesus, a previously unknown God, and to use as Scripture his own edited version of Luke's Gospel and some of Paul's letters. Marcion's radical proposal (which in time other Christians rejected as heretical), along with other deviant, and generally gnostic, teachings and writings,* prompted Christian leaders to begin to try to identify precisely the writings that were to be considered authoritative or canonical for the faith and life of their growing communities. Bishops and other church fathers such as Irenaeus, Tertullian, Origen, and Eusebius tried to distinguish canonical from noncanonical writings, beginning in the late second century and on into the first part of the fourth. Some authorities included writings that eventually were excluded from the canon, such as the *Gospel* and the *Revelation of Peter*, *1* and *2 Clement*, the *Shepherd of Hermas*, and the *Epistle of Barnabas*, while omitting several writings that ultimately were included, such as the Gospel according to John, Colossians, Hebrews, James, 1 and 2 Peter, 2 and 3 John, Jude, and Revelation. By the end of the fourth century, Christians had all but reached universal agreement that the New Testament (NT) canon would consist of its present twenty-seven books. At least officially, then and ever since, Christians have also agreed, against Marcion, that the OT would remain part of their Scripture as well.

Paul's letters, probably the earliest NT writings, were composed between A.D. 50 and 60. If a written source Q existed (see below), it may have been set down as early as ca. A.D. 40, but no such document is extant. The Gospel according to Mark could have been written as early as A.D. 60. The latest NT writings probably are 1 and 2 Timothy and Titus (the Pastoral letters), ca. A.D. 110–20; Jude, ca. A.D. 120–40; and 2 Peter, ca. A.D. 140. The other Gospels are generally dated between A.D. 70 and 100, and the other NT writings between ca. 90 and 110.

The NT writings eventually were arranged according to the following scheme. First, the Gospels, taken together, report on Jesus' birth,

---

*Several such writings turned up in Egypt in the late 1940s. See James M. Robinson, ed., *The Nag Hammadi Library in English* (San Francisco: Harper & Row, 1977). Extracanonical "gospels" have also been collected in modern editions of the New Testament Apocrypha (see p. 103).

public ministry or activity and teaching, and his trial, death, and early resurrection appearances. Next comes Acts, which describes Christianity's growth from Jerusalem and its environs into a universal religion, open to Gentiles (non–Jews) as well as Jews. Then follow Paul's letters—or those believed to have been written by Paul— arranged in approximate order of length: the longest (Romans) first, then the next longest (1 Corinthians), on down to the shortest (Philemon). (First and Second Timothy, however, are longer than some of the letters that precede them.) Next come letters attributed to other writers, again beginning with the longest (Hebrews), followed by the next longest (James), and ending with Jude, the shortest of the non-Pauline letters apart from 2 and 3 John, which are grouped with 1 John. These non-Pauline letters generally deal with problems arising in the churches a decade or more after Paul's time. Finally, the NT closes with the Book of Revelation, which probably was written in response to the persecution of Asian Christians ca. A.D. 96, and looks for the return of Jesus and the beginning of the new age of salvation in their near future.

The first three Gospels are called the Synoptic Gospels because when "read or seen together," they present similar accounts of Jesus' message and activity. Some interpreters urge that Matthew was the earliest Gospel, and that Mark and Luke based their versions on it. Most interpreters, however, view Mark as the earliest Gospel, and suggest that Matthew and Luke both used its narrative framework and many of its sayings when writing their own Gospels. Approximately two hundred verses consisting mainly of Jesus' sayings that do not appear in Mark are found in both Matthew and Luke. Most interpreters agree that these verses derived from an earlier written or oral source commonly called Q. The exact extent of the Q material is unknown, however, since, if there was such a source, we can only identify its contents when both Matthew and Luke drew from it. Neither Matthew nor Luke necessarily used all of it, and either may have drawn on it at times when the other did not. Thus some sayings found only in Matthew or only in Luke may also have come from Q. Many, but not all, interpreters believe that Matthew had an additional special source (M) and that Luke had his special source (L). Interpreters also generally credit the evangelists with the composition of some verses and the editorial revision or modification of others. The synoptic evangelists, then, may be seen not only as collectors and editors or redactors, but also as authors of some of the traditions we find in their Gospels. Luke is generally regarded as the author/editor of the Book of Acts. Evidently when the Gospel according to John was included, it was placed after the Synoptic Gospels, and so comes between the two volumes of Luke-Acts. John's Gospel has a few features in common with the Synoptics, but for the most part gives a rather different account of the course of events in Jesus' ministry, and a very different account of his sayings and his self-understanding.

Most of the Pauline letters were written to churches which Paul himself had founded, and dealt with problems there about which he had learned. The exceptions are Romans, his own theological letter of introduction to this significant church which he had neither founded nor, as yet, visited, and his letter to Philemon, a person who, under his influence, had converted to Christianity. Interpreters use the term Deutero-Pauline to refer to Ephesians, Colossians, and sometimes 2 Thessalonians: letters which purport to have been written by Paul, but may well have been composed by associates or followers of Paul, using his name. We learn from 2 Thess. 2:1–2 that people other than Paul had already been writing letters in Paul's name. Many interpreters think that Paul did write one or more of these letters. Few, however, believe that Paul wrote 1 and 2 Timothy and Titus. These may have been composed by someone who wished to invoke Paul's authority in dealing with problems of the early second century, notably those presented by deviant doctrines and questionable moral standards among the churches and their leadership.

Most of the non-Pauline letters were written as treatises or tracts for the guidance and instruction of Christians during the late first and early second centuries A.D. They are commonly called "catholic" or general epistles, since they were addressed, in effect, to all Christians everywhere. Possible exceptions are 1 Peter, which was addressed to churches in certain provinces of Asia Minor, 2 John, which may have been written to a particular church, and 3 John, which is in the form of a letter to a single person, Gaius. Revelation might be considered in this connection, also, since it was addressed to seven churches all in the Roman province of Asia, and may not have been intended for Christians elsewhere. Other than Hebrews, whose writer remains anonymous, the other non-Pauline letters purport to have been authored by (or were later attributed to) persons who had been apostles of Jesus (Peter and John), or else his brothers (James and Jude).

The term Christian is rarely used in the NT (only in Acts 11:26; 26:28; and 1 Pet. 4:16), and the term Christianity does not appear at all. The NT writers used a wide variety of terms to name the adherents of the new religion and the religion itself. Acts frequently refers to followers of "the Way" (Acts 9:2; 18:26; 24:14; cf. John 14:6; Heb. 10:20). Other common terms for Christians are "(the) brethren" (Acts. 15:1, 23; 28:14; 1 Cor. 7:29; 10:1; Phil. 3:1; 1 Thess. 5:25–27; Heb. 3:1; James 2:1, 14; 3:1; cf. Philem. 2, "our sister") and "the saints" (Acts 26:10; Rom. 1:7; 2 Cor. 1:1, 8; Eph. 3:18; Jude 3). Somewhat less common terms for Christians are "believers" (Acts 16:1; 1 Tim. 6:2; Heb. 4:3), "the elect" (2 Tim. 2:8; 2 John 1, 13), those "of the truth" (John 18:37; 1 John 3:19), "beloved" (1 Pet. 4:12; 1 John 3:2; 4:1; Jude vv. 3, 20), "children" or "little children" (1 John 2:1, 12, 28; 3:7), and "children of God" (1 John 3:1–2, 10; 5:1). Christians are also referred to as those "called to belong to Jesus Christ" (Rom. 1:6) and "friends" (3 John 15). Christianity is known variously as "the faith" (Col. 1:23; 2:6; 1 Tim. 3:9; Titus 1:13; Jude v. 3), or "our faith" (1 John 5:4), "the truth" (John 8:31–32; 2 Tim. 3:8; 2 John 4; 3 John 3–4, 8; Jude v. 3, "the mystery" (Eph. 3:3–4, 9; 6:19), "(our) religion" (1 Tim. 3:16; 2 Tim. 3:5), "the doctrine" (2 John 9), "the brotherhood" (1 Pet. 3:17), and "the way of truth" or of "righteousness" (2 Pet. 2:2, 21). As a convenience, we shall use the terms Christian and Christianity in the following chapters, *as if* these terms had already been current during the NT period.

THE NEW TESTAMENT

MATTHEW

Early Christian tradition attributes this writing to Matthew, presumably the apostle named at 9:9 and 10:3. Some time has passed between the events and this report: note the phrase "to this day" at 27:8 and 28:15. The author's apparent use of Mark (written ca. A.D. 60–70) and probable reference to the destruction of Jerusalem (22:7) date the book after A.D. 70, perhaps as late as A.D. 90. (Some modern scholars nevertheless urge that Matthew's was the earliest Gospel.) Its use by Ignatius of Antioch (ca. A.D. 110) and the prominence assigned to Peter (16:18–19) suggest that it was written in Antioch, Syria, where Peter may have been a leading figure.

Matthew evidently reproduces Mark's narrative, adding, at the beginning, Jesus' genealogy and stories about his birth, the wise men, and Herod (chaps. 1—2), and at the end, stories about the appearance of the risen Jesus to the Marys and to the eleven (28:9–20). Within Mark's narrative framework, Matthew presents five collections of Jesus' sayings, each concluding with an editorial statement marking the end of the sayings and the resumption of narrative (5:1—7:29; 9:35—11:1; 13:1–53; 18:1—19:1; 23:1—26:1). The first collection is the famous Sermon on the Mount (cf. the "sermon on the plain" in Luke 6:17—7:1). Matthew also has collected and arranged several subgroups of sayings, for example, the "antitheses" or sayings about the law ("You have heard that it was said, . . . But I say to you. . . ." 5:21–48), and sayings about practicing piety (6:1–18), John the Baptist and himself (11:2–19), the kingdom of God (13:18–50), and the coming judgment (24:36—25:46). Numerous sayings are given twice, usually with slight variations, such as sayings on the excision of bodily members that cause sin (5:29–30; 18:8–9; cf. 19:12); divorce and remarriage (5:31–32; 19:3–9); good and bad trees and their respective fruit (7:16–20; 12:33); God's desire for mercy rather than sacrifice (9:13; 12:7); the sign of Jonah (12:39–41; 16:4); and the disciples' authority to bind and loose (16:19; 18:18). These considerations indicate that Matthew meant his writing (later called a Gospel) as a complete account of Jesus' ministry and message, which could guide and instruct the Christian community for which he prepared it on matters of belief and conduct. Interpreters generally agree that this was a Jewish Christian community, that is, a community of Christians who had been, and in some ways still were, Jews.

All the earliest Christians had been Jews. Matthew's Gospel shows that the place of Jewish law in the Christian life of that age had not yet been resolved (cf. Galatians). Here, Jesus not only commands observance of the written law (5:17–19), but also requires obedience to the oral law (tradition) of the Pharisees (23:2–3, 23). At the outset (1:1) Matthew states that Jesus is descended from Abraham, thus a Jew, and from David, thus qualified to be the Messiah (Christ), a term that had meaning only in Jewish circles. Throughout the Gospel, Matthew sees events associated with Jesus as fulfilled messianic prophecies (e.g., 1:22–23; 2:5–6, 17–18; 3:3). Yet clearly Matthew rejects the leadership of the scribes and Pharisees (23:2–33); instead, the church is to be guided by the will of God as set forth in the words of Jesus (7:21–29), which require a standard of righteousness beyond that affirmed by the scribes and Pharisees (5:20–28). Interpreters suggest that Matthew organized Jesus' sayings into the five collections following the model of Moses' "five books" of the law. Thus Matthew's Jesus is a new or second Moses; he is the authoritative teacher as to what God requires of those who would enter his kingdom.

As in Mark, Jesus proclaims that the kingdom of God is near and calls his hearers to repent before the Son of man comes to judge the world (4:17; 24:29–44); he casts out demons, heals the sick (8:1–6), and sends his twelve disciples to extend this mission of preaching, exorcism, and healing to all Jews or "Israel" (10:1–15). Matthew 10:23 even suggests that Jesus expects the parousia (the coming of the son of man and beginning of the kingdom of God or messianic age) to occur before the Twelve return. Later, after their return, Jesus "feeds" his followers the meal of bread and fish in the wilderness (chaps. 14; 15), perhaps to consecrate them for the joys of life together in the coming kingdom (cf., e.g., Matt. 6:11; 8:11; 26:29, which refer to the prospect of eating and drinking together there). As in Mark, Jesus then turns to Jerusalem to purify the temple, preach, eat the Last Supper with the Twelve, suffer, die, and be raised from the dead (chaps. 16—28).

Matthew emphasizes Jesus' miraculous or supernatural power. Jesus *did not* do many mighty works in his own country (13:59; cf. Mark 6:5); when he "cursed" the fig tree, it withered *at once* (21:19; cf. Mark 11:20); and he fed not only five and four thousand *men* but also unnumbered *women and children* (14:21; 15:38; cf. Mark 6:44; 8:9).

Matthew also stresses the coming judgment and the fate of the unrighteous. He alone depicts the great judgment scene (25:31–46). More than any other gospel-writer, he underscores the punishment awaiting the condemned in eternal fire or "outer darkness," where there will be "weeping and gnashing of teeth" (8:12; 13:42, 50; 22:13; 24:51; 25:30, 41, 46).

A further characteristic is Matthew's concern to reinterpret certain problematic sayings found in Mark. Thus Matthew's Jesus does *not* deny that he is good (19:16–17; cf. Mark 10:17–18); it is the *mother* of James and John who asks that they be given special status in the coming kingdom (20:20–21; cf. Mark 10:35–37); divorce *is* allowed in cases of unchastity (5:32; 19:9; cf. Mark 10:11–12). In these and other ways, Matthew gave his community a record of Jesus' words and deeds that could guide their faith and life at that time and, as it turned out, in the following centuries. During the course of these centuries Christians placed it first not only among the Gospels, but among all the writings they came to call the New Testament.

MARK

This Gospel, written ca. A.D. 60–70, perhaps in Rome, was intended for gentile (non-Jewish) Christians, as is evidenced by the author's numerous explanations of Jesus' Aramaic expressions and of Jewish practices (e.g., at 5:41; 7:3–4, 34; 15:34). Although no writer is identified in the text, the book has been captioned "According to Mark" since the second century. (The term "gospel," meaning "good news," represents a later addition to the title.) None of Jesus' twelve disciples was named Mark (cf. Acts 12:12); interpreters sometimes suggest that the author may have been the young man mentioned at 14:51–52. The author is traditionally called Mark.

Mark describes Jesus' adult activity or career, beginning with his baptism by John and ending with the empty tomb (16:8). This Gospel is characterized by a sense of urgency and mystery. Terms such as "immediately" and "and" continuously drive the narration forward. Mystery and wonder are expressed not only in the Gospel's abrupt conclusion, but in the "messianic secret," the repeated amazement of the crowds (1:27; 2:12; 7:37; 11:18), the disciples' lack of comprehension (4:10–13, 38–41; 8:16–21; 9:6, 32), and Jesus' announcements of the impending suffering ("passion"), death, and resurrection of "the Son of man"—with whom he only indirectly identifies himself (8:31; 9:31; 10:32–34).

Mark describes two periods in Jesus' career. In the first, Jesus summons his hearers to repent, for the kingdom of God has come near (1:15). He teaches, casts out demons, and heals the afflicted; he sends his disciples to preach, exorcise, and heal; he feeds multitudes with bread and fish; and he argues with the Pharisees. Near Caesarea Philippi, he asks his disciples who they think he is, and Peter answers, "The Messiah," whereupon Jesus tells them "to tell no one about him" (8:27–30). He then begins teaching his followers that the Son of man—and perhaps many of them—must suffer and die before the kingdom of God and the Son of man will be revealed, but that the parousia will occur while some of them are still alive (8:31—9:1; cf. 13:9–32).

In the second phase, Jesus moves with his disciples toward Jerusalem, exorcising demons and teaching the twelve and others as he goes (chaps. 9—10). He enters Jerusalem on a colt amid his followers' enthusiastic shouts (11:7–10; cf. Zech. 9:9), takes charge of the temple area (11:15–17; cf. Mal. 3:1–3; Zech. 14:21b), and teaches there for several days, arguing with the religious authorities (11:27—13:1; cf. 14:49). A woman anoints him with ointment; and Judas leaves in order to betray him (14:1–11). Jesus eats the Passover with the twelve, looking forward to the time when he will drink wine in the kingdom of God (14:12–25). Then he goes to Gethsemane with the twelve and prays, and there he is betrayed by Judas, arrested, tried before a night session of the Council or Sanhedrin, and handed over to the Romans, who execute him in the morning as "King of the Jews" (14:43—15:30). On the cross, he begins to repeat the Twenty-second Psalm in Aramaic, and soon afterward, dies (15:33–39). He is buried, but on the third day, the women find his tomb empty, and flee in astonishment, saying nothing to anyone about it—"for they were afraid" (16:8).

The question of Mark's historical value has often been debated since it has come to be widely regarded as the earliest Gospel. Many scholars consider it a reliable account of Jesus' message and the pattern (if not precise sequence) of events during his public activity; others view it primarily as an expression of Mark's theological interests. Controversy has centered especially on the "messianic secret" (Jesus' warnings to tell no one about him, e.g., at 1:44; 3:12; 8:30); the passion pronouncements; and the Marcan "apocalypse" (chap. 13). Several warnings in chap. 13 indicate that although some time would lapse before the parousia (appearance or arrival) of the Son of man, he would indeed come before the complete passing of the generation of Jesus' followers (13:30; cf. 8:38—9:1). Mark evidently wanted his contemporaries (ca. A.D. 60–70) to understand that the Son of man could come at any time, so they must "watch" in constant readiness for that event (13:32–37).

Among Mark's concerns, two are particularly prominent: to encourage Christians to believe in Jesus', or God's, power to deliver the faithful from danger, demons, or illness (e.g., 1:32–34, 40; 4:37–41; 5:34, 36; 13:9–27); and to urge them to hope and prepare for the coming of the Son of man, the time of judgment, and eternal life in the coming kingdom of God (8:34—9:1; 10:17–31; 13:9–37).

Modern editions of the Bible sometimes include verses 9–20 at the end of chap. 16 (see the RSV marginal notes). According to these added verses, the risen Jesus appears to Mary Magdalene, then to two of the disciples, and afterwards to the eleven, commanding them to preach the gospel to "the whole creation" (cf. Matt. 28:16–20). He commends belief and baptism as the way to salvation (cf. John 3:5), and promises that his adherents will handle serpents (cf. Isa. 11:8–9) and drink poison without being harmed. Finally, he ascends to heaven (cf. Tob. 12:20; Luke 24:51; Acts 1:9–11). Some interpreters believe that Mark originally ended with 16:8; others think that more followed, but has been lost. Perhaps a majority of interpreters conclude that the Gospel originally ended at 16:8. The most reliable early manuscripts end here, and nearly all modern scholars agree that vv. 9–20 and the alternative or additional two verses contained in various other versions are secondary. The abrupt ending at v. 8 accords with the terse narrative style and the element of mystery seen throughout Mark's Gospel.

LUKE

This is the first of a two-volume history of Jesus and the early church, sometimes referred to as Luke-Acts. The author may have been the physician named in Col. 4:14, but this is not known. (Luke does not clearly show more interest in Jesus' healing procedures than the other evangelists do.) He probably was a Gentile, writing for gentile Christians and also, perhaps, for the edification of non-Christian gentile readers, symbolized by Theophilus (1:3; Acts 1:1). Luke evidently wrote after the destruction of Jerusalem in A.D. 70 (see 19:41–44; 21:20, 24), perhaps as late as A.D. 90.

Luke, a second-generation Christian (1:1–2), sets out to write an "orderly account" (1:3) and gives many dates and other pieces of information, some of which may be accurate (e.g., 2:1–2; 3:1–2, 23). Like Matthew, he follows Mark's narrative, though omitting more of it (e.g., all of Mark 6:45—8:10, sometimes designated "Luke's great omission") than Matthew does. He adds both a preface, which consists largely of traditions not found in the other Gospels (chap. 1—3), and a conclusion, which describes appearances by the risen Jesus near Jerusalem (24:13–53; cf. Matthew 28, where Jesus' main appearance is in Galilee). Luke inserts two collections of material, mainly sayings (6:20—8:3; 9:51—18:14), within Mark's narrative framework. Some of the sayings in Luke evidently derive from Mark. Those found only in Luke are commonly identified as L. Others that appear also in Matthew (but not Mark) may derive from a sayings source (Q) used by both of these later evangelists.

Like the Jesus depicted in Mark and Matthew, Luke's Jesus proclaims the kingdom of God and the need for repentance (4:43; 13:1–9), exorcises demons and heals the sick, sends the twelve (also seventy others) to extend this activity more widely (chaps. 9—10), and feeds the five thousand; then he turns to go to Jerusalem, enters it to the acclaim of his disciples, teaches in the temple precincts, and eats the Passover with the twelve, looking for its fulfillment in the coming kingdom of God; he is arrested by Jewish authorities, then tried and executed by the Romans, and afterward, is raised from the dead.

In various ways, Luke suggests that Christianity was meant for Gentiles (non-Jews) from the very beginning: Simeon quotes the "light to the Gentiles" passage from Isa. 49:6 in his psalm of blessing (2:32); Jesus' ancestry is traced back to Adam—the father of all humankind (3:23–38; cf. Matt. 1:1–2); Jesus points to God's care for Gentiles in ancient times (4:25–27); and two Samaritans exemplify neighbor-love and faith (10:29–37; 17:11–19). Luke also sets out to show that Christianity is no threat to Roman order, by reporting that the several Roman officials in charge of Jesus' execution found him innocent (23:4, 14–15, 22, 47; cf. Mark 15:5, 39).

Frequently, Luke omits traditions that might be difficult to understand: the derogatory comment of Jesus' friends (Mark 3:21), the request of James and John (or their mother) for special honors (Mark 10:35–40), the seemingly unintelligible fig-tree incident (Mark 11:12–14), and Jesus' "cry of dereliction"—which Gentiles might not recognize as the first words of Psalm 22 (Mark 15:34). Instead of the latter, Luke's Jesus prays for God to forgive those who are crucifying him, assures one of the criminals crucified with him that "today" they will both be in Paradise, and commits his spirit to God (23:34, 43, 46). Perhaps to demonstrate Jesus' physical (as opposed to merely spiritual or docetic) resurrection, Luke reports that the risen Jesus takes and eats a piece of broiled fish (24:36–43; cf. Tob. 6:5; John 21:9–14).

Luke's Jesus particularly insists that those who have wealth should use it to aid the poor, who are heirs to the promised kingdom. Those who respond to people in need may themselves hope for life in the kingdom of God, but those who keep their possessions to themselves have nothing more to hope for (6:20, 24; 12:15–21, 33; 14:12–14; 16:1–9, 19–31; cf. 19:1–8). As in Matthew and Mark, Luke's Jesus eats and otherwise associates with "sinners" (5:29–32; 15:1–2), and gives assurances that God will forgive those who repent (e.g., through the parables of the Prodigal Son [15:11–32] and the Pharisee and the Tax Collector in the Temple [18:9–14]).

The promised kingdom had not yet come when Luke wrote his Gospel. Consequently, he omits Jesus' announcement at the beginning of his ministry that it was near (Mark 1:15), adds that Jesus' disciples incorrectly supposed it near as they approached Jerusalem (19:11), and changes Jesus' words to the high priest accordingly (22:69; cf. Mark 14:62). Nevertheless, Luke preserves and adds sayings that urge his own contemporaries to continue to hope and prepare for the coming of the kingdom of God and the Son of man, for these parousia events could now occur at any time (9:27; 11:2; 12:32; 18:1–8; 21:29–36). Other NT authors who wrote toward the end of the first century A.D. likewise indicated their belief and expectation that the parousia was then near (e.g., James 5:7–9; 1 Pet. 4:7; Rev. 1:1–3; 22:7, 10, 12, 20).

JOHN

The author is commonly identified as John, though no disciple by this name is mentioned in the text (cf. 21:2, which refers to two unnamed disciples). The only John in the Gospel is John the Baptist, the first person named therein who "came for testimony" (1:7, 19–23; cf. 21:24). The anonymous writer's implicit source was "the

Counselor" (Paraclete) or Holy Spirit (14:25–26; 16:12–13). This account of Jesus' ministry and message differs considerably from that of the first three, or Synoptic, Gospels. To what extent John gives reliable historical information is still debated.

John's Jesus does not proclaim the kingdom of God or repentance, and exorcises no demons, but he does heal some who were sick. He typically speaks in long, complicated, and somewhat repetitious discourses about himself and his relationship to God. In particular, Jesus calls people to believe that he, himself, is the way to eternal life (3:36; 6:40). He performs "signs" or "works" in order to manifest his glory so that people may believe (2:11; 5:36; 14:11). In what is considered the original conclusion, the writer states that his purpose is to report the signs provided by Jesus in order to promote the reader's belief "that Jesus is the Christ, the Son of God," thereby enabling the reader to "have life in his name" (20:30–31). These emphases contrast with the Synoptic Gospels, where Jesus never calls on people to believe in him and never performs miracles, signs, or works to prompt belief. Instead of proclaiming the coming of the kingdom of God (as in the Synoptics), John's Jesus assures the faithful that he will come again and bring them to the place he will prepare for them in his "father's house," presumably in heaven (14:1–3). In the meantime, they will be guided by the Spirit or Counselor, who can come only after he, Jesus, goes (16:7–11); and they are to live in obedience to the "new" commandment, to love one another (13:34–35; 15:12–17; cf. Matt. 5:43–46, where Jesus commands his hearers to love their enemies as well as their neighbors).

Jesus is portrayed in terms of a high christology: he is identified in the prologue (1:1–18) as the Word that was with God and was God from the beginning (cf. Prov. 8:22–31); and elsewhere he is represented as identical or one with God (8:58; 10:30; 14:7–11; 20:28; cf. Mark 10:18, where Jesus distinguishes himself from God, who alone is good). John's Jesus is omniscient (4:17–18; 18:4) and omnipotent: he voluntarily lays down his life, and can regain it when he wishes (10:17–18); he, himself, assigns Judas the task of betraying him (13:21–26); and says "I thirst" on the cross only to fulfill Scripture (19:28). He has no need of others' advice, though sometimes he later does as they suggest (2:3–10; 4:31–32; 7:3–10). He prays aloud, not to be heard by God, who always hears him, but for the edification of those standing by (11:41–42). When he learns that his friend Lazarus is sick, he purposely delays coming until Lazarus has definitely died, so that he can raise him from the dead, and so be glorified that others may believe in him (11:1–44).

Interpreters generally regard the Fourth Gospel as a theological treatise in which the faith-understanding or theology of a particular Christian writer or church is attributed to Jesus himself. (Most of the NT treatises are in the form of letters or epistles, e.g., Hebrews and James.) Certain sayings clearly represent the perspectives of later Christianity (e.g., 3:11, 13; 4:22; 17:3). There is no messianic secret in John: Jesus is identified publicly and repeatedly as the Son, Son of God, Son of man, and Messiah (Christ) all through the Gospel (e.g., 1:41; 4:25–26; 9:35–37). Jesus' contemporaries are labeled indiscriminately "the Jews," and, from early in his career, they seek to kill him (5:16–18; 7:1). John even implies that "the Jews" did execute Jesus (19:12–16), though Pilate's sentence actually was carried out by Roman soldiers (19:23). Interpreters also find traces of anti-gnostic or anti-docetic interests in the Gospel: Jesus was the "true light" (1:9; 8:12), the word become flesh (1:14; cf. 1 John 4:2; 2 John v. 7), and "the truth"; and he experienced bodily resurrection (20:27). These polemical interests indicate that the Gospel was written toward the end of the first century A.D., probably in a Hellenistic-Gentile-Christian setting. Gnostics generally held that salvation came through secret knowledge (*gnosis*), and viewed the material world as inferior or evil. Those who were docetists urged that Jesus had only *appeared* to have a physical body, but was actually spiritual and immaterial. Gnostic and docetic motifs were emerging within Christianity (as is evidenced in the Nag Hammadi writings) by ca. A.D. 100.

Certain discrepancies also puzzle interpreters: Jesus baptizes (3:22), but does not baptize (4:2); he will not bear witness to himself (5:31), but he bears witness to himself (8:14, 18); disciples ask where he is going (13:36; 14:5), but he complains that they do not ask where he is going (16:5). These and other considerations have prompted various theories about possible editorial rearrangements and revisions of the text. Chapter 21 is commonly viewed as a later supplement, concerned, among other matters, with rehabilitating Peter by reporting his threefold pledge of devotion to Jesus (21:15–17; cf. 18:17, 25–27), and with the problem presented by the death of the beloved disciple prior to Jesus' expected return (21:20–23). Several other NT writings likewise attempt to account for the unexpected delay of Jesus' coming as Christ or Lord (e.g., Acts 1:6–7; 1 Cor. 15:12–58; and 2 Pet. 3:3–13).

ACTS

Here Luke continues the narrative begun in his Gospel (see Acts 1:1–2). The sections written in the first person plural imply that the author was, at times, a companion of Paul's (chaps. 16; 20—21; 27—28). Acts ends with Paul alive in Rome, which could mean that it was written before A.D. 64, when, according to early, extrabiblical tradition, Paul and Peter were executed there. Another possibility is that Luke may have wished to end his account on a more positive note, and brought this volume to its close where he did, even though he was writing after Paul's death. Luke-Acts is usually dated ca. A.D. 70–90.

The structure of Acts is straightforward: it describes the expansion of "the Way" (Christianity, first designated as such at 11:26) from its beginnings in Jerusalem and Judea into Samaria and to the end (or political center) of the earth (1:8)—Rome. Luke thematically reports increasing numbers of believers in Jerusalem (1:15; 2:41; 4:4; 5:14; 6:7); the persecution of the church there, causing its members to scatter throughout Judea and Samaria (8:1); Philip's preaching in Samaria and elsewhere (8:4–40); and, in particular, the mission of Paul (and others) to the gentile (non-Jewish) world, while converts continue to increase in number (9:31; 11:24; 16:5; 18:8; 19:20). Luke frequently reports that various women—including several of "high standing"—are among these growing numbers of believers (e.g., 5:14; 9:36; 16:14–15; 17:4, 12, 33).

Acts supplies many details not recorded elsewhere, such as those concerning the communal life of the Jerusalem church (2:42–47; 4:32–37), and the biographical information that Paul had studied with Rabbi Gamaliel (22:3), that he was a tentmaker by trade (18:3), and that he was a Roman citizen (22:25). Some features, however, seem legendary: angels appear frequently; apostles are miraculously rescued from prison on three different occasions (5:17–24; 12:6–17; 16:25–34); and they experience visions and perform signs and wonders, some approximating magic (5:12–15; 13:9–12; 19:11–12).

Luke especially wished to show that the eventual mission to the Gentiles was divinely inspired, as well as officially approved by the leaders of the church. The initial proclamation to Gentiles is endorsed by the apostles at Jerusalem, who send Peter and John to baptize Philip's Samaritan converts (8:5–17). An "angel of the Lord" sends Philip to instruct the Ethiopian treasurer, whom he then baptizes (8:26–38). An angel directs the Roman Cornelius to Peter, and in a vision and by order of "the Spirit," Peter is made to understand that not only Jews, but also Gentiles may become Christians, for "God shows no partiality" (10:34–35). Since the Holy Spirit sanctions the conversion of these uncircumcised persons, Peter sees no reason not to baptize them (10:44–48), and soon even the circumcisionist faction in Jerusalem is persuaded that Gentiles, too, may be received into the church (11:1–18). Acts states explicitly that God (or the Spirit) has initiated the gentile mission, in particular, Paul's activity among them (e.g., 13:2–4; 14:27). Paul's final statement epitomizes the point: "This salvation of God has been sent to the Gentiles; they will listen" (28:28).

The Jewish Christian faction in Jerusalem, however, is not initially convinced that Paul's gentile converts can be "saved" unless they are circumcised. Luke reports in Acts 15 that James (probably Jesus' brother, Gal. 1:18–19) and other apostles and elders there agree that circumcision will not be required of such converts. Instead, gentile Christians need only abstain from food that has been sacrificed to idols (cf. 1 Corinthians 8), blood, or animals that have been killed by strangling (cf. Gen. 9:4; Deut. 12:16), and refrain from unchastity (15:19–28, 28–29; cf. 21:25). Luke's threefold repetition of these terms indicates that he considers them important. Paul's own recollection of the agreement, however, is substantially different (see Gal. 2:1–10).

Paul is the main figure in Acts 13—28. Though formerly a zealous persecutor of "the Way," his experience on the road to Damascus (described three times: 9:1–22; 22:6–16; 26:12–18) turns him into the leading proponent of the gentile mission. In Acts, Paul typically begins by preaching (and arguing) in the local synagogue, persuading many Jews and God-fearers (converts to Judaism) to become Christians, but then "the Jews," prompted by jealousy, reject Paul and his message. After that, Paul condemns them, declaring that now salvation will be for the Gentiles (e.g., 13:42–47; 18:4–6; cf. Matt. 10:5–6, where Jesus tells the twelve to go only to Jews, but after his resurrection instructs them to make disciples of all nations, 28:19). As in the Fourth Gospel, "the Jews" generally appear as a hostile aggregation, here plotting against Paul—when not attacking him (9:23; 14:19; 17:5; 18:12; 20:3; 23:12; 24:9).

Luke evidently is also concerned with showing that Rome has no reason to view Christianity as a threat to its sovereignty. Paul is a Roman citizen and a beneficiary of Roman law. Jesus was innocent in the eyes of Roman officials (Luke 23:14–15, 47); in Acts Luke says repeatedly that Jesus really was killed by "the Jews" (e.g., 2:36; 3:14–15; 4:10; 10:39; cf. 13:28). Roman officials likewise pronounce Paul innocent of any crime (23:29; 26:31). As in the Gospel, so in Acts, Jesus' disciples heal the sick, cast out demons, and proclaim the kingdom of God and repentance; but here they also declare as a central article of faith that Jesus is the Christ (5:42; 18:28). Those who believe in Jesus will have their sins forgiven (10:43; 13:38–39), receive eternal life (13:48; cf. John, e.g., 3:36; 6:40), or be saved (16:31).

Several times Luke reports that many were baptized, suggesting the increasing importance of baptism in his time (e.g., 8:36; 9:18; 10:47–48; cf. John 3:5). Though the kingdom of God was still an important topic in Christian preaching, it is unclear in Acts what the reported speakers meant to say about it (e.g., 8:12; 14:22; 28:23, 31). Passages frequently quoted by Christians in later times include 5:29; 17:28; and 20:35.

ROMANS

Paul, "an apostle to the Gentiles," as he calls himself here and elsewhere (e.g., 11:13; Gal. 2:2, 8), has already traveled and preached widely in the gentile (non-Jewish) world. Now he plans to visit the Christian church in Rome on his way to Spain (15:18–29). In the meantime, he intends to deliver the contributions he has been soliciting from various gentile congregations to the Jerusalem church, in order to assist "the poor among the saints" there (cf. Gal. 2:10; 1 Cor. 16:1–4). Since he has not previously visited the church at Rome (1:10; 15:22), he writes at some length, describing his gospel (2:16; 16:25) or understanding of the substance of Christian faith and life. Thus Romans is the fullest statement we have of Paul's beliefs or "systematic theology." Frequently, he echoes or anticipates thoughts and concerns developed in his other letters, especially 1 Corinthians, Galatians, and Philippians. He did not found the church in Rome, but does not hesitate to mention, though somewhat delicately, his apostolic authority over it, while remarking graciously upon the faith and knowledge these Roman Christians already enjoy (1:5–6, 11–12; 15:14–16).

Romans is a real letter, written to an actual congregation in the course of Paul's busy life (see Acts 18—21), perhaps ca. A.D. 58. He begins, as he usually does in his other letters, by identifying himself and stating his authority and role as apostle (1:1–16), naming the community addressed, saluting the intended recipients in distinctive theological terms (1:7), and mentioning his thanks, constant prayers, and concerns for them (1:8–15). He concludes the letter with various personal comments, including a benediction (15:13), reference to his travel plans (15:14–32), another benediction (15:33), greetings and words of commendation for a number of acquaintances in (or bound for) Rome (16:1–15), further exhortations, and still another benediction (16:17–20), greetings from various companions, including his secretary (16:21–23), and the final benediction (16:25–27).

In between, the letter includes the following: his thematic statement that righteousness by faith is for both Jews and Gentiles (1:16–17); his reflections on the moral responsibility and destiny of Gentiles (1:18—2:16); his description of the situation of Jews in relation to the law and justification (2:27—4:25); his definition of the character of Christian existence under grace and faith (5:1—8:39); his assurance that salvation is for Gentiles as well as for "Israel" (9:1—11:36); various admonitions to right living (12:1—15:6); and a concluding affirmation that Gentiles as well as Jews are heirs to the promise of hope (15:7–12).

Several basic Pauline terms recur throughout the first eleven chapters: faith, grace, works, sin, death, wrath, justification, righteousness, and the law. In brief, Paul's argument is as follows. Those Gentiles who do "by nature" what the law demands "show that what the law requires is written on their hearts" (2:14–15). But Jews do not keep the law of Moses (2:17–24); indeed, all people, "both Jews and Greeks," are under the power of sin (3:9–18). The law brings "knowledge of sin," prompts disobedience, causes sin to be "counted," and so results in death (3:20; 4:15; 5:12–14; 7:7–11). Therefore, no one can hope to be justified (considered or accounted as righteous or acceptable) before God by doing the "works" of Jewish law (3:20). Yet without justification, there can be no deliverance from death. The good news is that God has manifested his righteousness apart from the law, as the gift of redemption in Jesus Christ, a gift that is to be received by faith (3:21–28; 10:1–13). Paul sometimes refers to this gift as the grace of God (e.g., 5:2, 20). The various elements of Paul's understanding are not always clearly integrated, and at times he seems to say that God justifies people because of their faith (e.g., 3:26; 10:9–10). Generally, however, Paul seems to mean that Jesus' death and resurrection overcome the power of sin for those who believe, by reconciling them to God, thus sparing them the wrath of God they otherwise deserve (4:23—5:11), and giving them assurance of eternal life (5:18–21; 6:22–23). Therefore, they can be confident of God's continuing care for them during the interim before the parousia, despite all tribulation and persecution (8:18–39).

As to the moral life, Paul insists that those "in Christ" are no longer "under law" but are "under grace" (6:15). This does not mean, however, that they are free to do as they please. Liberated from the power of sin, they should be obedient to the teachings they have received, becoming servants or slaves to righteousness and of God (6:1–23; cf. 1 Cor. 6:9–20; Gal. 5:1–26). Paul urges his readers to live according to the guidance of God's indwelling Spirit (8:2–14), in obedience to the Roman authorities, who are God's ministers (13:1–7; cf. 1 Pet. 2:13–17), and with love or concern for the good of their neighbors and fellow believers (13:8–10; 14:1—15:6; cf. 1 Corinthians 12—14; Phil. 2:1–4), conducting themselves as persons who know that the day of salvation is near (13:11–14).

1 CORINTHIANS

Like most of Paul's letters, 1 Corinthians was written to a gentile (non-Jewish) Christian church which he, himself, had founded (4:15), regarding problems he was concerned about there. Paul had established the church at Corinth ca. A.D. 40, and was now writing to them ca. A.D. 52 or 53.

First Corinthians treats matters Paul has learned about both from members of Chloe's household (1:11) and from a letter the church has sent asking his advice (7:1), and possibly also from other sources (5:1; 11:18; 16:15–18). As usual, he begins by stating his name (also that of his associate, "brother Sosthenes") and identifying the addressees; he adds a characteristic theological salutation and mentions his constant thanks and concern for them (1:1–9). The conclusion (chap. 16) refers to the collection which he is raising for the church in Jerusalem (cf. Gal. 2:10) and his travel plans, adds a summary exhortation peculiarly appropriate to this letter (16:13–14), and ends with various personal commendations and greetings, a final warning—or execration—(16:22a), an Aramaic prayer for the Lord's coming (v. 22b), a benediction, and one last affirmation about love—this time, his for them.

Paul's main concern is that some of these Corinthian Christians consider themselves better than others and are behaving in ways that are harmful to the church and to other members. In particular, they are "puffed up" with pride about their spiritual gifts, especially "knowledge," "wisdom," and "speaking in tongues." They like to boast about and show off what they consider their religious superiority.

All through the letter Paul reminds these self-styled spiritualists that their wisdom and knowledge are still imperfect (3:1–3; 8:2; 13:8–12); that what matters is the power of God, not the wisdom of men, which at best, by contrast, is foolishness (1:17—2:13; 3:18–21). Their knowledge should not be used to dazzle and confuse new converts, who may not know, for instance, that idols have no real existence. Instead, it should be tested and improved by love: " 'Knowledge' puffs up, but love builds up" (8:1–13; 10:23–33). In their zeal to claim superior status, the spiritualists have divided the church into factions which are "puffed up in favor of one against the other" (4:6), each pretending to be the only true Christians (1:10–15). Moreover, their sense of freedom has led some of these proud spiritualists to follow an anything-goes morality with respect to their bodily life (5:1–2). "All things are lawful," they claim; but, Paul counters, "not all things are helpful," either to themselves or to others (6:12–20). These factional spiritualists should recognize that there is one and the same Spirit, Lord, and God, who inspires all spiritual gifts alike (chap. 12). Those who have received such gifts—whether the ability to speak in tongues, prophetic powers, knowledge, and even faith and the ability to practice self-sacrifice—gain and give nothing, if they do not also have and act from love (13:1–3). Present knowledge is incomplete or imperfect, prophecy likewise; both will "pass away" when the "perfect" (parousia or kingdom of God) comes, but love never ends. In the coming age love, the greatest of the spiritual gifts, will abide, along with faith and hope (13:8–13).

Paul is particularly concerned about the spiritualists' practice of speaking in tongues (inspired, but incoherent utterance). He insists that this practice be restricted for the sake of "building up the church" (14:6–12). In their worship services, Paul urges, thematically, "let all things be done for edification" (14:26). Paul therefore especially commends the gift of prophecy (intelligible and inspirational discourse, 14:1–5); urges that those who speak in tongues also pray for power to interpret, so that others may be edified (14:13–20); recommends that not more than three persons speak in tongues during the course of a worship service, and then each in turn, but not at all, unless someone is present to interpret; and rules that those who prophesy do so only one at a time (14:26–33). He adds—without further explanation or rationale—that women should keep silent in church (14:33b–35).

Paul reviews several other questions as well. "The saints" (Christians) are "to judge the world" in the last days (cf. Matt. 19:28); there-fore, in the meantime, they should settle matters among themselves, rather than go before pagan law courts (6:1–8; cf. Matt. 18:15–17). Sexual and marital guidelines are given, along with advice to the circumcised and the uncircumcised, and to slave and free. All should remain in whatever state they are, if possible, for the present age is soon to pass away (chap. 7). Women are to have their heads (espe-cially their hair) covered when they pray or prophesy (11:2–16). It is unclear how Paul relates this requirement to his insistence that women keep silence in church (14:33b–35); perhaps he means that women might pray and prophesy (provided they cover their hair) so long as they do not do so in church. The Lord's Supper is to be observed with due regard for the feelings of others (11:17–22, 33–34). Paul recites the tradition he "received from the Lord" as to the Last Supper, which, unlike the Gospel's accounts, includes the "words of institu-tion": "Do this . . . in remembrance of me" (11:24–25). Thereby, Paul says, they will "proclaim the Lord's death until he comes" (v. 26).

Chapter 15 is devoted to concerns about Jesus' resurrection, and the future resurrection of Christians whose deaths will have occurred before his coming. (Paul never refers to Jesus' "second coming," but rather to his "coming.") Paul recalls the tradition he has received concerning Jesus' resurrection appearances, including an otherwise unrecorded report of the risen Jesus' appearance to some five hundred people, most of them still alive in the author's day (cf. Matt. 16:28; 24:34), to James (presumably the brother of Jesus, cf. Gal. 1:19), and finally, "as to one untimely born," to himself (15:1–8). Responding to their concerns, he declares that Christians who have died ("fallen asleep") will indeed be raised, with a "spiritual body," and that those who are still alive when "the man of heaven" comes likewise will be transformed ("changed"), and will thus put on immortality. Paul's writings reflect his expectation that Jesus would come and that the related parousia events would occur within his own lifetime and that of his contemporaries (15:51–52; cf. 1 Thess. 4:15–17). Appropri-ately, as he concludes the letter, he repeats the primitive Aramaic prayer, "Our Lord, come!" (16:22; cf. Rev. 22:20, "Come, Lord Jesus!"; Matt. 6:10 or Luke 11:2, "Thy kingdom come!").

2 CORINTHIANS

Several common themes appear throughout 2 Corinthians, but it is not clear whether we have here the letter as Paul wrote it, or whether the present writing is a composite of parts of two or perhaps three letters. Paul evidently visited and wrote to this fractious congregation at Corinth on several occasions. Interpreters sometimes suggest that 2 Cor. 6:14—7:1 is a fragment of an earlier letter, perhaps the one alluded to in 1 Cor. 5:9–11. The rest of 2 Corinthians may include all or parts of two other letters: a "hot" or agitated one (chaps. 10—13) and a calmer one, possibly written somewhat later, after the passing of the crisis in Paul's relation with this troubled and troublesome church (chaps. 1—9). When Paul's letters were collected—possibly several decades after he wrote them—these separate units might then have been put together to form the present writing. Or, it may be that chaps. 1—13 originally constituted a single letter, in which—as happened elsewhere—Paul's mood shifted somewhat abruptly. This theory could be supported by the fact that the two main sections share some similarities: chaps. 1—9 do reflect some strain between Paul and the Corinthians, and in chaps. 10—13 he does mention his love and concern for them; and in both sections, Paul refers to a previous visit (2:1–5; 13:2), and is sensitive to the charge of self-commendation or boasting. Thus a good case can be made for both the composite and the original integrity theories. Commentators agree that Paul authored all the contents of the letter.

Chapter 1 begins typically: Paul names himself (also Timothy, "our brother"), notes his own apostolic status, designates the addressees, and greets them with the double salutation, "grace and peace." There follows, atypically, a lengthy review of his relationship with the church, in which he reminds them of his own career, his apostolic role, and his hopes for the future, intermittently and uneasily justifying and commending himself (3:1; 4:2; 5:12; 6:3–10). His tone, generally, is conciliatory, especially in chap. 7, where he affirms his "great confidence" in them. His central concern is to declare that in Christ, God was reconciling the world to himself, and that, therefore, those "in Christ" can and must now be reconciled to God (5:16–20). Chapters 8—9 conclude this unit (which may have been a separate, perhaps later, conciliatory letter), urging the Corinthian Christians to contribute generously to the collection he is raising for the church in Jerusalem, a concern that often appears toward the end of Paul's letters (cf. Rom. 15:25–28; 1 Cor. 16:1–4; Gal. 2:6–10).

Paul's warning against association with unbelievers (6:14—7:1) interrupts his calling on the Corinthians to widen or open their hearts to him (6:11; 7:2). Conceivably this warning section may be a fragment from a letter of the sort Paul refers to in 1 Cor. 5:9–11, which had been preserved and was added to the present writing when Paul's letters were collected in later years. On the other hand, Paul sometimes does interrupt himself (see, e.g., 1 Corinthians 8—10), and may have done so here, as well. It is not clear whether 2 Cor. 6:14—7:1 refers to marriage with non-Christians (cf. 1 Cor. 7:12–16), or more generally, to associating with those who worship other gods and practice what from a Christian standpoint would be "iniquity" and "defilement."

In the unit that begins in chap. 10—possibly part of an earlier, agitated letter—Paul starts by identifying himself, but without adding any further preliminaries, angrily asserts his authority against those in the church who would belittle him. He notes that it was he who first brought the gospel to them, and indulges in some "foolish" boasting as to his Jewish credentials, his hardships, and his religious experience, in order to refute the "superlative" or false apostles who have tried to undermine his authority (10:7—12:13). That these false apostles claim Jewish descent (11:22) suggests that they may be Jewish Christians like the "circumcisionists" who troubled Paul's churches in Galatia and Philippi. Paul warns that he plans to come, hinting that he may have to use his authority severely (12:14—13:10). In a somewhat abrupt conclusion to this unit (if not to the original letter in its entirety), he tells the Corinthians that if they mend their ways, heed his admonitions, agree with one another, and live in peace, the God of love and peace will be with them (13:11). Such advice seems appropriate, given the factional character of this church as we know it also from 1 Corinthians. Paul then ends the letter with an unusual Trinitarian benediction (13:11–14; cf. Matt. 28:19).

In the course of the letter, Paul expresses several of his basic ideas, in particular, that believers are in Christ, or Christ is in them, that they are being transformed into his likeness and are thus already "new creatures" (3:18; 4:16; 5:17; 13:5; cf. Gal. 6:15); that they may look for an eternal dwelling in the heavens (4:17—5:5; cf. Phil. 3:20–21; John 14:2–3); but that they will be judged according to their deeds done "in the body" (5:10; cf. Gal. 6:7–9). Paul does not say when the parousia will take place, but as in 1 Corinthians 15, he evidently expects it in the near future, probably in the lifetime of some of those to whom he was writing (1:13–14; cf. 1 Cor. 13:12; 15:51–52). Two of Paul's often quoted affirmations are found in 2 Corinthians: "We have this treasure in earthen vessels" (3:7); and "We can do nothing against the truth, but only for the truth" (13:8).

GALATIANS

Paul is writing, ca. A.D. 55, to some churches in Galatia, which he himself apparently founded several years earlier (4:13). (Galatia was the Roman province situated diagonally across central Asia Minor.) The Christians addressed, as in all of Paul's letters, are Gentiles (i.e., former pagans rather than former Jews). Here as elsewhere, he describes himself as an apostle to the Gentiles (1:16; 2:2, 8).

We learn from Acts and from some of Paul's letters that he was one of the first and principal Christian missionaries to the gentile world. Paul confronts a major problem, for Christianity began entirely within the context of Judaism. That Jesus was the Messiah or the Christ would have made sense only in the thought-world of Judaism. All the first Christians had been Jews. According to Matthew, Jesus had told his followers that they must observe all of Jewish law, both written and oral (Matt. 5:17–19; 23:2–3); and according to Luke, Christians in Jerusalem had continued to worship in the temple there (Acts 2:46; 3:1). Whether Gentiles might also become Christians was an open question at first (see also Acts 10:1—11:18).

Paul's main concern as he writes to the Galatians is that some people have been telling these gentile converts that in order to be real Christians, they must first become Jews by being circumcised and observing Jewish holidays (4:10; 5:2–6). The circumcisionists seem to have been associated with, if not officially sent by, the "pillars" (leaders) of the Jewish Christian church in Jerusalem. Arguing against the position of the circumcisionists, Paul contends for the independence and authenticity of his understanding of the gospel: he had received it by revelation, not from others (1:11–17); only much later did he consult with Cephas (Peter), James (the brother of Jesus and leader of the Jerusalem congregation), and John, and then, Paul insists, they made no stipulations about circumcision (1:18—2:10). Paul's point is that requiring circumcision now is contrary to the understanding he and the "pillars" agreed to years ago in Jerusalem. The only condition then, Paul says, was that gentile Christians were to "remember the poor"—that is, contribute to the well-being of the "poor among the saints" in the Jerusalem church, a condition to which Paul gladly agreed (cf. Rom. 15:25–27; Acts 15:1–29).

In this context, Paul goes on to charge that Peter was unduly responsive to the wishes of the circumcisionists who came to Antioch "from James," insisting that Jewish Christians must not eat with gentile Christians (2:11–12). It is not certain exactly where Paul's summary of his earlier remarks to Peter ends and the statement of his present faith-understanding to the Galatians begins; but his argument is clear. Justification or righteousness before God is never attained by keeping Jewish law, but only through faith in Jesus Christ (2:15–16). If one tries to keep part of the law, he must keep all of it (3:10; 5:3). But no one is able to keep the whole law (3:21–22; cf. Rom 7:4–25; 2 Esdras 7). To try to keep even part of the law is to ignore the grace of God, who gives righteousness through faith (2:18–21; 5:4–5).

Paul insists that neither being circumcised nor being uncircumcised is important. What matter are faith and love. Through faith, all are children of God and one in Christ; externals such as being Jew or Greek, slave or free, male or female, no longer mean anything (3:26–28; 6:15). The only thing that counts is "faith working through love" (5:6; cf. 1 Corinthians 13).

But now another question arises. If gentile Christians are not obliged to follow Jewish law, what should be the basis for their moral life? Obviously reverting to their prior pagan standards will not do. Paul now argues that freedom from Jewish law does not mean license. Life is to be lived under the law of neighbor-love (5:13–14) and in accordance with the Spirit, not according to the lower nature or "flesh" (5:16–26). By "flesh," Paul means not only sensuality, but also, and more centrally, self-centeredness, that is, envy and selfish ambition. The "fruits of the Spirit" include love, joy, peace, patience, kindness, gentleness, and self-control. The standard by which people live, then, is crucially important. Those who live according to the flesh will not inherit the kingdom of God (5:19–21; cf. 1 Cor. 6:9–10); but those who live by love and the Spirit, he assures the Galatians, will receive the harvest of eternal life (6:7–10).

EPHESIANS

It is not certain whether Ephesians was written by Paul or by a later Christian who was familiar with Paul's thought. Some stylistic and conceptual features suggest authorship by someone other than Paul himself—see, for instance, such atypical expressions as "the heavenly places" and "forgiveness" (1:3, 7, 20), and the idea of Christ's uniting or filling "all things" (1:10; 4:10) or his self-giving love for the church (5:25–27). Secondary authorship is also suggested by the fact that many passages parallel and possibly were taken from Colossians, authorship of which likewise is in doubt. Paul does not elsewhere say that Christians have been "sealed with the Holy Spirit" (1:13; 4:30), or refer to the gospel he preaches as a "mystery" (3:3–4; 6:19; so also in Colossians; cf. 1 Cor. 13:2; 15:51). The idea that Christians were predestined "before the foundation of the world" (1:4–5) goes beyond Paul's claim to have been "set apart," before his birth, to be an apostle (Gal. 1:15; cf. Jer. 1:5). The letter makes no mention of the collection Paul was raising for the poor among the saints in Jerusalem or his travel plans—standard features of his genuine letters. According to Acts 19, Paul spent considerable time in Ephesus, but the author of Ephesians wrote it as if he had not been there before (1:15; 3:1–3). Early versions of the letter do not mention Ephesus, and it may be that it was written, like the catholic or general letters (e.g., Hebrews and Jude) to all Christians everywhere. If written by Paul, it would be the only such letter of his that we have.

On the other hand, a strong case can be made for Paul's authorship. Ephesians begins and ends in Paul's usual fashion (1:1–2; 6:21–24). Much of its substance resembles that of unquestionably authentic letters, especially Galatians and 1 Corinthians. The letter states, even more clearly than in Paul's usual fashion, that salvation is by the grace of God through, but not because of faith (2:4–9; cf. Rom. 3:21–26; Gal. 2:15–16). Emphasis is placed upon the unity of the church (4:3–6), as in the genuinely Pauline 1 Corinthians 12—14, though in Ephesians, the principle of unity applies to the church universal, rather than the local congregation. The author implies that he is in prison (3:1; 4:1; 6:20), which was Paul's lot several times. Here, as in unquestionably Pauline letters, the author presents himself as a missionary to the Gentiles (3:2, 8; cf. Gal. 2:8–9), and as only "least" of all the saints or apostles (3:8; cf. 1 Cor. 15:9).

The letter's main concern is to emphasize that Gentiles are no longer separated from Jews as they were before Christ, but are now fellow-heirs to the promise and members of the same body—the universal church—through the grace of God (2:1–22). This is the great "mystery" now revealed to the apostles, so that they might preach it to all men, and even to the "principalities and powers" (3:1–10). Paul elsewhere urged that Christianity was not only for Jews but also for Gentiles (see esp. Romans and Galatians). Not only the church, but all creation, is now under the lordship of Christ (1:20–23; cf. Phil. 2:1–11).

The writer is also concerned with encouraging his late-first-century readers to live worthily of their "calling" (4:1), recognizing their common unity in the church: there is one body, one Spirit, one hope, one Lord, one faith, one baptism, "one God and Father of us all"

(4:3–6). In this connection, the writer summons readers to live in accordance with their new "nature," in patience, peace, and love, "building up" the church (4:1—5:20; cf. 1 Corinthians 12—14). Such moral instruction was particularly important for gentile Christians who previously had known only paganism and its low moral standards. The admonitions to wives and husbands, children and fathers, slaves and masters, also are in the context of concern for the unity of the church, love and respect for one another, and the lordship of Christ over all (5:21—6:9).

Finally, the writer urges Christians to "put on the whole armor of God," in order to withstand the devil in "the evil day," and to pray "at all times in the Spirit" for all of God's people, including himself (6:10–20). Because they are sealed by the Holy Spirit, these readers may be confident that they will acquire possession of their "inheritance" on the day of redemption (1:13–14; 4:30; cf. Col. 3:24).

PHILIPPIANS

Paul is writing from prison, perhaps in Rome (1:13–14; 4:22), in which case this may be the last letter of his that we have. He looks back fondly on his long and special association with these good Macedonian Christians. The church at Philippi was the first he established in Europe; since early times they have supported his work (1:5; 4:15–16). Paul wants his friends in Philippi to know that his imprisonment should not cause them concern (1:12–26); even if he is put to death, they should rejoice (2:17–18). He wishes to reassure them as to Epaphroditus's health, and so sends him back to them, perhaps carrying this letter (2:25–30), urges two women there, his "fellow-workers," to be reconciled (4:2–3), and thanks them all for the gifts they have sent him by Epaphroditus (4:10–18). Twice he seems about to conclude the letter (3:1; 4:8), but each time he goes on, unwilling, it seems, to bid farewell to these people of whom he is so fond (1:8).

The most striking feature here is Paul's completely peaceful frame of mind. The verb "rejoice" is woven through the letter like a scarlet thread: he rejoices, and he calls on the Philippians to do so as well. He is in prison, but his imprisonment has served to "advance the gospel" (1:12–14). Some preach Christ for wrong reasons, yet he rejoices because Christ nevertheless is proclaimed (1:15–18). Whether he lives or dies, he looks forward to the outcome (1:19–26). Not even the circumcisionists upset him now (3:1–3; cf. Gal. 5:12). He reviews his Hebrew credentials, but refuses to claim merit or perfection (3:3–14;

cf. 2 Corinthians 10—12). Some may disagree with him, but he only urges that they all hold true to the understandings they have attained (3:15–16; cf. 1 Cor. 11:16; 14:36, where Paul disallows dissent). Lyrically, he urges his readers to rejoice always and have no anxieties (4:4–6; cf. Matt. 6:25–34).

As in most of his letters, Paul exhorts its recipients to live worthily of the gospel or the new life that has been given them, and so to be concerned not only for themselves but also for others (1:27—2:4). In this connection, perhaps quoting from an early Christian hymn or creed, he refers them to the example of Jesus' own self-giving love (2:5–11). "Work out your own salvation," he urges them; be confident that "God is at work in you" (2:12–13). Moreover, they are to live blameless lives, so that "in the day of Christ," he may be proud of them (2:14–16; see also 1:6, 9–11). He tells them to imitate him in striving for the goal of the "upward call" of God, sure of their "prize" or "end"—the transformed existence of life in the heavenly commonwealth, which will be theirs when Christ comes (3:12–21). As in 1 Cor. 15:50–53 and 1 Thess. 4:15–17 where Paul expresses similar hopes and assurances, he indicates an expectation that both he and those to whom his letter is addressed are to experience this great transformation soon, surely in their own lifetime; for "the Lord is at hand!" (4:5).

COLOSSIANS

This letter may have been written either by Paul or in Paul's name, perhaps after his death, by someone interested in advising Colossian (and Laodicean) Christians in the spirit of Paul (see 2:1, 5; 4:16). Since the author says he is Paul (1:1, 23; 4:18), we shall so name him here, leaving open the question of his actual identity.

Much of the letter is typically Pauline. The writer begins by identifying himself as "Paul, an apostle of Christ Jesus," and mentioning Timothy, his co-worker. He refers to his continual thanks and prayers for the church (1:3, 9), and bids these Christians live according to the new life (or nature) that is theirs (3:1–17). As in many of Paul's authentic letters, the concluding verses mention certain persons (4:7–17). Among these are Onesimus and several others named in Paul's letter to Philemon (see Philem. vv. 1, 10, 23–24). Only in Colossians is it said that Luke—who may or may not have been the author of Luke-Acts—is a physician (4:14). As in Ephesians, Philippians, and Philemon, Paul here is in prison (4:3, 10). He did not found the church at Colossae, but has heard of them (1:4), and writes to give them guidance and directions on various matters of faith and life.

Nevertheless, several features suggest that the author may have been someone other than Paul. The writer says nothing about hoping to visit the church (cf. Phil. 1:27; Philem. 22), and hints that Paul will be seen no more (2:1, 5). Certain basic terms here are not used in Paul's normal sense: the grace of God is something to be heard and understood (1:6); "the faith" means the substance of Christian teaching (1:23; 2:7); and, as in Ephesians, forgiveness replaces justification (1:14; 2:13; 3:13; cf. Rom. 4:25; Gal. 2:16).

Some passages in Colossians closely parallel parts of Ephesians (e.g., Col. 3:9–10, cf. Eph. 4:22–24, on the "old nature" and Christians' "new nature"; Col. 3:16–17, cf. Eph. 5:19–20, on Christian worship and conduct; Col. 3:18—4.1; cf. Eph. 5:21—6:9, on relations between husbands and wives, fathers and children, and masters and slaves. As in Ephesians, Paul refers to the substance of the gospel as a "mystery" in this letter (1:26–27; 2:2; 4:3). From these similarities, it might be concluded either that Paul—or someone else—wrote both, perhaps near the same time, when these concerns were on his mind, or that someone else copied from the earlier letter, while writing the other.

But Colossians and Ephesians also differ on significant points. In Ephesians, the author says that Christ has begun to unite and fill all things, and that this mission either was or will be accomplished in the "fulness of time" (Eph. 1:9–10, 16–23; 4:10). In Colossians, however, the author affirms that Christ ("the Son") "is before all things," the "first-born of all creation," "the beginning," in whom all things were created (1:16–18; cf. Prov. 8:22–31; John 1:1–3), and in whom "all things hold together" (1:17; cf. Wisd. of Sol. 1:7), and in whom "the fulness of deity dwells bodily" (2:9).

Other unusual ideas and expressions include "making peace by the blood of [the] cross" (1:20); the completion of the preaching of the gospel to "every creature under heaven" (1:23; cf. Mark 16:15; Pss. 148:7–10; 150:6; Jon. 3:6–8); and God's canceling the bond (of the law) by "nailing it to the cross," and disarming "the principalities and powers" (2:14–15). The idea that Christians' baptism represents their being buried with Christ (2:12) is not found in Paul's other letters (cf. 1 Cor. 1:13–17). Another unique idea is that the Son (Christ) is the image of the invisible God (1:15; cf. 2 Cor. 4:4; Gen. 1:26–27).

The writer's main concerns are to warn against various heresies and to urge readers to live up to the standard of their new Christian morality, putting aside old, pagan ways. The heresies include: philosophy based on mere human tradition or belief in the *stoicheia* ("elemental spirits") which, in Greek thought, gave structure to the universe (2:8, 20; cf. 1:15–19, where Paul says that Christ has this function); some sort of legalism, possibly of the sort Paul undertook to refute in Galatians (see Col. 2:13, 16, 20–21; 4:11); ascetic self-denial (2:18, 23; cf. Paul's rejection of asceticism and martyrdom in 1 Cor. 13:3); angel worship; and possibly a docetic belief that Jesus did not have bodily existence (1:22; 2:9, 18; cf. 1 John 4:2). Several moral admonitions characterize the way of the old or earthly nature which Christians are to "put to death" or "put off" (3:5–10), and the way of the new nature, which they are to "put on" (3:12—4:6). Those who conduct themselves properly, "making the most of the time" (4:5), will receive "the inheritance" as their reward at the parousia, when Christ appears (3:4, 6, 24; cf. Matt. 25:34; Gal. 5:21).

1 THESSALONIANS

The congregations in Philippi and Thessalonica probably were the first Christian churches established in Europe, at least the first established there by Paul. First Thessalonians is commonly regarded as the earliest of Paul's letters, though no evidence particularly compels this conclusion. The authors of the letter identify themselves as "Paul, Silvanus, and Timothy" (1:1) and generally write in the first-person plural, though Paul seems to be the principal spokesman (2:17–18). The letter begins and ends in Paul's characteristic fashion (1:1–2; 5:23–28), and critics generally agree that this is one of his authentic letters.

Paul has several concerns here. He wants to strengthen the Thessalonian "believers" in the face of persecution from their fellow countrymen (2:14). The afflictions they suffer, he says, are part of the tempter's (Satan's) efforts to undermine faith (3:3–5; cf. Matt. 6:13). Paul is encouraged now that Timothy has brought back good news about their steadfast faith (3:6–10). He urges them to live according to the moral standards he has taught them (4:1–12). Especially, he wishes to reassure them that fellow believers who have "fallen asleep" (died) have not perished forever, but will return with Christ when he comes (4:13–18; cf. 3:13). Paul expects this to happen while many, including himself, are still alive; at the same time, those who are still alive, "who are left until the coming of the Lord," will be "caught up together with them in the clouds" (4:14–17). Paul does not say here that those still alive would first be "changed" or transformed, so as to have "spiritual bodies" like the resurrected dead; but that understanding may be implicit: see 1 Cor. 15:35–52; Phil. 3:20–21.

When exactly the parousia will be is not known, but it will come "like a thief in the night" (5:1–4; cf. Matt. 24:34–44; Acts 1:7; Rev. 3:3), that is, unexpectedly, at any time. In the meantime, Christians are to live a life of faith, hope, and love (5:5–8; cf. Eph. 6:10–17), building one another up (5:11; cf. 1 Corinthians 12—14). Various other passages underscore the expectation of Christ's coming and likewise urge readers to live in the interim with faith, love, and hope (1:3; 2:19; 3:11–13; 5:12–23). These Christians are to love one another (4:9–10; cf. John 13:34–35), but love is not limited to "the brethren" or fellow believers; it is to be all-inclusive (3:12; cf. Matt. 5:43–48).

One peculiarity of the letter is the animus Paul expresses toward "the Jews." Here he says that they killed "the Lord Jesus" (2:15; cf. John 19:14–18), in contrast to Matt. 27:27–36 or Mark 15:16–25, according to which Jesus was crucified by Roman soldiers. Moreover, Paul reports that "the Jews" have interfered with his work among Gentiles (2:15–16; cf. Acts 14:1–2). (Evidently he is not referring here to Jewish Christians or "circumcisionists" of the sort that troubled the Galatian churches.) Another special feature of the letter is Paul's affectionate attitude toward these Christians (e.g., 2:8, 17–20; 3:9–10), equaled only, perhaps, in his letter to the Philippians. Here, as there, he calls on the readers to "rejoice always" (5:16). Though Paul may not have known that he was composing Scripture for all later Christianity, he did intend the letter as authoritative instruction for the whole church at Thessalonica (5:27; cf. Col. 4:16).

2 THESSALONIANS

Some interpreters consider this a genuine letter of Paul's. Most others, perhaps, regard it as Deutero- or pseudo-Pauline, that is, actually written by someone else, possibly as late as the A.D. 90s. At points, it is quite similar to 1 Thessalonians: for example, the opening (1:1–2a) duplicates 1 Thess. 1:1, and the concluding benedictions are nearly identical. Both purport to be from "Paul, Silvanus, and Timothy," and are written largely in the first person plural. Both refer to afflictions experienced by members of the church at Thessalonica.

But there are significant differences. In 1 Thessalonians, the parousia is characterized as a time of salvation for both the living and "those who have fallen asleep" (1 Thess. 4:13–17; cf. 1 Cor. 15:51–57). Here, on the other hand, it is represented as a time of vengeance, when Jesus and his "mighty angels in flaming fire" will inflict eternal punishment upon unbelievers and the disobedient (1:7–9), and Jesus will slay "the lawless one," a minion of Satan, "with the breath of his mouth" (2:8–9). The whole scene more nearly resembles what is anticipated in Revelation than anything found elsewhere in Paul's writings.

In 1 Thessalonians, Paul urges—and warns—that the parousia will occur without any prior signs or notice (5:1–3); but here, the author clearly and forcibly insists that there will be prior indications, namely, the appearance of "the man of lawlessness," "the son of perdition" (associated with Satan), whose coming will be marked by false "signs and wonders" (2:1–3, 8–9). A similar expectation is found in 1 John 2:18, but not in the letters of Paul that are generally recognized as authentic. In the meantime, the "lawless one" is being restrained, but will be revealed "in his time," when he will try to deceive unbelievers (2:6–7; cf. Rev. 20:1–3, 7–8). The specific meaning is uncertain; however, the writer's apparent point is that believers should not be among those deceived into believing that the Lord has come (2:2–3), but rather should hold fast to truth and righteousness (2:9–12). We hear for the first (and only) time in the NT of Christians assembling to meet Jesus when he comes at the parousia (2:1); perhaps the reason some have stopped work and are living in idleness (3:6, 11–12) is that they suppose that the kingdom of God either has come or is on the verge of doing so. (Numerous OT and intertestamental texts suggest that in the coming age, food and drink would abound; from these, it could have been inferred that working would no longer be necessary in that age.) Alternatively, these idlers may have been prompted by ordinary laziness. In any event, the writer admonishes them to earn their own way in the interim: "If anyone will not work, let him not eat" (3:6–12).

There are other hints that someone other than Paul wrote the letter. The "reminder" of what Paul said while still with them (2:5) and the admonitions to keep "the tradition" he taught (2:1; 3:6) suggest that the letter was written after Paul's time. References to Paul's giving commands (3:6, 10, 12) also suggest secondary authorship, since Paul only once so characterized his instruction in the authentic letters (1 Cor. 11:17; commands are also referred to in the Pastoral Letters). The writer's unparalleled insistence on Paul's "mark" (3:17) as proof of his authorship may protest too much.

Whoever the writer may have been, his intent, certainly, was to encourage Christians at Thessalonica to endure their present sufferings (cf. 1 Peter and Revelation), looking for vindication at the parousia, which was still to come—and would not come until after the appearance of "the man of lawlessness"—and to urge them to remain steadfast in the meantime, each one earning his own living, rather than depending on the others. Unlike Paul's (other) letters, 2 Thessalonians contains virtually nothing else in the way of moral instruction or guidance. There is no indication whether the suffering or affliction the Thessalonians were experiencing was at the hands of their pagan neighbors, hostile Jews (cf. 1 Thess. 2:14), or perhaps, Roman authorities, as in the case of those addressed by the authors of 1 Peter and Revelation.

1 TIMOTHY

Most modern interpreters see 1 and 2 Timothy and Titus as treatises by an anonymous Christian pastor concerning problems common among the churches in the first quarter of the second century A.D. These Pastoral Letters, as they are usually called, are written in the form of instructions by Paul to his associates Timothy and Titus. Implicitly, the writer is proposing, in Paul's name, to advise the rising generation of church leaders, symbolized by these two former companions of Paul's, as to how they should conduct their ministries and deal with problems arising in their own time. Above all, they are to train themselves in "godliness" (4:7–8). The letters offer guidance on such issues as the importance of "guarding" or preserving "sound doctrine" and of avoiding theological disputes and speculations, the duties and qualifications of bishops and deacons, and the care of widows. In the ancient world, writers frequently attributed their own compositions to honored predecessors. It is understandable that someone concerned about these matters would have written in Paul's name, since Paul was the most important authority figure in first-century gentile Christianity.

All the Pastoral Letters reflect Christianity's emergence as a gentile religion. No longer do we find references to Judaizers or Christian circumcisionists. "The law" is now viewed favorably as a restraint upon "the lawless" and "the ungodly," and as the moral dimension of "sound doctrine" or "the glorious gospel" which the writer espouses (1 Tim. 1:7–11). The first and perhaps second generation of apostles and other early church leaders have all died. Now there arises the problem of maintaining not only correct doctrine, but also proper moral standards within the churches. As yet there is no "canon," or authoritative collection of Christian writings; there are no creeds; and there is no recognized structure of church governance, other than local bishops and lower orders of clergy—whom we find mentioned for the first time in these letters.

Several passages in 1 Timothy have to do with preserving orthodoxy ("right teaching") and right conduct, as over against different doctrines and practices (1:3–11; 4:1–5, 7; 6:1–2). References to "endless genealogies" and "silly myths" (1:4; 4:7) may indicate that early gnostic versions of Christianity were current in the author's time. The writer urges that prayers be offered "for all men," because "God our Savior . . . desires all men to be saved" (2:1–4; so likewise 4:10; Rom. 5:18; 1 Cor. 15:22; but see 2 Thess. 2:9–12). Women are to dress modestly, adorning themselves not with braided hair or costly attire, but with good deeds. They are to be silent and submissive to men (cf. 1 Cor. 14:34–35; Eph. 5:22–24), since woman, not man, was deceived by the serpent (2:9–14; cf. 2 Esd. 7:7, 118, which give the man, Adam, full credit for this primordial transgression. Milton's *Paradise Lost* reflects the account found in 1 Timothy). Notwithstanding this great error, a woman may be saved if she bears children, provided she also maintains the virtues of faith, love, holiness, and modesty (2:15). Bishops and deacons should be good husbands and fathers and men of reputable character, and neither drunkards nor lovers of money (3:1–13). Women also have some place as church leaders, possibly as deacons (3:11). Ministers are advised on how to handle responsibilities and various delicate situations that arise from time to time in their congregations (4:11—5:22), and what to teach (6:2). Somewhat intolerantly, the writer condemns those who would teach otherwise (6:3–5; cf. Phil. 3:15–16).

The writer is particularly concerned that widows be provided for— at least those who are "real widows" (5:3–16). Ruling "elders" may possibly represent still another new category of leadership; but see Titus 1:5–9 where the terms "bishop" and "elder" appear to be used synonymously. Those elders who preach and teach (cf. 1 Cor. 12:28), are worthy of special honor (and due remuneration), and may not be charged with offenses unless at least two witnesses testify against them (5:17–19; cf. Susanna). Evidently such elders were understood to have authority to ordain ministers by the laying on of hands (4:14; cf. 5:22).

In keeping with the writer's affirmation that "everything created by

God is good" (4:4; cf. Gen. 1:31), he commends use of "a little wine" for the sake of one's health (5:23). Christian slaves should not be disrespectful toward their Christian masters just because now "they are brethren," but "must serve all the better" (6:1–2; cf. Philem. vv. 15–17). Christians should be content if they have food and clothing, and not desire wealth, for such desires "plunge men into ruin" (6:6–10). In this connection, the writer sets forth what becomes an oft-quoted warning: "The love of money is the root of all evils" (6:10). Ministers should "fight the good fight," holding on to the eternal life that is already theirs, looking for the coming of Christ "at the proper time," and should charge wealthy members of their congregations "to be rich in good deeds" and generosity, setting their hopes on God, not on "uncertain riches," and thereby "laying up for themselves a good foundation for the future" (6:11–19; cf. Matt. 6:19–20 and parallels, and Luke 16).

Like the author(s) of Ephesians and Colossians, the present writer refers to the substance of the Christian faith as "the mystery" (3:8, 16). Like the author of the Gospel according to John, the writer of 1 Timothy declares that those who believe in Jesus already have eternal life (1:16; cf. John 6:40). Like the author of Hebrews, this writer represents Jesus as "mediator" between God and humanity (2:5). There is no mention of the coming of, or of entry into, the kingdom of God.

A number of passages and expressions have been absorbed into later Christian liturgy and hymns, such as "The saying is sure and worthy of full acceptance, that Christ Jesus came into the world to save sinners" (1:15); the characterization of God as "immortal, invisible, the only God" (1:17); and the admonitions to "fight the good fight," and "take hold of [the] eternal life," and "be rich in good deeds, liberal and generous" (6:12, 18).

2 TIMOTHY

This letter (or treatise), like 1 Timothy and Titus, probably was written well after Paul's lifetime by a church leader who wished to encourage Christian pastors to practice their ministries bravely and effectively, upholding "the truth" against false teaching and myths (1:6–8; 4:1–5). "Timothy" is a third-generation Christian (1:5) who represents such pastors. "Paul" mentions his own appointment as preacher and teacher, and his consequent suffering as an example and encouragement to later preachers and teachers who—in the writer's time—might expect to "share in suffering for the gospel" (1:8–12; 3:10–12; 4:5). The letter is written as if from Rome, where Paul is a prisoner (1:8; 2:9), expecting soon to die, having fought the good fight (cf. 1 Tim. 6:12) and kept the faith (4:6–8).

As in 1 Timothy, the writer offers advice for pastors in coping with their tasks and responsibilities. He is particularly concerned that ministers should "guard" the teaching received from earlier times and avoid being confused by other teachings (1:13–14; 2:2, 14–18, 23). They should pursue their aims single-mindedly and conscientiously, like good soldiers, athletes, farmers, and workmen (2:3–6, 15). The "man of God" (Christian minister, 3:17) is to use Scripture in his work. This, being inspired by God, is a sure guide to faith and righteousness (3:16). "Scripture" here probably refers to the Greek Old Testament (Septuagint or other versions), which would have included most of the OT Apocrypha. There was, as yet, no NT.

The author warns that in "the last days" men will be lovers of self, money, and pleasure (3:1–9). Such people, he writes, are to be avoided (cf. 1 John 2:15–17). Implicitly, he believes that he and his readers are living in the "last days" (cf. 2 Pet. 3:3; 1 John 2:18). He opposes the "realized eschatology" of those proponents of the idea that the resurrection has already occurred (2:18; cf. 2 Thess. 2:1–5, where "Paul" cautions against the notion "that the day of the Lord has come"). The writer also looks in hope for "that Day" when Christ Jesus will appear "to judge the living and the dead" (4:1, 8), language later reflected in the Apostles' and Nicene Creeds. He is also confident of the salvation already manifested in the One who "brought life and immortality to light" (1:9–10). Like Paul and the author of the Fourth Gospel, the present writer evidently expected that salvation would be experienced in heaven—the apparent meaning of the new expression "heavenly kingdom" at 4:18 (cf. Phil. 3:20; John 14:1–3).

TITUS

Here we find many of the same themes and expressions as in 1 and 2 Timothy. Interpreters generally agree that all three of these Pastoral Letters were written by the same person. The author probably understood that he was stating what he believed Paul would have said about problems confronting the churches' ministers, a generation or two later. Timothy and Titus stand for or symbolize such ministers. The three Pastoral Letters or treatises are usually dated ca. A.D. 110–20.

Again the writer urges that Christian leaders maintain sound doctrine and refute contrary teachings (1:9—2:1). At the same time, they are to avoid "stupid controversies, genealogies, dissension," and the like (3:9). Genealogies may refer to gnostic myths about divine emanations (cf. 1:14; 1 Tim. 1:4; 4:7). References to circumcisionists (1:10) and arguments about "the law" (3:9) suggest the existence of a problem with Jewish Christian legalism—though this is not indicated in the other Pastoral Letters (cf. Galatians). In any event, Christians are to adhere to "the faith"—meaning, evidently, Christian doctrine or tradition—also referred to as "the truth" (1:13–14; cf. Col. 1:23; 2:6).

We again see several basic ethical concerns: pastors and all Christians are to be "zealous for good deeds" (2:7, 14; cf. James 2:14–22), helping those in urgent need (3:14; cf. Matt. 25:31–46; Luke 10:30–37). Bishops or elders—here evidently two names for the same thing—must be able to manage their own households and otherwise be qualified as worthy leaders (1:5–9; cf. 1 Tim. 3:1–7). "Paul" advises how ministers should instruct different kinds of people in the congregations: older men and women, younger women and men, and slaves (2:2–10). As in 1 Tim. 6:1–2, the writer says nothing here as to masters' obligations to slaves (cf. Eph. 6:9; Col. 4:1). He declares God's intent to save all mankind (2:11; cf. 1 Tim. 2:3–4), but also refers to "the elect" (1:1; cf. 2 Tim. 2:10), an expression which implies God's choice to save only some.

As in most NT writings, hope for the future is associated with the parousia or appearing of Christ, which the writer and his readers await (2:13). Christians have already been saved or justified by God's mercy or grace and are therefore "heirs in hope of eternal life" (3:5–7; cf. 1:2). In the meantime, pastors should use their authority to insist that all live "sober, upright, and godly lives in this world" based on the mercy and grace of God (2:11—3:8). Also, during this interim, Christians are to be submissive to "rulers and authorities," meaning, probably, Roman rulers of the time (3:1; cf. 1 Tim. 2:1–2; Rom. 13:1; 1 Pet. 2:13–17).

PHILEMON

When the NT writings were collected, beginning sometime during the second century A.D., the letters then ascribed to Paul were arranged by order of length, Romans first and Philemon last. Philemon may also have been the last letter Paul wrote. As in Philippians, Paul is a "prisoner" (vv. 1, 9), perhaps in Rome, ca. A.D. 62. Paul's

other letters are to churches; this one is to a single individual, Philemon, though indirectly also to others and the church in Philemon's
house (vv. 1–2).

Paul begins much the same way he does in his letters to churches:
he names himself and his "brother" Timothy and the addressees, sets
down his customary salutation (v. 3), and states that he thanks God
always in his prayers for Philemon because of his love and faith. He
closes with greetings from his fellow workers and a characteristic
benediction (cf. Phil. 4:23; 1 Thess. 5:28).

Paul's apparent purpose in writing is that he wants Philemon to free
his slave Onesimus. He puts the matter graciously but firmly. He
begins by saying that although he might command, "for love's sake"
he prefers to appeal to Philemon's free will, so that his "goodness
might not be by compulsion" (vv. 8–14). Though he would be glad to
have Onesimus continue to serve him, Paul sends him back to Philemon: not it seems, so that Philemon might send him back again to
resume serving Paul in prison, but in order that Philemon might
receive him "no longer as a slave" but "as a beloved brother" (v. 16).
Paul here makes operative his understanding that in Christ "there is
neither slave nor free" (Gal. 3:28). He offers to pay anything that
Onesimus may owe Philemon, but reminds Philemon that such pay-
ment would not really be fitting, since Philemon owes his "own self"
to Paul (vv. 18–19). Apparently both Philemon and Onesimus have
been converted to Christianity through Paul's efforts. Paul states that
he is confident of Philemon's obedience, and that Philemon will
do ever more than Paul expressly asks, namely, give Onesimus his
freedom. At the same time he adds, not too subtly, that Philemon
should prepare a guest room for him, hinting that he plans to come for
a visit to see whether Onesimus has in fact been freed (vv. 21–22).

Interpreters sometimes state as an established fact that Onesimus
was a runaway slave who had stolen money or property from Philemon. The text of this letter—our only information on these matters—
does not necessarily support such conclusions. It seems as likely that
Philemon had sent Onesimus to wait upon Paul during his imprisonment—which is just what Onesimus was doing—but that after
Onesimus's conversion, Paul determined that he should become a free
man, and so wrote Philemon to this effect. That Onesimus might have
done Philemon any wrong or owed him anything could be interpreted
in terms of damages to Philemon's property or debts incurred in the
course of Onesimus's servitude, which would need to be settled in
connection with his manumission.

Paul did not categorically call for the abolition of slavery—nor did anyone else in the ancient world. Paul did believe that the present age would soon pass away, and with it, such institutions as slavery and even marriage (1 Cor. 7:17–31; cf. Matt. 22:30). In the meantime, Paul urged people in all his churches, including slaves, to remain in whatever estate or condition God had called them (1 Cor. 7:17–24). Either Paul or, more likely, one or two later Christian writers, who still looked for the parousia in the near future, subsequently added that in the interim, Christian slaves should be obedient and serve their masters with good will, while Christian masters should be considerate of their slaves, "knowing that he who is [the Master of both] is in heaven, and that there is no partiality with him" (Eph. 6:5–9; Col. 3:22—4:1). A still later author, who likewise apparently expected the parousia in his and his readers' lifetime, rather more harshly insisted that slaves be required to be submissive, "give satisfaction in every respect," not be "refractory" or pilferers, and that they "show entire and true fidelity" to their masters, not presuming upon the fact that masters and slaves were now "brethren" (Titus 2:9–10, 13; 1 Tim. 6:1–2). The author of these Pastoral Letters did not include anything about the equality of masters and slaves in Christ, or any advice or admonitions to masters as to how they should treat their slaves. By contrast, in Philemon, Paul says nothing about Onesimus's owing obedience as a slave; instead, it is Philemon who is to be obedient to Paul, by giving Onesimus his freedom (v. 21).

HEBREWS

Although a few verses (13:18–19, 22–25) parallel the substance and format of typical Pauline letters, Hebrews is generally regarded as a treatise by someone other than Paul; indeed, it constitutes a distinctive interpretation of the essence of Christianity. Those who eventually arranged the NT canon placed it as the first (since it was the longest) of the non-Pauline letters or "catholic epistles." Like the other catholic epistles, it was written for Christians of its author's time generally, not addressed to particular congregations or individuals. Its emphasis on holding fast "the confession" (2:1–3; 4:14) and eschewing "strange teaching" (13:9) suggests that it was composed during a period when the defense of orthodoxy against variant doctrines was a serious problem, perhaps ca. A.D. 100–120 (cf. 1 Tim. 1:3–6; 2 Pet. 2:1–3; and the gnostic Christian writings of the early second century found at Nag Hammadi in the 1940s). Although the author writes as if Jewish priests were still offering sacrifices in the temple (which the Romans destroyed in A.D. 70), his knowledge of Judaism seems to have been based on OT Scriptures or "testimonies" rather than on first-hand acquaintance with ongoing Jewish or Jewish Christian practices and concerns (e.g., 9:1–10). There is no mention of circumcision or keeping Sabbaths or other holy days. His references to the OT are sometimes vague (2:6; 4:4) and fanciful (11:26; 12:17). Hebrews is written in excellent Greek. Notwithstanding the traditional title, there is no indication that the treatise was written to or for Jews or Jewish Christians.

The author's main concern was to set out an understanding of the meaning of Christianity for gentile Christians of his time. These Christians had inherited as their Scripture the Greek OT. (There was as yet no NT.) Central beliefs and institutions in the OT, however, meant little to gentile Christians, who were largely unfamiliar with Jewish traditions. Hebrews renders OT traditions relevant to the author's era, by showing how Christianity was grounded in the OT, and at the same time, how it was something new, indeed, the *fulfillment* of the hopes and promises set down in the OT. The author uses several strategies in this connection. He invokes the Platonic distinction between shadow and reality (10:3). Basically he contrasts earlier Israelite/Jewish persons and institutions with Christ, who is presented as superior to, or the fulfillment and perfection of, all earlier persons, practices, and promises. Thus the Son is superior to biblical angels (1:4—2:8), Christ to Moses (3:3–6), Jesus, as "high priest," to the whole Levitical priesthood (5:1—7:19), and the heavenly sanctuary to the earthly (8:5; 9:1). Christians enjoy a better covenant (7:22), better promises (8:6), better sacrifices (9:23), and ultimately, a better country (11:16) than those afforded their precursors in the OT.

The Christology (understanding of Christ) set out in Hebrews differs in significant respects from the understandings found elsewhere in the NT. Not only were all things created through Christ (1:2; cf. John 1:1–3), though God was "the builder" (3:4), and the universe upheld by Christ's word (1:3; 2:10; cf. Col. 1:15–17); all things were created for him (2:10), and he is the appointed "heir of all things" (1:2; cf. 1 Cor. 15:28). By suffering death, he tasted death "for every one" (2:9), and through his death, destroyed the devil, thereby delivering all who were in bondage (to the devil?) through fear of death (2:14–15; cf. Rom. 6:23; 1 Cor. 15:24–26, 54–57; Rev. 20:14).

Most characteristically and distinctively, Hebrews' christology focuses on Christ's role as the new and ultimate high priest. Various

OT passages, especially in Psalms, are read as testimony by the Holy Spirit (3:7; 9:8; 10:15) to Jesus' priestly mission in the role of "high priest for ever after the order of Melchizedek" (6:20; cf. Gen. 14:18–20; Ps. 110:4). The author explains that Melchizedek's name means "righteous king" and "king of peace," and that Melchizedek, unlike later Levitical priests, was a priest forever. In these respects, he says, Jesus is like Melchizedek (chap. 7). Perhaps the author also meant to relate Jesus to Melchizedek because Jesus did not have any Aaronic or Levitical ancestors (7:14; cf. Matthew 1 and Luke 3). His main point is that whereas the Levitical priests had to offer sacrifices daily, Jesus "did this once for all when he offered up himself" (7:27; 10:10–14). Jesus is now enthroned as high priest in the heavenly sanctuary (8:1–2); there he mediates a new covenant, the one promised by Jeremiah (8:6–12; 9:15; 12:24). In this connection, he also makes intercession for those who "draw near to God," thereby saving them "for all time" (7:25).

Several passages indicate the writer's belief that the "present age" was coming to an end, and that Christ soon would come again. The writer refers to his own time as "these last days" (1:2) and urges his readers to live rightly as they "see the Day drawing near" (10:25). He quotes from Habakkuk to the effect that in "yet a little while . . . the coming one shall come and shall not tarry" (10:37; cf. Hab. 2:3; Mal. 3:1; Luke 18:8), and promises that Christ will appear a second time "to save those who are eagerly awaiting him" (9:28). This is the only text in the Bible to speak of Christ's "second" coming. Christian hopes for the future are also described in terms of the true "rest" promised the fathers of old (3:7—4:11) and as the "heavenly city" which is to come (11:16; 13:14; cf. Rev. 21:2–27). Christians should "strive to enter" or "seek" (4:11; 13:14; cf. Matt. 6:33; Luke 13:24) this "rest" or "city" by faith and righteous living.

Hebrews also contains several other distinctive ideas and texts. Here we find the famous definition of faith as "the assurance of things hoped for, the conviction of things not seen" (11:1), but "faith" also seems to mean doing or acting rightly in accordance with the divine intent (cf. Gal. 5:6; James 2:18–26), as is illustrated by a series of OT personalities and scenes (11:4–38). The need for authoritative leadership is indicated in the admonition, "Obey your leaders and submit to them" (13:17; cf. Titus 2:15). (There was, as yet, no overall church hierarchy.) The book also tells of some Christians' habit of neglecting common meetings, presumably for worship (10:25). The writer addresses the problem of whether Christians who lapse into apostasy or sin may be restored to the community and have any hope of salvation. The answer given here is no (6:4–8; 10:26–31; cf. James 5:19–20). In Hebrews, God's promise is characterized in striking language, as "a sure and steadfast anchor of the soul" (6:19)—an image that may have been important to later Christian catacomb artists, who adopted the anchor as one of the earliest Christian symbols. Passages from Hebrews, more than from most other NT writings, are commonly repeated in later Christian preaching, liturgy, and aphorism (e.g., 4:12, 14–16; 10:31; 11:1; 12:1–2; 13:8, 20–21).

Several concluding exhortations set forth the kind of life befitting those who aspire to enter the heavenly city or promised rest. They are to accept the Lord's discipline; strive for peace with all men; let brotherly love continue; show hospitality to strangers (cf. 3 John vv. 5–8); remember those in prison and the ill-treated (cf. Matt. 25:31–46); honor marriage; renounce love of money (cf. 1 Tim. 6:10); share possessions (cf. Acts 2:44–45); and obey their leaders (12:1—13:17).

JAMES

Like Hebrews, James is a tract or treatise, written for Christians everywhere ("the twelve tribes in the Dispersion," 1:1). Though not claiming to be an apostle, the writer gives authoritative advice and instruction on several subjects. Some interpreters see traces of Jewish Christianity here, and suggest that the author was James, the brother of Jesus (cf. Matt. 13:55; Galatians 1—2). But Jewish Christian interests, such as circumcision and Sabbath observance, are lacking. The writer does not commend works of the Jewish law, but the laws of liberty and love (2:8, 12), and "works" that complete faith and give expression to love (2:14–26; cf. 1:27). James may be the work of a gentile Christian pastor who wrote it ca. A.D. 90–100.

He particularly wishes to correct the notion that faith or belief is all that matters. Interpreters sometimes call this notion "fideism." Such a misunderstanding perhaps was prompted by Paul's emphasis on faith. Like Paul, however, James insists that what matters is faith working through love (2:14–26; cf. Gal. 5:6; 1 Cor. 13:2). In addition, James is concerned with urging Christians to be humble, peaceable, and gentle, rather than proud, jealous, ambitious, and judgmental (3:13–18; 4:2, 6, 10–12). He warns against misusing the tongue—that "little member" which is "a fire," and a "restless evil, full of deadly poison"—urging that it be controlled and directed toward right speaking (1:26; 3:2–12; cf. Mark 7:14–23). Similarly, he warns that passions or desires, if not restrained, lead to sin, strife, and death (1:14–15; 4:1–3). Christians must keep themselves from "friendship with the world" (4:4; cf. 1 John 2:15–17); but this does not mean indifference to those in need. On the contrary, "religion that is pure and undefiled" includes visiting "widows and orphans in their affliction" (1:27). Such, indeed, is the test of faith: whether it is helpful to those in need (2:15–17; cf. Luke 10:25–37). It is a question of doing, not simply hearing, the word (1:22–26; cf. Luke 6:46–49). The author's attitude toward the rich is related to this: they busy themselves with the pursuit of gain and luxury, not only ignoring, but even exploiting laborers and killing the righteous (5:1–6; cf. Wisd. of Sol. 1:16—2:20). Therefore, Christians should not defer to the rich or humiliate the poor. Indeed, the poor are heirs to the kingdom of God (2:1–5; cf. Luke 6:20, 24; 16:19–31).

Like most NT authors, James understands that the "coming of the Lord is at hand," indeed, "the Judge is standing at the doors" (5:8–9). But he admonishes readers to be patient and steadfast in the meantime (5:7, 10–11). Those who suffer should pray, and those who are cheerful should sing praise (5:13). If one is sick, he should summon the church elders (cf. 1 Tim. 4:14; Titus 1:5), who are then to pray over him and anoint him with oil (5:14). This text may have given rise to the later Christian rite or sacrament of anointing the sick and dying. Christians, according to James, are to confess their sins to one another, and pray for one another (5:16, a text that later may have led to the Christian rite or sacrament of confession—though here there is no suggestion of offering one's confession to a priest). Elijah is then presented as an example of the efficacy of prayer (5:17–18). In contrast to Hebrews, James holds that sinners and those who wander from the truth can indeed be brought back, and, in effect, offers indulgences to those who help rehabilitate them (5:19–20). Several passages in James echo sayings of Jesus in the Synoptic Gospels, especially in Matthew. James may have been familiar with one or more of these Gospels, or may have known the sayings through oral tradition. Examples include 1:22 (cf. Matt. 7:24–27); 2:13 (cf. Matt. 6:14–15; 18:23–35); 3:11–12 (cf. Matt. 3:17–18); 4:10 (cf. Matt. 23:12); 4:11–12 (cf. Matt. 7:7); and 5:12 (cf. Matt. 5:34–37).

1 PETER

The writer identifies himself as Peter, an apostle (1:1), and sends greetings from the church at "Babylon" (probably Rome, 5:13; cf.

Rev. 17:1—18:24). The letter might have been written by the apostle Peter, who, with Paul, was executed in Rome ca. A.D. 64, according to extrabiblical tradition. Many interpreters, however, think that it is more likely the composition of a later Christian, and that its references to sufferings and trials should be understood in connection either with the experienced persecution of Christians in Asia Minor ca. A.D. 96 (see Revelation 1—3), or with the common apocalyptic expectation that the messianic age would be preceded by a time of severe suffering or tribulation (see, e.g., Dan. 12:1; Mark 13:7–23). The author also identifies himself as an elder (5:1), a kind of Christian leader found only in NT writings of the late first century. First Peter's several affinities to Ephesians, the Pastorals, Hebrews, and James also point toward probable post-Petrine authorship. The author begins in the fashion of Paul's letters, addressing certain persons or communities, here "the exiles of the Dispersion" (cf. James 1:1), specifically, Christians located in several of the Roman provinces of Asia Minor (1:1). These probably were first- or second-generation converts from paganism to Christianity (1:14, 18). Christians in two of these provinces, Galatia and Asia, are also addressed, respectively, in Paul's letter to the Galatians, and in the Book of Revelation. "Peter" likewise concludes in terms reminiscent of Paul's letters (5:12–14). According to Paul (Galatians 1—2), Peter (or Cephas) was a missionary to Jews and was associated with Jewish Christian concerns in Jerusalem and Antioch. The present letter gives no indication of these connections or concerns. To this writer, Christians are "a chosen race" and "holy nation" (2:9). When he mentions Gentiles, he seems to mean non-Christian Gentiles (2:12; 4:3). Jews are not mentioned at all.

The writer is particularly concerned with encouraging Christians in Asia Minor to remain steadfast despite the trials they are suffering or may have to undergo (1:6–7; 3:14; 4:12–19). Suffering is associated with the evil designs of the devil (5:8–9; cf. Matt. 6:13), but not with Roman persecution, in contrast to Revelation, where both Satan and Rome are implicated in the tribulation experienced by Christians. Here readers are instructed to be subject to and honor the emperor (2:13–17; cf. Rom. 13:1–7).

Like most other NT writings, 1 Peter warns then-contemporary readers that the present age was soon to end. Christ's previous coming has marked the beginning of the end of the old era (1:20); now "the end of all things is at hand" (4:7); "the time has come for judgment" (4:17; cf. 1:5; 2:12; 4:5). Evidently the writer expects God to be the Judge (1:17; 4:5). Afterward, those whose previous conduct has been found sufficiently righteous will receive the imperishable "inheritance . . . kept in heaven" for them (1:4). Whether that inheritance will be experienced in heaven (cf. John 14:2–3; Phil. 3:20–21) or on earth (cf. Matt. 6:10; Heb. 12:22; 13:14; Rev. 21:2) is not indicated. In the meantime, "for a little while," Christians may have to suffer various trials (1:6; 5:10).

During the interim, Christians should live soberly and righteously, above all, with love for one another (1:22; 2:16; 3:8; 4:8; cf. John 13:34–35; Heb. 13:1). Love, the writer urges, "covers a multitude of sins" (4:8; cf. James 5:20). In this connection, Christians should "practice hospitality ungrudgingly to one another" (4:9; cf. Heb. 13:1–2; 2 John vv. 10–11; 3 John vv. 5–8). Like Paul, the present writer understands that this new life of love has been made possible by the death and resurrection of Christ, in whom Christians are now "born anew" (1:3, 22–23; cf. John 3:3). Righteous living is essential, for at the Judgment, God will judge each person "impartially according to his deeds" (1:17; 2:12; cf. 1 Cor. 6:9–10; Gal. 6:7–9). So important is the matter of right living that the author devotes most of chaps. 2—5 to moral advice and instruction. Such advice was particularly important since the gentile Christians to whom he was writing had grown up in the midst of degraded pagan culture without the benefit of guidance from biblical law. Particularly, the writer is concerned that Christians should control the "passions of the flesh" (2:11; 4:2; cf. 1 Cor. 6:9–20, where Paul confronted the same kind of problem). Though formerly not God's people, now through God's grace, Gentiles have become his people (2:9–10; cf. Hos. 1:6—2:23). But they must live up to the standard of their new being. Therefore they should "put away" malice and envy, and use their gifts for one another's good (2:1; 4:10–11; cf. 1 Corinthians 12—14). Many other specific precepts and guidelines are enumerated (e.g., in 2:11—3:17; 4:15; 5:1–6).

First Peter has a number of unique or unusual features. The idea that the Spirit of Christ inspired OT prophetic utterances (1:10–11) is not found elsewhere (cf. Heb. 3:7; 9:8; 10:15, where the Holy Spirit is said to have done so). Only in 1 Peter do we find the idea that when Christ died he was "put to death in the flesh" but remained or became "alive in the spirit" (3:18). This spiritual Christ then "preached to the spirits in prison," namely, the dead in Hades (3:19–20; 4:6; cf. Eph. 4:8–10). These texts probably were the basis for the later creedal affirmation that after he was buried, Christ "descended into Hell." Here the idea is that he did so in order to make salvation possible for the dead of earlier generations. Like some other post-Pauline writings, 1 Peter calls on servants (here "house servants") to be submissive to their masters (*despotai*), showing "all respect," "even to the overbearing," thereby "following" in Christ's "steps." The author says nothing about how masters should treat their servants (cf. Eph. 6:5–9, which does; and Titus 2:9–10, which does not). Likewise, the author calls on wives to be submissive to their husbands, evidently so as to "win" (convert) those who are pagans (3:1–6)—a rather extraordinary missions strategy (cf. 1 Cor. 7:12–17). He does call on husbands to be considerate of their wives (3:7; cf. Eph. 5:22–30, which also gives such advice; and Titus 2:4–5, which does not), honoring them "as the weaker sex" (an expression found earlier in 4 Macc. 15:5), since they are "joint heirs of the grace of life."

Some form critics (interpreters tending to place biblical traditions in possible cultic settings within the early Christian communities) generally suggest that 1 Peter was originally a baptismal sermon. Baptism is mentioned, somewhat indirectly, at 3:21, where the deliverance of Noah (and others on the ark) "by water" is compared with baptism, which saves "as an appeal to God for a clear conscience through the resurrection of Jesus Christ" (cf. John 3:5). Most NT writings do not refer to baptism; it is not clear to what extent this rite was considered important within the NT period (cf. John 4:2; Acts 8:36; 1 Cor. 1:13–17). At all events, baptism does not seem to be one of the central interests indicated in 1 Peter.

Implicitly, elders are seen as "shepherds," charged to care for their flocks (5:1–3; cf. Ezekiel 34). Elders are also referred to as church leaders in Acts and the Pastorals. Perhaps the principal leaders in each congregation, or possibly each town, were known as elders or bishops (see Titus 1:5–9). In 1 Peter, Christ is twice designated the Chief Shepherd (2:25; 5:4; cf. Ezek. 34:11–15, where God is his people's Shepherd), an unusual christological title in the NT. See also John 10:1–4, and Heb. 13:20.

Finally, "the devil" plays a special role in 1 Peter. He "prowls around like a roaring lion, seeking someone to devour" (5:8). The devil, Satan, or "the Evil One" is associated with tribulation or the suffering of the faithful, and regarded as a danger to be reckoned with in several other NT writings (e.g., Matt. 6:13; Eph. 6:11; 1 John 5:19; Rev. 12:7–12). This understanding contrasts with that in Heb. 2:14–15 which seems to say that Jesus has already destroyed the devil (cf. Mark 3:23–27).

2 PETER

Though the writer presents himself as Peter the apostle (1:1, 16–18), NT scholars generally agree that this letter was written well after Peter's time, possibly as late as ca. A.D. 140. The generation of the "fathers" (apostles) has passed away (3:4; cf. John 21:20–23). Paul's letters have been collected and are considered authoritative writings if not Scriptures (3:15–16). The writer notes that some things in Paul's letters are hard to understand, a word of consolation to later interpreters of Paul, as well. Since Paul's letters are well known, the present author does not write in his name, as some earlier NT writers did; instead, so that his advice would carry weight, he writes to "remind" Christians what "Peter" said they should remember or recall in years to come (1:12–15; 3:1). Another (or possibly the same) author undertook to offer fellow Christians much of the same advice, writing under the name of Jude (see infra). Like other "catholic epistles," such as Hebrews, James, and 1 John, 2 Peter is a general letter or tract, which was written for all Christians of the time, not for a particular congregation. It emphasizes three related concerns.

First, Christians should live godly lives, supplementing their faith with virtue, so that they might indeed enter into the kingdom of Christ (1:3–11; 3:11, 14). The author does not use the term Christian or Christianity, but refers to the latter as "the way of truth" (2:2) and "the way of righteousness" (2:21). "Knowledge" and "godliness" are recurrent expressions characterizing the Christian life (e.g., 1:3–8). Self-control, steadfastness, and brotherly affection (*philadelphia*) are also commended (1:6–7). Second Peter has a distinctive theory of salvation: Christians are to "become partakers of the divine nature" (1:4; cf. 1 Cor. 15:35–54). Implicitly, they will do so when they enter "the eternal kingdom" of their "Lord and Savior Jesus Christ" (1:11; cf. the usual term in earlier NT writings, kingdom of God, e.g., at Mark 1:15; 1 Cor. 6:9–10; and Gal. 5:19–20.) The writer suggests that by their holiness and godliness, Christians can hasten the coming of the parousia (3:11–12; cf. Acts 3:19–21).

Second, the writer urges his readers to beware of false prophets and teachers who promote heresies and entice or exploit men with their licentiousness and greed (2:1–3). These deviants have been promoting "cleverly devised myths" and other heresies (1:16; 2:1). Christians should recognize that the interpretation of Scripture is not a matter for each individual's opinion (i.e., heresy, 1:20–21). False teachers and prophets also promote ungodly wickedness (2:2–22). The writer refers frequently to the "destruction" that awaits such persons (2:3, 12; 3:7). Unlike other NT writers, 2 Peter looks for their punishment not only on the day of judgment, but in the meantime, as well (2:9–10).

Finally, the writer attempts to explain why the promised parousia or coming of Christ has not yet occurred. "Peter" anticipated that in the last days, "scoffers" would raise this question (3:3–4). Evidently the writer believed that his readers were then living in these "last days," for such scoffers have evidently appeared. He suggests several explanations. For one thing, God has created and destroyed the earth before by his word (3:5–6); he will "by the same word" destroy the heavens and earth that now exist (3:7), and make new heavens and a new earth (3:11–13). In other words, God did it before, and he will surely do it again, as the scoffers and the ungodly will discover to their sorrow on the day of judgment. Next, the writer suggests that God reckons time differently than humans do: "with the Lord, one day is as a thousand years" (3:8; cf. Ps. 90:4). Therefore, the passing of two or more generations since the parousia was to have occurred need not be a matter of concern, despite earlier promises and expectations (e.g., Matt. 24:33–34 = Mark 13:29–30 = Luke 21:31–32; 1 Thess. 4:13–17; Rev. 1:1–3; 22:10, 12, 20). Another explanation is that this delay is to be understood as God's forbearance, so that none should perish and all might reach repentance (3:9, 15). Nevertheless, "the Day" may come at any time, "like a thief" in the night (3:10; cf. Matt. 24:43–44; 1 Thess. 5:2–3; Rev. 3:3; 16:15); therefore Christians must be ready, awaiting it in "lives of holiness and godliness" (3:10–14). The idea that the old heavens and earth would be completely destroyed at the time of the parousia (3:10–12) is unusual; the OT prophets typically looked for the transformation or restoration of the earth, when humans and other creatures would live together on earth in peace under the sovereignty of God (e.g., Isa. 11:6–9; 19:19–25; 25:6–9; Hos. 2:18–23; Mic. 4:1–4). In Revelation (21:1—22:5), which shares the expectation that the present world is to "pass away," as here (3:13), the redeemed are expected to inhabit a new earth.

1 JOHN

Here again, we have a treatise for all Christians of the author's time, rather than a letter to a particular congregation. It is, the writer says, "the message" he proclaims (1:3, 5). Both in style and substance, 1 John resembles the Gospel of John so closely as to suggest that the same author might have written both. There are, however, important differences, and the question of authorship remains open. The letter and the Gospel probably were written ca. A.D. 100. Some interpreters think that the same person who wrote 1 John also wrote 2 and 3 John, but this theory is still less well founded.

Both 1 John and the Gospel use the term "abiding" prominently (see, e.g., 1 John 3:23–24; John 15:4–10); and both make much of the contrast between light and darkness, and the ambiguous character of the world. Both refer frequently to the truth as the essence of Christianity (1 John 3:19; John 18:37) and to eternal life (rather than the kingdom of God) as the ultimate blessing for those who believe in Jesus (1 John 5:13; John 20:30–31). Both stress the commandment to love one another or "the brethren" (1 John 2:7–10; 3:23; John 15:12–17). Both refer to believers as "children of God" (1 John 3:1; John 1:12). Unlike most NT writings, each mentions the forgiveness of sins (1 John 2:12; John 20:23); and each twice records the unusual promise that God will grant those who pray whatever they wish (1 John 3:22; 5:14–15; John 14:13–14; 16:23–24; cf. Matt. 7:7–11; Mark 11:23–24). Both insist that Jesus was "in the flesh," evidently in order to counter some incipient docetic heresy which regarded him only as a spirit or spiritual being (1 John 4:2; John 1:14; 20:27; cf. Luke 24:39–43; Phil. 2:5–8).

Many features, however, contrast with those of the Gospel according to John. The author of 1 John consistently addresses his readers rather condescendingly as "little children" or "children" (e.g., 2:1, 18, 28), a mode of address found only in the appendix to the Fourth Gospel (John 21:5). First John is the only NT writing to say that those who commit sins are "of the devil" (cf. Wisd. of Sol. 2:24), or that Jesus "appeared to destroy the works of the devil" (3:8, 10; cf. 3:5, which says that he appeared "to take away sins"; and Heb. 2:14). Only in 1 John do we find a distinction between "mortal" and "non-mortal" sins (5:16–17). Somewhat in passing, the author of the letter cautions against believing "false prophets" (4:1) and worshiping idols (5:21)— concerns not present in the Gospel. First John also diverges from the Fourth Gospel in its understandings that the world is dominated by "the evil one" (5:19) and that the parousia is imminent (2:18).

The basic purpose of the letter (or treatise) is to urge Christians both to hold fast, or believe, the Christian message (1:5), particularly that Jesus is the Christ or Son of God (5:1, 5), and to live in accordance with the love commandment; in short, to believe and love (3:23). Various "antichrists" (heretics) have split off from the church, denying that Jesus is the Christ (2:18–23). Anyone who denies this is a "liar"

(2:22). So is anyone who claims to "know" Christ but disobeys his commandments (2:4); thus "if any one says 'I love God,' and hates his brother, he is a liar" (4:20). The test of love is whether it prompts one to help his brother who is in need (3:17–18; cf. James 1:27; 2:14–17; Matt. 25:31–46). Love is "of God"; indeed, "God is love" (4:7–8, 16)—the only biblical passages to say this in so many words. Those who abide in love "may have confidence for the day of judgment" (4:17).

The writer is mainly concerned with the moral life of his Christian contemporaries. Repeatedly, he urges them to live according to Christ's commandment to love one another. Those who do so may thereby know and show that they are "children of God" (3:10). First John holds that Christians (those "born of God") do not sin (3:4–9; 5:18). Yet he insists that those who say they have no sin deceive themselves, and he urges Christians to confess their sins so that God may forgive them (1:8–10). Indeed, he says that his reason for writing is so that his intended readers may not sin (2:1).

Like most NT writers, the author of 1 John expected the coming of Christ in the near future. According to apocalyptic doctrine, "antichrist" was to come first (see, e.g., Mark 13:21–23; 2 Thess. 2:3–4). Since many antichrists have now come, the author logically concludes, it must be "the last hour" (2:18; cf. 4:3). Like Paul, 1 John anticipates that when Christ comes, believers will be transformed, becoming like him (3:2; cf. 1 Cor. 15:49; Phil. 3:21). In the meantime, those who so hope should live in purity of life, in love, and in righteousness, renouncing sin (3:3–10) and "the world," which "passes away" (2:15–17; cf. 1 Cor. 7:29–31) but in the meantime continues to be "in the power of the evil one" (5:19; cf. 1 Pet. 5:8–9). Implicitly, perhaps, as in John 14:1–3 and some of Paul's letters (e.g., Phil. 3:20 and 1 Thess. 4:15–17), the future realm of salvation was thought to be in heaven, not on earth (cf. Matt. 6:10; Rev. 21:2—22:5).

2 JOHN

Second John is written in the form of a letter from "the elder" (or "old man" or "presbyter") to "the elect lady and her children." The Greek term for church (*ekklesia*) is feminine; the "elect lady" evidently stood either for some particular church and its members, or for the whole church. If the latter, it would have been in effect a catholic or general letter, like 1 Peter, James, and 1 John. The writer could have been the same person who wrote 1 John (ca. A.D. 100), or may have been a somewhat later church leader writing, perhaps, near the time the Pastoral Letters were composed (ca. A.D. 110–120). "Elders" are mentioned as church leaders in the latter chapters of Acts, in the Pastorals, and in James 5:14, and seem to have been local leaders or bishops. The author or authors of the Gospel of John and of 1, 2, and 3 John are all anonymous: none of these writings itself states that it was written by a person named John. Third John likewise purports to have been written by "the elder." No single person is so named or identified in the other Johannine writings or elsewhere in the NT.

Like 1 John, 2 John addresses those who already know "the truth," meaning, in effect, sound doctrine (vv. 1, 4). Second John also uses the term "abiding," but does so with reference to maintaining true doctrine (v. 9), in contrast to what we find in 1 John 4:13–16, where it is a question of abiding in love and in God, and of God's abiding in believers (cf. John 15:4–7). Nothing is said in 2 John about light and darkness or the world—which are central themes in 1 John. Concern with maintaining sound doctrine is characteristic of NT writings composed somewhat after A.D. 100, notably the Pastoral Letters, Jude, and 2 Peter. Language used in urging adherence to the love commandment here (vv. 5–6) suggests some literary relationship to 1 John (cf. 1 John 2:7; 3:11; 5:3), though the instruction to "follow love" (v. 6) is unparalleled. The salutation (v. 3) may have been borrowed from one of Paul's letters, several of which were familiar to Christians by the time of 2 Peter (2 Pet. 3:15–16), and probably somewhat earlier. Compare 2 John 3 with Romans 1:7 and 1 Cor. 1:3, for instance.

The main concern in 2 John is to warn Christians against heretical teachers or "deceivers," who deny that Jesus came in the flesh (v. 7; cf. 1 John 2:22–23; 4:2). These docetists presumably held that Jesus only "seemed" (*dokein*) to have been in human form. Like the author of 1 and 2 Timothy and Titus, this writer exhorts his readers to hold to "the truth" or traditional "doctrine." He warns especially against offering hospitality to such heretics and thereby contributing to their "wicked work" (vv. 10–11). The question of offering hospitality was a difficult or delicate one. Given the absence of a central structure of church government which could issue credentials, and the lack of any common creedal standards, it might well have been unclear at first encounter whether a newly arrived traveling missionary was heretical or not. Nevertheless, Heb. 13:2 and 3 John vv. 5–8 advocate offering hospitality to strangers. Unlike the author of 1 John, the writer of 2 John does not construe the appearance of many deceivers or "antichrists" as a sign that the parousia was near (v. 7; cf. 1 John 2:18). The letter ends with greetings from the children of "your elect sister," presumably another church. The terms "elect lady" and "elect sister" are not used in other NT writings; if they refer to particular churches or congregations, we have no way to identify them.

3 JOHN

As in 2 John, the writer identifies himself as "the elder," or "presbyter." The "beloved disciple" to whom the Gospel of John is attributed, implicitly, via its epilogue or appendix, presumably lived to a considerable age (John 21:20–24). The assertion in 3 John v. 12 that its writer's "testimony is true" seems intended to associate him with this disciple, of whom the same is said in John 21:24. That disciple might have been known as "the elder," in view of his age; and no doubt would have been acknowledged as a person of some authority (see 3 John 9; cf. Matt. 18:18). So it is possible that the author of the Fourth Gospel also wrote 3 John; but it is by no means certain. No disciple or writer named John is mentioned in either the Gospel or any of the letters of John, but ascriptions to John appear in the earliest NT manuscripts. Like 2 John, 3 John mentions truth several times; the expression "follow the truth" appears in both (v. 4; 2 John v. 4); and some concluding remarks are nearly identical (2 John v. 12; 3 John vv. 13–14). Unlike 1 and 2 John, 3 John mentions neither heretics nor the love commandment. Interpreters generally think it likely that the same person wrote 2 and 3 John, but are less certain as to whether this person was the author of 1 John.

The writer's main concern is to encourage Gaius (and perhaps others in his church, v. 9) to show hospitality to traveling Christian missionaries, support their future travels, and resist efforts by a certain misguided Diotrephes to the contrary. Interpreters suggest that 3 John was meant to correct a misreading of the warning in 2 John against welcoming heretics (2 John vv. 10–11). Other NT writings also encourage hospitality (Heb. 13:2; 1 Pet. 4:9). Whether strangers or traveling missionaries were heretical or orthodox might not have been immediately apparent. Thus the writer wishes to vouch for the credentials of Demetrius, a well-attested Christian, perhaps a missionary, and possibly the bearer of the letter, and evidently asks Gaius to receive him hospitably (v. 12).

Gaius was a common Roman name. We know nothing about him. Like Philemon, in Paul's letter by that name, he may have been an actual person. Or, perhaps like Theophilus in Luke 1:3 and Acts 1:1, he may have been a symbol standing for readers generally. References to Diotrephes and Demetrius suggest that this letter may have been a genuine one, that is, to and about real persons. The concluding greeting to and from "the friends" (v. 15) is distinctive, and may have been the basis for the Quakers' later self-designation as the Society of Friends.

JUDE

The author describes himself as the brother of James (v. 1). Jesus had brothers named James and Judas (Jude in Matt. 13:55 = Mark 6:3), but the letter's concern about ungodly heretics (vv. 4, 8–9) suggests a setting after the time of the generation of Jesus' contemporaries, perhaps during the period when 2 Timothy and Titus were composed, ca. A.D. 110–20. Similar concerns are prominent in these Pastoral Letters. The present writing probably was ascribed to Jude in accordance with the later Christian practice of attributing authoritative writings to figures of the apostolic age, namely, to Paul, the twelve apostles, or Jesus' brothers. If Jesus' brother James was thought to have written a letter for the guidance of all Christians, why should his brother Jude not have done so as well? But the writer reveals that the age of the apostles was already over by calling on readers to remember their predictions (v. 17). Jude and 2 Peter are so similar that one must have drawn from the other: compare Jude 3–8, 10–13, and 17–18 with 2 Pet. 2:1–17 and 3:1–3. If used by 2 Peter, Jude would have been written by ca. A.D. 140.

This general letter or tract for all Christians urges "those who are called" to defend "the faith" given to their holy predecessors from certain heretics who have infiltrated the churches (vv. 3–4). As in Col. 1:23 and 2:6, and Titus 1:13, "faith" here refers to the body of authoritative doctrine that the present generation of Christians received from those before them. Here only in the NT do we find the expression "holy faith" (v. 20). Like the wicked men and angels of old, the worldly and licentious people of the writer's time would surely be punished severely. (Among other things, they have been carousing during church love feasts, v. 12; cf. 1 Cor. 11:20–22.) But those who are "beloved in God the Father and kept for Jesus Christ" (v. 1) should confirm their "most holy faith," remaining in the love of God, awaiting Christ's mercy "until eternal life" (vv. 20–21). The fact that "scoffers following their own ungodly passions"—a phenomenon of "the last times"—have now already appeared (vv. 17–19; cf. 2 Pet. 3:3–6; 2 Tim. 3:1–9; 1 John 2:18) can be construed as evidence of the writer's belief in the imminence of this mercy.

The author shows a tendency to incorporate and expand upon earlier legends and lore. He seems to have drawn upon Wisd. of Sol. 10:6 as to the destruction not only of Sodom and Gomorrah, but also of neighboring towns, adding that they were all punished by eternal fire (v. 7; cf. Genesis 19; Deut. 29:23). His use of the *Book of Enoch* suggests that he considered it authoritative as Scripture (vv. 6, 13–15; cf., e.g., *1 Enoch* 1:9; also *1 Enoch* 6–10 and 86–88). His reference to the archangel Michael's debate with the devil over possession of Moses' body comes from some other extrabiblical tradition, possibly a lost fragment of the pseudepigraphic *Assumption of Moses*.

The unusually elaborate benediction or doxology at the end of the letter (vv. 24–25) may derive from earlier Christian liturgy, or may have been composed by the author of the letter. Its reference to God's being "before all time" is unparalleled in biblical tradition, though possibly implicit in the Genesis creation stories.

REVELATION

The writer identifies himself several times as John, but does not claim to be one of the apostles. Reference to his bearing witness and testimony (1:2) might suggest a connection with the "beloved disciple" of John 21:24; but probably was intended to authenticate the "words of prophecy" set forth in the rest of the book. The "revelation" (i.e., apocalypse) is in two parts: a group of letters by John to seven churches in the Roman province of Asia in western Asia Minor (1:4—3:22), and a series of apocalyptic visions and auditions experienced by the author while "in the spirit" (4:1—22:5). A concluding section affirms the validity and importance of "these words." For the most part, the words of the "prophecy" or "revelation" are attributed to Jesus himself, either directly (1:10–19) or through his "angel" (1:1; 22:16). Revelation is the only NT work apart from the Gospels and Acts 1:7–8 to attribute verbatim statements to Jesus.

In Rev. 1:4–20, John writes a "cover letter" introducing the separate letters that follow, which are addressed to the "angels" of each of the seven churches. Intertestamental tradition (influenced by Persian religion) visualized seven angels as intermediaries between "the saints" and God (e.g., Tob. 12:15; cf. Rev. 1:4), and the fact that seven churches, each with a separate angel, are named here is suggestive of that tradition. On the other hand, Jewish thought of the time also understood that God had appointed a patron angel (or "prince") to have charge over the affairs of each nation (e.g., Dan. 10:13; 12:1). Revelation seems to extend the idea of patron angels to local cities. In the context of Revelations 2—3, however, the angels appear in the role of corresponding secretaries, receiving the message of revelation which God had given to Jesus, who then gave it to John (1:1), who then writes to the angels of each of the churches. These seven "letters," along with the apocalyptic visions and prophecies that come later in the apocalypse, have one common theme: they call on their intended first-century Christian readers to endure all trials and tribulations they must suffer, remaining faithful despite persecution, for Jesus is coming soon to deliver them and punish both their persecutors and any who succumb to pressure and worship the image of the emperor. The visions and prophecies go on to promise that all forces of evil will be overcome and that the heavenly city, the New Jerusalem, will come down and be established on a new or completely transformed earth.

The writer sums up the purpose of this book: "Here is a call for the endurance and faith of the saints" (13:10; 14:12; cf. 1:9; 3:10). John knows that his readers are suffering persecution and tribulation, or expects that they are about to do so (2:10; 3:10). They are urged to "hold fast" to what they have (2:25; 3:11), meaning both the traditions they previously received (3:3; cf. 2 Tim. 1:13–14; Jude v. 3), and the words of the present book (1:3; 22:7). They can do so with hope for the future because—John declares repeatedly—Jesus is coming soon (3:11; 22:7, 12, 20), "like a thief" in the night (3:3; 16:15; cf. Matt. 24:42–44 = Luke 12:39–40; 1 Thess. 5:2; 2 Pet. 3:10). The book is written to show Christians "what must soon take place" (1:1; 22:6). "The time is near" (1:3; 22:10; cf. Matt. 4:17 = Mark 1:15); there will be "no more delay" (10:6; cf. 2 Pet. 3:3–10; 2 Esd. 16:37–39, 74). And the book ends with the eager prayer: "Come, Lord Jesus!" (22:20; cf. Matt. 6:10 = Luke 11:2; 1 Cor. 16:22).

Satan either already has been, or soon will be defeated in heaven (12:7–11), but for a short time he will cause much grief among the faithful on earth (12:12–17). Satan (sometimes identified here as "the devil" and "the dragon") is associated with various beasts which evidently represent the Roman Empire and certain of its emperors (chaps. 13; 16). Rome is also pictured as "the great harlot," "Babylon," seated on seven mountains (i.e., the seven hills of Rome), which persecutes "the saints" (i.e., faithful Christians) (chap. 17). But "Babylon" is soon to fall (chap. 18) and Satan will be bound, while those martyred for their faith will come to life and reign with Christ a thousand years, literally, a millennium (20:1–6; cf. 2 Esd. 7:28, which looks for a four-hundred-year interregnum during which the Messiah will be manifested). After that, Satan will be loosed for a while, but then be destroyed forever, along with Death, Hades, and all unrighteous persons (20:7–15; cf. 1 Cor. 15:23–26). The old heaven and earth will pass away, and new ones will come in their place. The glorious New Jerusalem will come down from heaven to earth (cf. Matt. 6:10). Here the faithful and righteous shall dwell forever in the presence of God and the Lamb (Christ), by the river of life with trees of life on either side (21:1—22:5; cf. Ezek. 47:12). There will be no temple in this new era (21:22; cf. Ezekiel 40—48, Haggai, and Zechariah, which looked for a new temple as the central feature of the coming or messianic age). By the time Revelation was written, the Jerusalem temple had been destroyed, and both Jews and Christians were adjusting their beliefs and practices to its absence. Here, the writer says that all Christians (who remain faithful) are "priests" (1:6; 5:10), an understanding that anticipates the Protestant idea of the "priesthood of all believers."

Many interpreters think that Revelation was written to strengthen the faith of Christians in the Roman province of Asia during a persecution by Roman authorities there ca. A.D. 96. Several passages suggest that Christians had been required to worship the emperor's image on pain of economic sanctions or death, and that many had been persecuted for failing to do so (6:9–11; 13:13–17; 17:6; 20:4). Little is known about this persecution, which may also have been the historical setting for 1 Peter, likewise addressed to Christians in Asia (and other Roman provinces in Asia Minor). In the second and third centuries A.D., Romans persecuted Christians after plagues broke out or barbarians (Western Europeans) defeated the legions, apparently on the theory that the Roman gods were displeased at not receiving the homage due them from their Christian subjects, and that something had to be done about it. Such seems to have been the case here. The "image of the beast" probably was an image of the current Roman emperor Domitian. The emperor Augustus had introduced the cult of the deity of the emperor and revived the worship of the old Roman gods a hundred years earlier, in order to cement the loyalty of Roman citizens and subjects from many ethnic backgrounds to the empire and its emperor or Caesar. The number 666 (13:18) probably stands for Nero Caesar, the first and most flamboyant persecutor of Christians. His name, like that of Haman in Esther, might then apply to latter-day persecutors, in the way that Zimri's name is applied to a latter-day traitor at 2 Kings 9:31. The author of Revelation uses Jezebel's name in this way, referring to a contemporary idolatress at 2:20. In Asia in the 90s, Christians apparently were required to offer a pinch of incense or a libation of some sort to the emperor's image. Those who did so would receive a "mark," perhaps a tattoo, to show they had met this requirement, so that they would be spared persecution (13:16–17; 14:9-11; 19:20; 20:4). Christians confronting this requirement faced a terrible choice: either they would be persecuted by the Romans, or else they would suffer eternal torment in fire and sulfur (14:9–11). The experience of persecution may partly account for the writer's lurid interest in the torment in store for both the unrighteous and the apostate (9:1–21; 14:9–11, 14–20; 19:17–21).

Use of the number seven is typical of the writer's interest in mysterious and symbolic meanings (cf. the seven visions of 2 Esdras). Another special characteristic is the composition or incorporation of numerous Christian hymns or psalms of praise (e.g., 4:8, 11; 11:15; 14:13; 15:3–4; 19:6–8). Handel later drew on some of these as texts for his famous *Messiah*, as did later Christian hymn writers. Chapter 18, a psalm of rejoicing over the prospective fall of Rome, echoes similar OT texts, such as Ezek. 26:17—28:23 and the Book of Nahum.

Modern readers sometimes view the Book of Revelation as a series of "Bible prophecies" meant for "us" and unfolding in our time "before our very eyes." It is clear, however, that Revelation was written to give hope and encouragement to readers in its author's time: the faithful could withstand Roman persecution for Jesus was coming soon, and both Satan and Rome would soon be overthrown. But Jesus did not come; martyred Christians did not rise from the dead; there was no thousand-year reign of Christ; if Satan was bound, tragedy and evil were not noticeably diminished during the "dark ages"; and it was more than three hundred years before the Roman Empire in the West began to collapse. The fact that the anticipated course of events did not materialize does not, of course, justify the invention of some modern, imaginative substitute scenario. Yet the underlying hopes and assurances expressed in Revelation need not be taken as inextricably tied to the specific circumstances and expectations of that time. Revelation 21—22 in particular look for the reconstitution of the conditions of life: a transformed existence much like that which, according to Genesis 1—2, God had intended mankind to enjoy forever. Once more God would dwell on earth with people; death would be no more; a river and the tree(s) of life would again be there to bless the human race, which would embrace the full range of descendants of the first human couple—the nations. Such hopes accord with much else that is central in the biblical tradition. Moreover, like Daniel in the OT and many other biblical writings, the Book of Revelation expresses supreme confidence in God's almighty power to deliver his people from seemingly hopeless circumstances.

THE BOOKS OF
THE BIBLE IN CONTEXT

1. THE HISTORICAL CONTEXT: MAIN EVENTS AND DEVELOPMENTS, 1500 B.C. TO A.D. 100

Most of the biblical drama took place on a stage just slightly larger than the state of Vermont, known first as the land of Canaan (the Canaanites had been there since ca. 3000 B.C.), then Israel, and later as Palestine (so named by the Romans in honor of the Philistines). Portions of the land also went by other names during the biblical period, such as Judah, Judea, Samaria, and Galilee. North to south, "from Dan to Beersheba," was 150 miles, while the greatest width, from Gaza to the Dead Sea, was barely sixty miles. Located on the southeastern end of the Mediterranean Sea, the land served as a corridor between the great empires of the the Tigris-Euphrates Valley and periodically powerful Egypt. A number of smaller nations or peoples were situated nearby: the Philistines, Edomites, Moabites, Ammonites, Syrians, and Phoenicians, for example. To a considerable extent, the history of Israel, Judah, and the Jewish people is the story of the interactions between them and these occasionally friendly but generally intrusive and often dominant neighbors. The biblical traditions, however, are more interested in the internal history: the events and meaning of events from the perspective of the faith-understanding of Abraham's descendants.

Abram and Sarai, the first of the fathers and mothers of Israel, migrated from Babylon (Chaldea) and sojourned in Syria (Aram) before going on into Canaan. The stories of Abraham and Sarah, Isaac and Rebekah, and Jacob, Leah, and Rachel—the principal "patriarchs" and "matriarchs" of Israel—may recall real persons and events from the fifteenth century B.C., or even earlier. As the story is told, Jacob was renamed Israel, and became the father or grandfather of those persons for whom the twelve tribes of Israel were named. A number of names and practices mentioned in biblical narratives are corroborated by archaeological evidence, though the stories themselves may be somewhat legendary.

The Joseph saga brought the people of Israel, still a large family or clan, into the land of Egypt. Time passed, probably more than one generation; the Hebrews multiplied, and the Egyptians, fearing their growing numbers, subjected them to slavery, probably during the reign of the famous Pharaoh Ramses II. Under Moses' leadership, the Israelites escaped from Egypt into the Sinai wilderness, perhaps ca. 1230 B.C. Here they wandered "forty years," receiving, through Moses, God's law or covenant. The Canaanites and various other peoples had already occupied most of the fertile lowlands of Canaan. The invading Israelites, led by Joshua, only succeeded in conquering or settling the central hill country of Canaan, along with some of the plateau land east of the Jordan River. Unhappily for the Israelites, the Philistines arrived about the same time (ca. 1200 B.C.) and quickly proceeded to occupy the fertile southern coastal plain and, within two centuries, nearly the entire land of Canaan.

The time between 1200 and 1000 B.C. is known as the period of the judges. During that period, the tribes of Israel (which included Gilead and Bashan, besides the traditional twelve) were, at best, loosely united in a confederation led, occasionally, by able charismatic judges and prophets, the last and perhaps greatest of whom was Samuel. The judges seem to have been mainly local heroes who came forward in times of crisis and singlehandedly, or with volunteers from, at most, a few tribes, tried to cope with neighboring marauders or oppressors. An editor of the Book of Judges comments from time to time, after describing particularly chaotic and gruesome scenes, "In those days there was no king in Israel; every man did what was right in his own eyes." In retrospect, it is clear that the political structure of the confederation proved inadequate to cope either with internal dissension and, at times, fratricidal conflict between or among the tribes of Israel, or with external threats to the nation's existence, in particular, the Philistine menace. Around 1000 B.C., after the Philistines had decisively overwhelmed Israel at Shiloh and captured the ark of the Lord, Samuel was induced to anoint Saul, a Benjamite, as king of Israel. Saul began his career after the fashion of the judges, leading a volunteer guerrilla army to rescue the village of Jabesh-Gilead from besieging Ammonite invaders. For a while, Saul succeeded in establishing a precarious kingdom on Israelite soil, but his kingship was weakened by internal problems, and the Philistines eventually proved too much for Israel, defeating Saul and his army at Mount Gilboa.

David, a Judahite, had earlier been anointed by Samuel to replace Saul, but became king only after Saul's death. He was then anointed by the leaders of Judah, his own people. Only after surmounting certain obstacles was he also made king of Israel. Under David, the people of Israel and Judah were united (for the greater part of his reign) into one nation, and succeeded in both throwing off Philistine domination and compelling other nearby nations to keep their distance. In after years, David's reign was seen as the golden age, and later hopes for the future often took the form of longing for another king or messiah (i.e., anointed one) from the house (i.e., lineage) of David. Yet David was strangely incapable of dealing with problems occasioned by the lust and ambition of his own sons — which nearly recapitulated his own offenses against Bathsheba and Uriah, if not also against the house of Saul. One son raped a half-sister and afterward was murdered by her brother, who later led the Israelites in revolt against David. David became old and senile, without having arranged for someone to succeed him. When he failed to install his surviving oldest son as king in his place, Solomon became king through a palace revolution engineered by his mother and the prophet Nathan.

Solomon became famous both for his wisdom and for the material splendor of his reign. But Solomon's luxury was paid for, in part, by the forced labor of his northern subjects, the Israelites, who resented this oppression by a southern (Judahite) ruler. A later commentator also condemned Solomon for his apostasy and worship of foreign deities. When Solomon died, his son Rehoboam arrogantly rejected the appeal by Jeroboam and the elders of Israel for relief from the heavy yoke of Solomon. Thereupon, the Israelites renounced Rehoboam and the house of David, and established their own separate kingdom, Israel, with Jeroboam as king, ca. 926 B.C. This marked the end of the united kingdom, and the beginning of the period of the divided monarchy.

The Northern Kingdom, Israel (also known as Ephraim or Samaria), continued under its own kings — who came from nine different, mostly short-lived, dynasties — down to 722 B.C., when Assyria took it over. The Southern Kingdom, Judah, was ruled by David's descendants (with one exception, Queen Athaliah) and continued as a separate and more or less independent nation until 586 B.C., when it was annexed by Babylonia, then the dominant power in the Near East. The period of the divided monarchy was complicated and sometimes chaotic, as the period of the judges had been earlier. At its beginning, ca. 926 B.C., Israel and Judah were at war with each other, and soon the latter was raided by Egypt (ca. 922). At times, Israel and its northern neighbor Syria warred against each other; once, at least, Israel and Judah were allied against Syria. Toward the end of the period (ca. 734), Syria and Israel combined against Judah, intending to compel the latter to join in a triple alliance against Assyria in order to try to check that empire's advance, as the three small kingdoms had done before in 853 B.C.

Some prophets had appeared before the time of the divided monarchy: Moses, Miriam, Balaam, Deborah, Samuel, and Nathan, for example. Now many others came forward. Micaiah, Elijah, Elisha, and others played prominent parts in the early years of the Northern Kingdom, advocating worship of Yahweh (God), and condemning Baal and other "foreign" (non-Israelite) gods and the kings, priests, prophets, and people who served them. The first two classical prophets, Amos and Hosea, also appeared in the North, ca. 740 B.C. These two denounced the people and particularly the leaders of Israel for their apostasy (i.e., turning from Yahweh), their worship of other gods, and their violations of the covenant requirements of kindness and justice within the community. Each declared that Yahweh would bring Israel to an end. That end came, at the hands of Assyria, in 722 B.C.

Judah survived, paying tribute to Assyria as the price of independence. The reign of Manasseh (ca. 687–642 B.C.), the longest of any of the kings of Israel or Judah, was marked by religious syncretism, cruel oppression, and compliance with Assyrian domination. But hope dawned with the accession of Josiah to the throne of Judah in 640. Josiah sponsored a major religious institutional reform (ca. 622 B.C.) inspired by the requirement set forth in the newly discovered "book of the law" that God should be worshiped in only one place. This requirement, along with several institutional accommodations necessary to implement it, appears in Deuteronomy 12—19. It apparently was not known in earlier biblical traditions (which reported, without misgiving, sacrificial worship at several different places). Many interpreters suggest that it was added to the text of Deuteronomy sometime during the seventh century B.C. in order to counter the persistent tendency of Judahites to worship other gods at the old cult shrines outside of Jerusalem. Josiah ordered the renovation of the Jerusalem temple and the destruction of all other places of worship, and also asserted Judah's independence from Assyria. But now the Babylonians were on the move. By 598, Judah had become a Babylonian vassal. After Judah tried to rebel in 586, a Babylonian army stormed into Jerusalem, burned the city, destroyed the temple and much of the city's system of walls, and carried away most of the remaining leaders as captives.

The Babylonian conquest of Judah in 586 B.C. marked the beginning of the period of the exile. The terms Jew and Jewish came into use at this point in the biblical tradition, for there was no longer a kingdom of Judah. Now it was their religion and their culture that gave the people identity. Though the prophets Jeremiah and Ezekiel encouraged the exiles to believe that God was still with them, the life of some exiles was bitter and anguished (see Psalm 137), as was that of those Jews who had remained in their homeland (see Lamentations). Persia, in the meantime, had become the preeminent power in the Middle East. By defeating the Babylonians in 540 B.C., Cyrus, the Persian emperor, became the liberator of the Jewish people. Judah and Jerusalem were still part of the Persian Empire, but in 538 Cyrus decreed that exiled peoples might return to their homelands, and many exiled Jews did so. Thus the exile ended in 538 B.C.

The Jewish exiles who returned to what had been their country at first busied themselves with rebuilding their homes and trying to reestablish their livelihoods. But crops failed, and many suffered from continuing poverty. Eventually the temple was rebuilt (ca. 515), but despite assurances by the prophets Haggai and Zechariah, conditions did not improve greatly. The walls and gates of Jerusalem were rebuilt ca. 444 under the direction of Nehemiah, a redoubtable Jewish leader commissioned by the Persians as governor. Malachi, the last of the biblical prophets, appeared about this time, insisting that Yahweh required full tithes and unblemished sacrificial animal offerings. By ca. 400 B.C., the Jewish law (Exodus through Deuteronomy) was codified and promulgated, evidently under the auspices of temple priests and Ezra the scribe. This written law, or Torah, was to be the basic standard for all subsequent Jewish faith and life.

Led by Alexander the Great, the Greeks rapidly expanded into a world empire, overwhelming the Persians in 333 B.C. By 331, the Jews were living under these new masters. For several centuries afterwards, Greek (Hellenistic) culture was a major influence upon Judaism — and also upon Christianity. Following Alexander's death in 323, his leading generals contended for supremacy, dividing the empire among themselves. One of them, Seleucus, established himself in Syria and began a dynasty there to the north of Israel. Another, Ptolemy, did the same in Egypt. From 301 to 198 B.C., the Jewish people were ruled by the Ptolemies; after 198, by the Seleucids. The Seleucid emperor Antiochus IV ("Epiphanes" the illustrious, as he named himself), moved, it seems, by enthusiasm for Greek culture, decided to stamp out Judaism and require Jews to worship Greek gods. Many Jews were persecuted for their religion, and in 168 B.C., a group of Jews took up arms against their Syrian oppressors. Judas Maccabeus was the most famous of the leaders of that era of resistance and eventual independence (of sorts), which came to be known as the Maccabean or Hasmonean period. Religious freedom was restored, and the title "king" reinstituted—though none of the Maccabean kings was descended from David. The period was marked by constant plotting and intrigue.

The independent Jewish kingdom ended, however, in 64 B.C., when the Roman general Pompey annexed Judea as part of the Roman Empire. Jews continued to have religious freedom under Roman rule, largely through the influence of a series of shrewd Edomite (Idumean) powerbrokers: Antipater, his son Herod the Great, and the latter's son Antipas and grandson Agrippa. Herod the Great rebuilt the temple (which had fallen into disrepair since 515), making it into a magnificent edifice (sometimes referred to as the temple of Herod), and presided over a period of material prosperity. Many Jews, however, resented his harsh ways and the fact that he was an Edomite and an agent for foreign overlords. At his death in 4 B.C., Herod's jurisdiction was divided among his sons. Antipas was made tetrarch of Galilee, and Archelaus tetrarch over Samaria, Judea, and Idumea. Archelaus proved incompetent and was replaced by a succession of Roman officials known as procurators, who were not particularly capable either. The fifth of these, Pontius Pilate, was removed from office in A.D. 36. The Romans later put Agrippa over these provinces. He was popular with the Jewish people, but when he died in A.D. 44, a second series of procurators took over. Some of these deliberately provoked Jewish religious sensibilities. In A.D. 66, under the leadership of "the Zealots," the Jewish people revolted against Rome. Under the emperor Titus the Romans laid siege to Jerusalem, and in A.D. 70 overran it and destroyed the temple (see the depiction on the Arch of Titus in Rome). The Jewish sectarian community at Qumran (where the Dead Sea Scrolls had been copied and preserved) was also overrun at this time. With no temple, there was no longer a place for sacrificial worship, and the Sadducees, who had been associated with the temple priests, lost their leadership role. Instead of the offering of sacrifices, knowing and observing other aspects of the law became the central features of Judaism. The Pharisees, with their teachers (rabbis), developing oral law or tradition, and synagogues, became the main authorities for later Judaism.

From its beginnings in Galilee and Judea, Christianity spread over the Mediterranean world, in large part through the efforts of Paul. All of the first Christians had been Jews, and many continued to observe Jewish law and tradition. Paul insisted that the gospel was for Gentiles (non-Jews) as well as Jews, and personally established numerous gentile congregations. James (Jesus' brother) and Peter (also known as Cephas) were the main leaders of the early churches in Jerusalem and Antioch, respectively, where certain Jewish practices evidently were retained for some time. Paul and Peter may have been executed in Rome at the time of the emperor Nero's persecution of Christians there in A.D. 64. Christians in Jerusalem abandoned that city shortly before or during the war of A.D. 66–70, after which Christianity became increasingly a gentile religion.

Several other kinds of problems arose among second- and third-generation Christians. One of increasingly urgent importance was that of defining and identifying correct or sound teachings and proper moral standards in the absence of an overall structure of church governance, any generally accepted creeds or doctrines, or even consensus as to which Christian writings should be considered authoritative. False teachers, heresies, and immoral conduct were central concerns in the NT writings dating from ca. A.D. 110 to 140. Another recurrent problem throughout the NT period was the fact that the expected parousia or return of Christ had not yet occurred. Christians in Asia Minor, particularly in the Roman province of Asia, faced another serious problem in the A.D. mid-90s: Roman authorities there were enforcing a requirement that everyone, including Christians, make a show of worshiping an image of the Roman emperor (perhaps the current emperor, Domitian). Those who failed to do so were subjected to severe persecution. Christians in post-NT times also were subjected, periodically, to similar persecution. That, and much else, of course, changed radically, when toward the end of the first quarter of the fourth century A.D., the emperor Constantine converted to Christianity and established this faith and its developing institutions as the official religion of the Roman Empire.

2. THE BIBLICAL
LITERATURE

The Bible comprises the preserved traditions and writings of a series of communities, reflecting the full range of their experiences and concerns during more than twelve hundred years. We find here what we might call biographies and histories; "last words," dirges, and eulogies; sermons and parables; folk songs, hymns, and love songs; architectural plans and military strategies; diaries, detective stories, melodramas, and romances; ritual and criminal laws; blessings and curses; moral admonitions and advice; prophecies and political commentaries; scientific and psychological observations; genealogies; aphorisms; theologies of history; fragments of myths; letters and tracts; apocalyptic visions; and even a few prayers. The variety and richness of this literature may confuse readers who expect to find only "religious" material in the Bible. Nevertheless, the Bible tells one story: the story of God, creation, humanity, and God's special peoples. A number of categories or genres of writing can be identified.

ARRANGEMENT OR
ORDER OF APPEARANCE

Approximately the first half of the OT consists of historical narratives (along with other kinds of traditions) that set out the main events and periods from earliest times to around 400 B.C. in story form—mainly prose composition. Interpreters commonly identify three main collections or sets of writings: the Tetrateuch (Genesis through Numbers, "four books" edited under P or priestly auspices, ca. 400 B.C.);

the Deuteronomic history book (Deuteronomy through 2 Kings, edited ca. 550 B.C.), and the Chronicler's history book (1 Chronicles through Nehemiah, edited ca. 350 B.C.). The Pentateuch (the first "five books" of the Bible) includes both narratives (from the creation stories to the death of Moses) and, in Exodus through Deuteronomy, the basic law codes. It concludes with the Israelites still in the wilderness, but moving toward the land of Canaan. The books from Joshua through 2 Kings continue the story of Israel and Judah, starting with their occupation of Canaan and continuing into the beginning of the exile. First and 2 Chronicles recapitulate and revise the narrative from Adam to the end of the exile, while Ezra and Nehemiah carry it forward to about 350 B.C.. The OT writings from Esther through Malachi all were written or are set in the context of the historical period described in the last two of these three sets of works.

The story of Esther is placed in the Persian period, but probably was written somewhat later. The Psalms, some of which date from pre-exilic times, served as hymns or liturgical prayers in the second temple. (The Prayer of Manasseh and the Prayer of Azariah and the Song of the Three Young Men, also psalmlike, probably were written after the Book of Psalms was completed.) The wisdom writings—Job, Proverbs, Ecclesiastes, Wisdom of Solomon, and Ecclesiasticus—reflect Persian and Hellenistic influence and probably were composed between the fifth and second centuries B.C. The Song of Solomon is grouped with Ecclesiastes and Proverbs because these writings were popularly believed to have been written by Solomon. Three collections of relatively early prophets' oracles and reported activities are then set out at some length: Isaiah, Jeremiah, and Ezekiel. Lamentations was inserted after Jeremiah because it was commonly thought that Jeremiah wrote it. Lamentations, like the apocryphal writings Baruch and the Letter of Jeremiah, gropes with the meaning of the exile and related events. Daniel, also set in the time of the exile (though probably written much later), follows Ezekiel. The OT closes with the Book of the Twelve, namely, twelve relatively brief writings consisting largely of prophetic oracles, attributed to or concerned with the twelve prophets, Hosea through Malachi. These were probably all inscribed on a single scroll, originally, thus "the book" of the twelve. The Hebrew canon, on the other hand, closes with its third section, the Holy Writings, commonly placed in the following order: Psalms, Job, Proverbs, Ruth, Song of Songs (or of Solomon), Ecclesiastes, Lamentations, Esther, Daniel, Ezra-Nehemiah, and 1-2 Chronicles. The Law or Torah (Genesis—Deuteronomy) and the Prophets (including not only the prophetic books but also Joshua, Judges, and 1 Samuel—2 Kings) constitute the first parts of the Hebrew or Jewish Scriptures.

First Esdras reviews the history of the Jewish people from Josiah to Ezra, while 2 Esdras is a philosophical treatise in the form of an apocalypse. Several stories written between the fifth and second centuries B.C. give indications of Jewish life and interests during these years: Daniel, Tobit, Judith, Additions to Esther, Susanna, and Bel and the Dragon. These works are principally concerned with encouraging traditionalist Jews to keep from becoming too much like their friends and neighbors, in particular to refrain from worshiping the gods and from adopting the moral standards and customs of non-Jews. The Books of 1, 2, 3, and 4 Maccabees pick up Jewish history and lore from the time of Alexander the Great, reporting in some detail, if not always accurately, on events and intrigues during the years from about 170 to 125 B.C..

The NT begins with four accounts of Jesus' ministry, words, death, and resurrection: the four Gospels. The first three—the Synoptic Gospels—are quite similar: Matthew and Luke apparently followed Mark's narrative framework and drew many of Jesus' sayings from another common source, the hypothetical Q (from the German *Quelle,* meaning "source"). Luke continues with a second volume, Acts, which describes the early church's, and especially Peter and Paul's activities.

Epistles or letters purportedly written by Paul are arranged in order of length, from Romans to Philemon. Paul's letters date from the 50s A.D. and contain his thoughts and advice, usually for churches he himself had founded. Many interpreters attribute Ephesians and Colossians to a Deutero-Pauline author, 2 Thessalonians to someone else, and the Pastorals (1 and 2 Timothy; Titus) to a still later editor or follower (ca. A.D. 110). Epistles thought to have been written by other early Christian authorities follow next, again in approximate order of length, from Hebrews to Jude. Those not addressed to particular churches or persons are called "catholic" (general or universal) letters or epistles. Last, appropriately, comes the Revelation to John, known more simply as Revelation or the Apocalypse. It begins with a series of admonitions in the form of seven short letters to seven churches in Asia Minor and includes numerous reported visions and psalms or hymns, all concerning the imminent deliverance awaiting Christians who remain faithful despite persecution.

MAJOR CATEGORIES
OR LITERARY GENRES

Poetry

A few books consist entirely of poems, some of which were also songs or hymns, for example, Lamentations, Psalms, and Song of Solomon. Poems, songs or hymns, and prayers are found embedded in many other books, such as Genesis 49; Exodus 15; Numbers 24; Deuteronomy 32; Judges 5; Jonah 2; Tobit 13; Judith 16; Luke 1; and Revelation 19. Ordinarily, prophetic oracles, wisdom sayings, and prayers are in poetry. Biblical poetry takes the form of a short statement followed by reiteration or repetition in different terms of all or part of the idea first stated: in effect, A/A, B/B, etc. There is no rhyme, but some critics at times believe they can distinguish meter or cadence.

Law

Many biblical laws are similar to those of other ancient Near Eastern peoples: Babylonian, Hittite, and Assyrian codes, for instance. But most are distinctively Israelite in their understanding that it was God who gave the law to his people through Moses for their own good—to maintain the right relationship between God and people, and to preserve the welfare of the community (cf. Deut. 10:12–13). The laws as such are in the form of authoritative pronouncements stating what is to be done and what is not to be done. Those that specify what is or is not to be done under certain circumstances are sometimes called casuistic laws. From time to time, the laws were collected and to some extent organized by topics. These collections are known as codifications or codes. Exodus 34:10–26 may be a fragment of a quite early Israelite law code, sometimes called the Ritual Decalogue. The first complete law code is the Covenant Code or Book of the Covenant (Exodus 20—23). This is reproduced with modifications and additions in the Deuteronomic Code, or D (Deuteronomy 5, and most of 12—26). Leviticus 17—26 records a somewhat similar code, commonly called the Holiness Code or H. The Priestly Code (sometimes labeled PC) includes most of the other ritual and sacrificial laws in Exodus, Leviticus, and Numbers. These collections probably were codified at different times in various circles within the Israelite-Judahite-Jewish communities between ca. 1200 and 400 B.C.

Prophets

The prophets were spokesmen and spokeswomen for God to the people of their time. Some of the earliest prophets were women: Miriam and Deborah. Typically, a prophetic oracle begins with the declaration "Thus says the Lord." The oracles or prophetic declarations themselves are usually in poetic form. Several of the prophetic books also contain descriptive or narrative prose. Early prophets included cultic, court, or group prophets, as well as individuals. Balaam, an early non-Israelite (Numbers 22—24) in some respects was a prototype of later Israelite prophetism. Several prophets have prominent roles in 1 and 2 Samuel and 1 and 2 Kings, such as Samuel himself, Nathan, Elijah, Micaiah, Isaiah, and Huldah. Several of the prophets to whom whole books are dedicated are called "classical prophets" because of their emphasis on Yahweh's requirement both of fidelity to him, and of justice and mercy in dealings with other persons in the community. Hosea, Amos, Isaiah, Micah, Jeremiah, and sometimes Ezekiel and Second Isaiah are regarded as the classical prophets. "Postclassical" or other prophets (Joel, Obadiah, Nahum, Habakkuk, Haggai, Zephaniah, Zechariah, and Malachi) tend to emphasize Judah's special status vis-à-vis foreign nations or the importance of properly offering sacrifices in the temple.

Wisdom

Wisdom was an international type of literature, as is evidenced by comparing biblical with extant Egyptian, Babylonian, and Edomite wisdom writings. Several biblical wisdom books are traditionally associated with Solomon, an internationalist par excellence. The typical literary form is the aphorism, a short admonition or comparison. Interests include court etiquette, prudential and moral advice, and observations about natural phenomena, particularly human motives and behavior. The main writings are Proverbs, Ecclesiastes, Job, Wisdom of Solomon, and Ecclesiasticus (or Sirach). Certain psalms, such as Psalms 34 and 37, and various sayings in Tobit 4 and 12 and the Synoptic Gospels also exemplify typical wisdom interests and format. Such sayings are sometimes called "proverbial" or "gnomic."

Apocalyptic

The apocalyptic writers generally state that they are revealing secrets communicated earlier in the form of dreams or visions either to the author (e.g., Revelation) or to some person in antiquity (e.g., Daniel, 2 Esdras). These secrets give meaning to persons living in the period in and for which they are revealed—usually a time of tribulation or persecution. Typically apocalyptic writers vividly describe what is to take place in the last days of the present age, and picture the glorious conditions of life in the new, coming, or messianic age. The characteristic apocalyptic message is that those who are persecuted (Daniel, Revelation) or troubled (2 Esdras) should endure their trials and tribulations in hope and confidence, for God or supernatural power of some sort will soon intervene and deliver those who remain faithful to God and live rightly in the meantime. The main biblical examples are Daniel, Revelation, and Matthew 24 = Mark 13 = Luke 21 (the "little" or "synoptic apocalypse"). Other biblical writings, such as Isaiah 24—27, Joel, Amos 9, Zechariah 14, 2 Esdras, Additions to Esther 11, 2 Thessalonians, and 2 Peter also contain apocalyptic passages. Several other apocalypses are found in the Pseudepigrapha: *1* and *2 Enoch,* the *Sibylline Oracles,* and *2* and *3 Baruch,* for example.

Other literary types or genres amply represented in biblical tradition include narrative and epistolary compositions. The former category is illustrated throughout the biblical writings, for example, in J and E narratives from Genesis to 1 Kings, in numerous stories such as Ruth, Esther, Tobit, Judith, the Books of the Maccabees, and Acts. The letter or epistle appears commonly in the NT in virtually every writing from Romans to Revelation. Epistles, or writings in formal letter style, are also found in other biblical literature (e.g., Jeremiah 29, the Letter of Jeremiah, and Additions to Esther).

SOURCES AND
EDITORIAL UNITS

Many of the traditions were remembered and passed on by word of mouth perhaps for generations or even centuries, before being written down. Later writers or editors occasionally added to earlier writings in order to correct, clarify, or supplement them. Some of the earliest biblical writers may have been more collectors and editors of tradition than authors. These editors may have either been single individuals or comprised schools of interpretation.

The earliest such editor was the Yahwist (designated J), who gathered and set down a wide range of material, some of it probably dating from much earlier times, ca. 950 B.C. This writer regularly used the divine name YHWH or *Yahweh* (*Jahwe,* in German, hence the symbol

J), which is translated as "the LORD" in the RSV and NEB, and as "Jehovah" in some earlier translations. J apparently lived in Judah, and the material he collected probably represents Southern or Judahite tradition. Some interpreters suggest that he may have been a court archivist in the time of David or Solomon. The J material appears in Genesis, Exodus, Numbers, Deuteronomy, Joshua, Judges, 1 and 2 Samuel, and early chapters in 1 Kings. Later Southern tradition, sometimes designated A, then follows in the rest of 1 and 2 Kings. The J theology of history may be seen particularly in Genesis 2—4; 6—13; in 2 Samuel 11—20; and 1 Kings 1—2. J's critical appraisal of human pretension and cruelty, and his interpretation of events in terms of Yahweh's sovereign justice and mercy prompt some modern interpreters to view J as a precursor to the kind of prophetic understanding of human affairs that is found later in the classical prophets such as Hosea, Amos, Isaiah, and Jeremiah.

The Northern traditions were collected about the same time, ca. 950–850, by E, so called because the divine name *Elohim* ("God," RSV, NEB) is used regularly here. A later Northern editor, sometimes called B, may have completed the collection around 722 B.C. The E or B material is found intermittently from Genesis 20 through Exodus, in Numbers, Deuteronomy, Joshua, and in 1 Samuel through 2 Kings 17. In E traditions, God often is said to communicate with people through dreams. Northern traditions characteristically take a negative stance toward kingship in Israel, holding that God alone is Israel's king.

Sometime after the fall of the Northern Kingdom in 722 B.C., perhaps ca. 650, its traditions were combined with those of Judah into what is commonly called JE, by a redactor or editor referred to generally as R[JE]. By then, it may have become clear to people in Judah that the Northern Kingdom, Israel, was extinct. Southern writers had already begun to use the name Israel when referring to the surviving kingdom of Judah. In effect, Judah had inherited the name of Israel, and probably also many of the traditions of the North. JE represents the incorporation of these Northern into existing Southern traditions. Modern critics hesitate to differentiate between the J and E components of JE in many parts of the text. The fact that the combination took place under Southern auspices may account for the relatively fragmentary character of E, compared to J.

The presence of duplicate or conflicting versions and details in the writings from Genesis through 2 Kings may be understood by recalling that the editors, J, E, and R[JE], were collectors of traditions (and sometimes of earlier collections), some of which had come down in variant forms. These editors evidently were more concerned to preserve what they had collected than to iron out discrepancies. Editors may have occasionally added their own interpretations and comments as well. Not all modern interpreters regard J and E as early writings or documents. Many, particularly Scandinavian scholars, see the presently so-called J and E material primarily as oral traditions that were remembered, modified, and passed along by word of mouth until finally set down, perhaps as recently as ca. 400 B.C. It should also be recalled that the "documentary hypothesis," which posits the existence of early documents, J and E, then D, and finally P, is just that: a hypothesis. It may be the best current explanation of the process by which the present biblical traditions in Genesis through 2 Kings came together, though it is not unchallenged. None of the "documents" it posits, however, has been found; and it may be that in time a new scholarly consensus or model will develop to better account for the data.

The Priestly tradition (P) includes both narrative and legal materials. The legal portion, known as the Priestly Code (PC), is concerned primarily with procedures to be followed by priests in offering sacrifices in the temple or its portable predecessor, the tent or tabernacle. P material appears in all of the first four books (the Tetrateuch), which may have been put into their present form by the P editor or editors (R^P) ca. 400 B.C. P, unlike traditions dating before 450 B.C., consistently distinguishes between priests and Levites. In P, priests are characterized as the sons of Aaron, while Levites are relegated to the role of assistants to the priests. P traditions assume that Israelites always worshiped in one place at a time—first the portable tent, and later the Jerusalem temple—and include more numerous sacrificial offerings and more elaborate ritual procedures than are to be found in the earlier law codes.

Following the Tetrateuch, the next major editorial unit is the Deuteronomic history or Deuteronomic history book, which includes Deuteronomy, Joshua, Judges, 1 and 2 Samuel, and 1 and 2 Kings. At its core is the Deuteronomic Code, or D (Deuteronomy 5, 12—26), much of which may date from the time of the judges. The commandment in Deuteronomy 12 that Israel must worship in only the one place (implicitly, the temple in Jerusalem) was probably added in the seventh century B.C. in order to curb the worship of Canaanite gods, which continued to be associated with the numerous shrines throughout the land. Earlier traditions contain no strictures against worship at these places. Chapters 12—19 of Deuteronomy provided for a number of adjustments in cultic practice that were necessary in order to implement the new requirement of worship in only the one place: for example, Israelites (more precisely, Judahites, if the innovation occurred in the seventh century) might now slaughter farm animals for food in their local towns without offering them in sacrifice; rural Levites (who previously had earned their livelihood by officiating as priests at the local shrines) were now added to the list of persons to be cared for—along with orphans, widows, and sojourners—because they had no means of support and, in theory, were accorded the same status and perquisites as the Levites who were priests in the Jerusalem temple; since for many it was a long way to Jerusalem, Judahites might now sell the tithes of their harvests, carry the proceeds with them, and buy food and offerings in Jerusalem, rather than haul the heavy loads of tithes there. The dating of D before P is the keystone of the documentary hypothesis set forth late in the nineteenth century by J. Wellhausen. Since the D tradition requires, but P tradition assumes Israel's worship in one place, and for various other reasons, it seems likely that P represents a later perspective or understanding.

The Deuteronomic editor or historian (designated DH or R^D), writing ca. 550 B.C., interpreted the past in accordance with the prophetic theory of history, but with particular attention to the requirements of Deuteronomic law: that only Yahweh should be worshiped, and that such worship was to take place—once the temple was built—only in Jerusalem. DH thus structures the period of the judges in terms of a repeated cycle of Israel's apostasy, God's punishment ("he gave them over to plunderers") and deliverance through the prowess of a judge, who judges all Israel for so many years, then dies, and the cycle of apostasy begins again. DH rates the kings of Israel and Judah according to their exclusive devotion to Yahweh and their diligence in destroying the "high places" (shrines of Canaanite and other foreign gods). No Northern and only a few Southern kings receive good marks.

The third main editorial collection is the Chronicler's history book: 1 and 2 Chronicles, Ezra, and Nehemiah. History and religion are reviewed with special attention to David, Jerusalem, the temple, priests and Levites, and the "books of the law" (here perhaps the PC or the whole Tetrateuch, but more likely the whole legal corpus from Exodus through Deuteronomy). Critics suggest that the Chronicler may have been a Levite, a singer, or perhaps Ezra himself. The Chronicler's viewpoint is similar to that of P, in that the offering of sacrifices is the central interest, and that only priests may officiate at such ceremonies, while Levites are relegated to lower status. The Chronicler's collection probably was assembled and edited ca. 400–350 B.C.

Additions to and combinations of other material within single books, as in the case of Isaiah, Zechariah, and 2 Corinthians, along with other types of editorial activity, such as borrowing and interpolation, are noted in the introductory chapters on the separate books of the Bible.

CANON, MANUSCRIPTS, AND TRANSLATIONS

At what point did the biblical writings come to be regarded as canonical, that is, officially scriptural? The Covenant Code (Exodus 20—23) possibly was the law of the land as early as 1200–1000 B.C. The Deuteronomic law was authoritative for the Judahites by the seventh century B.C. (2 Kings 22—23), if not earlier; and the Priestly Code was so regarded for Judaism by ca. 400 (Nehemiah 8). A Greek translation of the Pentateuch known as the Septuagint (designated LXX) was made ca. 250 B.C., and supplemented in following centuries by other writings. According to Jewish tradition, learned rabbis at Jamnia, ca. A.D. 90, decided to retain as Scripture only those writings then known in Hebrew or Aramaic, perhaps on the assumption that these were more ancient and consequently more authoritative than those in Greek or other "modern" languages. The latter were excluded from the Jewish canon. In time, these excluded writings, and a few others, came to be known as the OT Apocrypha.

Early Christian communities apparently preferred to use the Greek Bible and preserved the apocryphal books as part of their Scriptures. Catholic and Eastern Orthodox Bibles still include most of the apocryphal writings, but beginning with Martin Luther in the sixteenth century, Protestants reverted to the Hebrew canon of Jamnia for their OT (see introduction to Part 2). The early churches did not yet have a NT, but some of their writings evidently were intended to be authoritative at least for their particular readers (e.g., Mark 13:14; John 20:30–31; 1 Cor. 14:37–38; Rev. 22:18–19). Possibly a collection of Paul's letters was circulating as early as A.D. 90. Such a collection may have served as the model for the collection of seven letters at the beginning of the Book of Revelation, composed ca. A.D. 96. Second Peter, ca. A.D. 140, refers to Paul's letters as authoritative "writings" or "scriptures." The earliest known NT canon was Marcion's (ca. A.D.

140). This was selected and edited in accordance with Marcion's own heretical views. By the end of the second century A.D., more orthodox Christian leaders began listing the writings they thought scriptural or otherwise, and achieved some consensus as to the same. The present NT canon was generally agreed to by ca. A.D. 400.

No original biblical manuscripts survive. What we have are copies of copies. Aside from the Dead Sea Scrolls (ca. 150 B.C.–A.D. 70), extant OT manuscripts date no earlier than the ninth century A.D. Copyists, including the Masoretes (scribes who added Hebrew vowel points or symbols during the period from A.D. 600 to 950), generally exercised great care, with the result that relatively late OT manuscripts may be fairly reliable renditions of much earlier copies. There are, however, numerous textual errors and multiple versions. Translators have to choose among Hebrew, Aramaic, Syriac, and Latin texts, and sometimes must finally resort to conjecture. (See alphabetized notes at bottom of pages in the RSV and NEB.) Some NT manuscripts found in 1931 date as early as the late second and third centuries A.D., but most NT manuscripts are more recent. Early NT manuscripts are in Greek, Latin, Syriac, Ethiopic, and other languages. Some four hundred thousand textual variants appear among the NT manuscripts; but the probable meaning of most passages is fairly clear.

Around A.D. 390, a scholarly monk, Jerome, produced a Latin translation of the OT and NT which was to become the standard Bible of most Western Christians for more than a thousand years. This was called *The Vulgate,* because it was written in the "vulgar," that is, common language of the time: Latin. It was based on Jerome's judgment as to the reliability of the manuscript versions then available to him. The Vulgate was later translated into English (the OT at Douay, in 1607; the NT at Rheims, in 1582) in order to counter the influence of Protestant English Bibles. The last 160 years of textual and linguistic discoveries and research have yielded substantial information not previously available. Modern versions such as the RSV, NEB, Jerusalem Bible, and New American Bible reconstruct and translate the text using the results of this scholarship.

The editors of the RSV tried to preserve as much of the familiar language of the King James Version (1611) as is both intelligible to modern readers and accurate in the light of modern knowledge. The KJV itself was a revision of earlier versions going back, for example, through the Bishop's Bible (1568) and the Coverdale translation (1535) to Tyndale's translation (1526–34). Many of Tyndale's phrases still may be found in the RSV. The NEB editors, on the other hand, decided to recast the meaning of the text in different language, adopting many modern British idioms. The RSV (1952) and NEB (1970) were translated by Protestant scholars, but have since been endorsed by American and British Catholic authorities. The Jerusalem Bible (1966) is an English version of a new (1956) translation by French Catholic scholars in Jerusalem. The New American Bible (1970) is a fresh translation by American Catholic scholars. A new inclusive-language version of the NT portion appeared in 1987 (The Revised New Testament of the New American Bible), replacing the 1970 version.

3. BASIC THEMES AND ISSUES IN BIBLICAL FAITH AND UNDERSTANDING

Mainline biblical faith affirms one God as creator and source of all that is; as the one whose merciful bounty provides for the needs of all his creatures; as the Sovereign over the history of nations and the little histories of individual persons; and as the one who in his own good time will restore and transform the world that has been disfigured and degraded by human depravity into that realm where all creatures shall flourish before him, doing his will and enjoying his blessings forever. Yet it would be a mistake to assume that the biblical peoples were always or inevitably devoted to the one God. Again and again, Hebrews, Israelites, Judahites, and Jews pursue their love affair with other gods: the golden calf, the gods of the Canaanites (whose favor was closely linked with successful agriculture and animal husbandry), the gods and goddesses of other nations, and the little man-made godlings or idols of hearth and home. From Moses to Elijah, to Hosea and Second Isaiah, to the Letter of Jeremiah and the stories of Bel and the Dragon in the Apocrypha, religious leaders and writers called on their people to choose which god they would serve. Thus one of the core issues in biblical faith is this continuing struggle between proponents of faith in the one God, and the popular and persistent worship of other deities. Such worship was not only an affair of the masses. At times it was abetted by leaders, for example, by Aaron, Moses' brother, and by kings of Israel and Judah (such as Solomon, Ahab, and Manasseh); and sometimes ordained by foreign overlords (as in Daniel, 1–4 Maccabees, and Revelation).

The biblical writings are nearly all theocentric: if human figures are on the stage, it is always God who is the director. God is not thought of abstractly, as a being in or by himself, but always in relationship to the world, which God created and rules; to human beings and other creatures; and in particular ways to Israel; and, in the New Testament, to Jesus and the church, and the world. These relationships—in the past, the present, and the anticipated future—are at the center of the biblical faith and understanding.

THE CREATION

In many Oriental and gnostic religions, the material world is regarded as evil, an illusion, or a mistake to be endured or overcome. Not so here: God created the heavens and the earth, and found all that he had made very good (Genesis 1). In the story of the flood, God spares not only a core of human survivors, but also the progenitors of all other species of life, and not just those useful to people. All living creatures were to "breed abundantly . . . and be fruitful and multiply upon the earth" (Genesis 6—9). The whole created order of beings is tended by God's wondrous power and good will; its existence occasions awe and celebration (Job 38—39; Psalms 104, 148; Isaiah 40; Song of the Three Young Men). Life in the world, including sexuality and material prosperity, is affirmed as good. Hopes for the future center first on coming into the promised land, a "land flowing with milk and honey," and later, on life in a fruitful and peaceable kingdom on a renewed or transformed earth, commonly visualized with Jerusalem or Zion in its midst (Isaiah 2, 11, 19; Jeremiah 33; Ezekiel 47; Hosea 2; Amos 9; Revelation 21—22). Only in the NT is it sometimes suggested that the fulfillment of life is to be in heaven (John 14; Philippians 3).

THE HUMAN CONDITION

Humanity is part of the good world of beings created by God. The creation story attributed to the Priestly source (P) in Genesis 1 declares that God made male and female in his own image and gave them dominion over other creatures of the earth. The Yahwist (J) tradition is less optimistic: in the J creation story, the first human, *adam*, like other creatures, is made from the dust of the earth (*adamah*) and, as a result of disobedience, is destined to return to the dust (Genesis 2—3). The P and J versions together encompass the biblical appreciation of the ambivalence of human nature and destiny. Humanity is "little less than God" (Ps. 8:5), but is not God. When human beings try to put themselves in God's place or ignore God's commands, catastrophe results, usually for others as well as themselves (Genesis 3—4; 6—9; 11). The number of persons characterized as righteous in the later biblical traditions is quite small: Abraham (perhaps), Kings Hezekiah and Josiah (2 Kings 18:5; 22:2), Job, Tobit, Judith, Esther (of the Additions), Susanna, and a few people commemorated in the books of Maccabees. Even the writings that are most pessimistic about human nature and destiny (Ecclesiastes and 2 Esdras), however, understand that people have the capacity to respond faithfully to God and considerately and justly to other persons—and must bear responsibility for failing to do so.

Death, Resurrection, Eternal Life

Since Adam's disobedience, all of humanity has had to face death. The hope for the resurrection of the dead appears only in a few late OT texts: Dan. 12:2, perhaps Isa. 26:19 and Ezekiel 37, and in 2 Macc. 7:9–14. In the NT, it is generally expected that those who have died will be raised when the Son of man, or Christ, comes. They will then face divine judgment, along with those who are still alive at the time, after which the righteous will enter into the kingdom of God or of Christ. Paul sometimes states that those still alive will be "changed" or transformed before entering their heavenly commonwealth. Throughout most of the biblical period, hope for the future was expressed mainly in terms of the continuation of one's name and family and of the people of Israel or Judah in coming generations. Hope for eternal life after death or the immortality of the soul is found a few times in the Bible (Isaiah 25; Wisdom of Solomon 3—6; 8; 4 Maccabees 7; 9—10; 14—15; 17—18; John 6; cf. Luke 16:19–31). Most NT texts that give expression to the hope for life in the coming kingdom of God (or of Christ) suggest that life there will be eternal life (e.g., Matthew 25; Mark 10; 1 Corinthians 6; 15).

Good and Evil

All creation, including humanity, was made good by God. Why then is there disobedience, fratricide, homicide, injustice, suffering, and death? In some biblical traditions, what may seem evil is attributed to God's acting for his own purposes, for instance, hardening Pharaoh's heart (Exodus 10) or tormenting Job. Usually, however, in the OT, evil is understood to arise out of the anxious and arrogant will of people to gain power and glory over others or to put themselves in the place of God. "The imagination of man's heart is evil from his youth" (Gen. 8:21), but people also can obey God and love their neighbors.

This dual capacity is the basic dynamic of the biblical story of mankind's, and particularly of Israel's, life under God's sovereignty. Many OT prophets looked for the time when God would transform the human heart, so that obedience, love, and the knowledge of the Lord would prevail on earth (Jer. 31:33–34; Ezek. 36:26–27; Hos. 2:19–20). But in the meantime, the story of mankind and of Israel is one of faithfulness and obedience, but also—and more typically—of mistrust and disobedience, and of God's varied responses of judgment and steadfast love. In the NT, Satan and his demons emerge as instigators of illness and suffering, as well as of faithlessness and wrongdoing. Satan is also known here as "the Evil One," and sometimes, though not always, as "the devil." In a few NT writings, the present world is said to be under his power (1 John 5, Revelation). Nevertheless, the NT writings all maintain that human beings are accountable for their decision whether to serve God or other masters, and responsible before God for how they act in relation to other persons.

ISRAEL AND OTHER NATIONS

Chapters 1—11 of Genesis tell the story of early mankind: his and her creation, and that of the rest of the world and its other various inhabitants, the first human pair's eating of the forbidden fruit, the first fratricide, a subsequent homicide, the flood, and the building of the city and the tower. Thereafter, according to the stories, people were scattered abroad over the earth, separated by nations and languages, alienated from one another and from God. In this inauspicious setting, Abraham is called both to be blessed, and to become a great nation and also, somehow, to "be a blessing" to all the families of the earth (Gen. 12:1–3; cf. 17:15–21, which adds that the promises are to be fulfilled through Isaac, who would be born to Sarah, Abraham's wife). The rest of the biblical story represents a series of fulfillments or partial fulfillments of these promises and tasks. In some traditions, the emphasis is on the role of Abraham's descendants as a blessing to other nations or peoples; in others, the blessings seem reserved more, or even exclusively, for Israel, Judah, or the Jewish people.

The former emphasis is exemplified in many prophetic and narrative traditions. Thus the "floating oracle" of Isa. 2:2–4 and Mic. 4:1–3 looks forward to a wonderful era of international peace and other blessings. Isaiah 19 visualizes Israel in the latter days as "a blessing in the midst of the earth," along with Egypt—God's people—and Assyria—the work of his hands. Zechariah looks for a time when the survivors of all nations will go up to worship Yahweh in Jerusalem each year (chap. 14). Through the evil scheme of Joseph's brothers, God brings it about that people from many nations are kept alive in time of famine (Genesis 50). Jonah's grudging message enables the Ninevites (Assyrians) to be spared otherwise certain destruction. Ruth, a Moabite, is a model for fidelity and devotion, and King David's great grandmother. Two of the most righteous people in the OT were non-Israelites: Noah and Job. In the NT, Jesus refers to a Samaritan as exemplar of responsive neighbor-love (Luke 10), and promises that men will come from all the earth to sit at table in the kingdom of God (Luke 13). A Roman centurion testifies to Jesus' divine status (Mark 15:39); an Ethiopian is among the early converts to Christianity (Acts 8); and, at least after Paul, Christianity becomes open to believers from all nations and races.

There was also a narrower, more exclusive point of view. When Israel enters Canaan, the indigenous peoples are to be slaughtered (Deuteronomy 7), or, failing that, made slaves (Judges 1). Ammonites and Moabites are forever to be barred from the congregation of Israel (Deuteronomy 23). Ezra and Nehemiah ruthlessly "cleansed" Israel of foreign wives and children for the sake of the "holy race" or ancient grievances (Ezra 9—10; Nehemiah 13). Xenophobia—fear of the foreigner or stranger—surfaces particularly in writings reflecting the experience of persecution or defeat (e.g., Esther; Psalm 137; Nahum; 3 Maccabees). Some of the prophets look for a messianic age in which other nations (i.e., Gentiles) either have been destroyed, or are made to serve the Jewish people (e.g., Joel, Obadiah, Haggai). Is Israel chosen by God for special, even unique, privilege; or is it chosen to be a blessing, a "light to the Gentiles" (Isaiah 49)? Both kinds of understandings are found in the OT. A similar issue arises in the NT: are Christians to love and do good to their enemies, or to only fellow-believers? Both kinds of answers appear here, as well.

THE GOD OF PAST,
PRESENT, AND FUTURE

The Past

God was not known through philosophical speculation. He was known and remembered, rather, through his actions and interactions in history. God had called the fathers and mothers, used the evil intentions of Joseph's brothers for the good of many peoples, and led

Israel, through Moses, out of Egypt, thereby showing not only his good intentions toward Israel but also his power to make good his will and word in the world. Through Moses, God had given Israel his law, and under Joshua, brought them into the land of Canaan, true to his promises to the fathers (Josh. 21:43–45). The Deuteronomic editor of Judges reports that because of Israel's apostasy, God periodically subjected them to oppressors, but would then send deliverance through the various judges (Judg. 2:11–23). Hosea looked to the past to understand the present relationship between God and Israel: "Out of Egypt have I called my son." But because the Israelites had forgotten God, "they shall return to the land of Egypt" (Hos. 11:1, 5). The prophet known as Second Isaiah saw in the exodus from Egypt a clue to a new deliverance in store for the exiles in Babylon (Isa. 43:14–21). Not only was the God of Israel the same as the one who had acted in the past; the people identified themselves with those who had gone before: "A wandering Aramean was my father. . . . And the Egyptians . . . laid upon us harsh bondage. . . . And the Lord brought us out of Egypt . . . and gave us this land" (Deut. 26:5–9; cf. chap. 6). The NT writers not only tell the story of Jesus and the early church, but also claim to be part of the continuing story of Israel that began with Abraham.

The Present

The present was understood with reference to both past and future. God who acted before is the same who now rules and overrules Israel and the nations. God's law, given to Moses, is the law for "this day" (Deuteronomy 5—11), for God's will and purpose are unchanged. Emphasis in the Law and the Prophets alike is always upon the here and now. Now is the time for faithfulness to God and for keeping God's commandments! Similarly, in the NT, Paul and John stress the present decision of faith in relation to what God has already done in Christ, and the possibility and demand for a life now lived according to the Spirit in the way of love.

The Future

The promises to Abraham and Sarah (Genesis 12 and 17) pointed toward a future fulfillment. The OT prophets expected God to act in judgment both against foreign nations because of their pride and cruelty, and particularly against his own people—Israel and Judah—who had forsaken the covenant. They also looked for God's action in restoring the fortunes of his people—and sometimes those of other peoples as well. This expectation was decisive for the present: if the people returned to the Lord, they might avert his wrath; if they looked to the Lord for deliverance, they need not despair. Some visions of hope for the future included the promise of a new king or messiah from the house of David (Isaiah 9, 11; Ezekiel 34); others do not (Isaiah 2, 19; Jeremiah 31; Daniel 7; Hosea 2; Zechariah 14). Jesus also called on his hearers to repent, for the kingdom of God and the time of judgment were near. Most of the NT writers also summoned their readers to right action then, while there was still time, before the coming of Christ. At that time, God would make all things new. Those found fit for the kingdom would then enter into the blessings of life together and with God in a transformed heaven and earth.

TOPICAL INDEX